Jones, George

Excursions to Cairo, Jerusalem, Damascus and Balbec

Inktank publishing

Jones, George

Excursions to Cairo, Jerusalem, Damascus and Balbec

Inktank publishing, 2018

www.inktank-publishing.com

ISBN/EAN: 9783747768778

EXCURSIONS

TO

CAIRO, JERUSALEM, DAMASCUS AND BALBEC,

FROM THE

UNITED STATES SHIP DELAWARE,

DURING HER RECENT CRUISE.

WITH AN

ATTEMPT TO DISCRIMINATE BETWEEN TRUTH AND ERROR IN REGARD TO THE SACRED PLACES OF THE

HOLY CITY.

BY GEORGE JONES, A. M.

CHAPLAIN U. S. NAVY; AUTHOR OF SKETCHES OF NAVAL LIFE.

NEW-YORK:

VAN NOSTRAND AND DWIGHT.

1836.

TO

COMMODORE D. T. PATTERSON,

U. S. NAVY,

THIS MEMORIAL

OF SOME INCIDENTS IN A VERY AGREEABLE CRUISE

UNDER HIS COMMAND,

IS INSCRIBED,

WITH THE RESPECTFUL AND GRATEFUL REGARDS OF

THE AUTHOR.

PREFACE.

THE Author had no intention during the cruise of writing such a book. His reasons for now engaging in it are, in addition to those common on such occasions, a belief that the public take a very deep interest in the countries which he has visited, and would be pleased to have further means of information respecting them. The circumstances under which his excursions into Egypt and Syria were made, though limiting his observations to a few cities, gave him some unusual advantages in examining those to which he was allowed access.

The reader, he believes, will be surprised to see the changes which the energetic government of Mohammed Ali has wrought in Egypt and Syria; and these are only the beginning of changes. The whole East seems destined before long to a wonderful revolution, if not political, at least mental and moral. It is pleasing to see the present dawnings of light upon two countries the most celebrated in the world; the one for its ancient science, the other for its religion. The night appears to be past, and the day-spring at hand.

The Author has given a chapter on Jerusalem, which may appear to some of his readers better suited to a book of romance than of travels. His object was to place vividly before the reader the ancient city, which he believes to have had a splendor and a beauty of which few persons are aware. Though the scene is supposed to be raised up by a spell of fancy, yet there is nothing presented in

1

the picture for which there is not authority in ancient writers, with the single exception of the arrangement of the hymns at the Paschal sacrifice.

The author, for reasons not necessary to be stated here, kept no journal during this cruise; but the events and scenes occurring in these visits made an impression so deep that the memory has kept a record of them sufficiently faithful. At the commencement of his attempt to put them on paper, he wrote to Commodore Patterson to ascertain whether such a design would meet with his approbation; and the Commodore, in a very kind letter in reply, was good enough to offer him the use of his own private journal and of his official letters. From these he has drawn much valuable statistical matter as well as hints on other subjects; and he takes this mode of publicly making his acknowledgments for the favor.

Through oversight, the year of these visits has not been mentioned in the body of the work; they were made in the year 1834.

INDEX.

EGYPT.

CHAPTER I.

CHAPTER II.

CHAPTER III.

CHAPTER IV.

CHAPTER V.

CHAPTER VI.

CHAPTER VII.

SYRIA.

CHAPTER XIII.

CHAPTER XIV.

CHAPTER XV.

CHAPTER XVI.

CHAPTER XVII.

CHAPTER XVIII.

CHAPTER XIX.

CHAPTER XX.

CHAPTER XXI.

CHAPTER XXII.

CHAPTER XXIII.

CHAPTER XXIV.

CHAPTER XXV.

ERRATA.

The Reader is requested to make the following corrections:

Page	105,	line	12,	for	" ten"	substitute one hundred.
	106,	..	14,	..	" case" ..	cause.
	111,	..	13,	..	" are" ..	were.
	114,	..	2,	..	" water" ..	lake.
	153,	..	22,	..	" extensive"	extreme.
	155,	..	26,	strike out " thirty miles from Jerusalem."		
	159,	..	27,	for	" whirling" read wheeling.	
	311,	..	29,	..	" filled" read piled.	

EGYPT.

EXCURSIONS

TO

CAIRO, JERUSALEM, &c.

CHAPTER I.

Approach to Egypt. Plague in Alexandria. Determination to visit Cairo and the Pyramids. Boghaz Bey. Canal of Mahmoudieh. Policy of Mohammed Ali. The abject state of his subjects, and his apology for it. Night on the Canal. First view of the Nile. Angelina's opinion of it. Ex-Dey of Algiers.

"Land O!" was cried from our mast-head on the morning of the 13th of July; and at the end of an hour, a dim yellow line, resting on the southern horizon, might be discovered from our elevated decks. When another hour had expired, a high misty object, that had drawn our attention, had taken distinctness of outline, and was known to be Pompey's Pillar. By this time also the narrow strip of sand forming the coast had begun to be ruffled, and soon after the city of Alexandria, its domes, minarets, palaces, and shipping, came into view. Notwithstanding the evidence of life and activity that had now presented itself, the scene was a melancholy one. Far off on either side stretched the low, sandy coast, its uniform outline unbroken except by a few insignificant ruins; not a tree or shrub, not a speck of verdure, was to be anywhere seen; while back from the coast the atmosphere seemed to be on fire; a deep

2

red glare, covering all the land, and ascending far up towards the zenith.

This was our first impression with regard to Egypt, and the second was by no means a more favorable one. Our ship was anchored about three miles from the shore, and the schooner Shark, our consort on this occasion, was directed to proceed into the harbor, with an invitation to the U. S. consul, Mr. J. Gliddon, to come on board. When he arrived, he informed us that two cases of what seemed to be the plague had appeared eight days previously in the Greek convent, and had excited some alarm: he added, however, that the building had been put in strict quarantine, and as the disease had extended no further, and the symptoms were not of a decided character, their fears had subsided, and that they were in hopes of enjoying their usual health. Their expectations were encouraged by the fact that the country had for many years been exempted from this dreadful disease.* Mohammed Ali was at this time in Syria, whither he had been called to assist in putting down a rebellion, which had suddenly burst out there. Mr. Gliddon strongly urged the Commodore to await his return; and informed us, that in

* They were too sanguine. Soon after our visit the plague broke out at Alexandria, and raged with a violence that has scarcely ever had a parallel. In the town of Atfour on the Nile, which, when we passed it, had 40,000 inhabitants, in the course of a few months only 1500 remained. Some had fled, but far the greater part had been carried off by the disease. It swept quite through the land from the sea-coast to the interior, sparing neither city nor village, and was everywhere unusually fatal.

the mean time we could visit Cairo and the Pyramids with perfect safety, as that city and the intermediate country were free from sickness, and our route would not carry us through Alexandria or expose us to contact with its inhabitants.

It was with the most sincere pleasure that we learned that Commodore Patterson had decided in favor of this excursion. Dim land of embalmed and faded greatness, that, from the searments of the tomb, dost murmur to us in solemn and mystic language, we should see thee then! we should stand on the banks of the Nile, where even Nature herself is shrouded in unusual obscurity: we should look down from the summits of the Pyramids, those monuments on which all ages have gazed with wonder, and where they have speculated in vain. I had myself just been living in a squatter's cabin in Indiana, and anticipated with keen relish the strong contrast that would here be presented. I had come from witnessing the first elements of society forming into order, to see the monuments of a people ancient even in the most ancient times; from watching the conflicts of separate individual interests, to behold the "vast expanse of ages and nations;" from wandering amid the primeval solitudes of nature, to wander amid the solitudes of deserted cities; and from witnessing the first efforts for human greatness to contemplate its end.

Mohammed Ali had left as his representative, Boghaz Bey, an Armenian of talent and energy, who enjoys his highest confidence; and while preparations were making for our journey, the Commodore, with Capt. Nicolson and Mr. Gliddon, went to pay him a visit of ceremony. On application being made to him for passports to Cairo, he replied, that they would be unnecessary; that he would consider Com. Patterson as the guest of the Pasha, and, as soon as we should start, would forward orders by telegraph to the river, to have boats provided, and to Cairo to have the party treated with every attention.

On the 16th we transferred ourselves, together with conveniences for cooking and sleeping, to the decks of the schooner, and were landed towards evening near the mouth of the great canal of Mahmoudieh. This canal was the first of the many proofs which our journey led us to witness of the wonderful enterprize and energy of Mohammed Ali, whom the reader, when he has followed us further, will, I think, agree with us in considering one of the greatest sovereigns of the age. In some respects we must also allow his government to be marked by singular short-sightedness and weakness; but on this point it is only fair to let him speak for himself, which we shall presently allow him to do.

The traveller through Egypt is constantly struck with two things: one, the high state of improvement in all public institutions, and the energy with which they are conducted; and the other, the vassalage, the extremely abject state of the people. No subjects in the world are in such a wretched condition as those of the Egyptian Pasha. They have the appearance of freedom, but throughout the whole country every man is a slave to the royal master. They till the land and may call the produce theirs; but when it is gathered in, he compels them to carry it to his store-houses, and there he purchases it at his own prices, which are just sufficient to keep them from a miserable death. The stores thus accumulated he sells all over Europe, wherever a good market can be procured; the money is laid out chiefly in the support of his army and navy, and thus the avails of their labor are returned to the poor wretches in the shape of the "nezzam," or soldiers to keep them in subjection. Of course they hate both the Pasha and all his armed forces most cordially; but for this he cares nought, and thus we have the spectacle of a nation apparently prosperous, but in reality extremely miserable. He is so severe in his exactions, that if a cultivator wishes to plant a tree, he must provide an equivalent for the ground it may occupy; and in one village up the Nile, where we stopped to get vegetables, they informed us that they had none for themselves. The last season their grounds, they said, had not yielded the quantity of grain required, and this year they had been compelled to convert their gardens into wheat fields, in order to make up the deficiency.

The annual revenue of the Pasha from all these sources amounts in ordinary seasons to twenty-five, and in very fruitful years to thirty millions of dollars. In his own personal expenses he may be considered very moderate; and nearly the whole of this immense income is expended in public improvements, and in the pay and equipment of his army and navy. The former consists of 80,000 men, well disciplined, and efficient, and strongly attached to their duties and to the Pasha; the navy at present consists of 11 one hundred gun ships and as many frigates, afloat, and is to be increased to 40 vessels, chiefly of the largest class. The public improvements throughout the country evince an enlargement of mind and an energy of character that in an eastern sovereign is wonderful, especially when we consider that in most of his operations the Pasha has no one to second him, but devises and executes by the force of his own individual energy; and very often has to give a personal superintendence to his operations. With regard to the abject state of his subjects, he says it is a necessary one, and is lamented by himself as much as by any other person. His power is unstable; he has lately gained a kind of slippery independence, is closely watched by his former master, the Sultan, and, without a large army and navy, his throne would soon slide from under him. His improvements, too, he says, must be carried on with untiring assiduity, or they will result in little good. His own life will probably not be continued much longer, and if they are not well advanced towards completion before his death, they will all be an abortion, and the country will retrograde to its late state of inferiority, and be again behind the character of the age. And in this he is correct; for his step-son, Ibrahim Pasha, who will doubtless be his successor, is altogether devoted to military affairs, and cares little for manufactories, unless they be of arms and munitions of war. "Therefore," argues the Pasha, (or thus at least argued the governor of Cairo for him at our first interview,) "therefore I must drive matters with the utmost speed, and to do this I must have a large revenue, and to obtain this I must lay heavy burdens on my subjects." He says, however, that as soon as the cause of these exactions is removed, and his power secured, and his improvements sufficiently advanced to fear no relapse, he will make his people comfortable; and that in the interval, by means of schools and his own example, he is endeavoring to inform them, and to stimulate them to higher views of things than they have hitherto had, and greatly to increase the resources of the country. Thus speaks the new monarch of Egypt, and I have thought it best to give the reader at once an insight into his views, in order that he may be able the better to judge of them as we proceed through the country.

We now return to the canal of Mahmoudieh. Fifteen years ago there was a scarcity of grain in Europe, but a great abundance in Egypt, and the merchant-sovereign had an opportunity of realizing an extremely handsome profit on the products of his soil ; but the Nile happened at that season to be unusually low, and vessels found it so difficult to load at the mouth of the river, that his harvest of gain was in a great measure lost. He then conceived the idea of a canal to unite the river with the secure and excellent harbor of Alexandria. With him there is but a short interval between planning and executing. He sent his soldiers into the country with requisitions on the various governors for men, according to the size of their villages or districts. The poor natives were hunted up, and being fastened to long poles by iron collars around the neck, forty to a pole, were thus driven down to the line marked out by his engineer, and there set to work. Mr. Gliddon, who saw the work in progress, informed me that there were 150,000 men employed upon it at one time. In six months the canal was completed, with the exception of a little masonry, and was opened for use. It is sixty miles in length, ninety feet wide, and eighteen in depth, including six feet of water. The workmen had no tools, except a few hoes to break the hard upper crust : when this had been done, they scraped the earth together with their fingers, formed it into balls, and passed them by hand to the sides of the cánal, a large portion of the wet mass often escaping between their hands while on the way. Exposed to the sun, and without shelter at night, and probably without sufficient food, disease crept in among them ; and I was credibly informed that during the digging, 30,000 of the workmen perished :

their bodies, as soon as life was extinct, were tossed upon the growing heaps of earth at the side, and this was their burial. The canal follows the line of that dug by Alexander the Great, till near Damanhour, when it unaccountably makes a great bend to the south. The engineer has made another blunder in the grading, in consequence of which it is too shallow to be navigable during the two months when the river is at the lowest.

Mr. Gliddon, whose kindness on this and other occasions has placed us under many obligations, had secured boats for us, and towards sunset our arrangements for the inland voyage were completed. We then hoisted the American ensign at the peaks of our little flotilla, and dropping the large sails to a fresh and favorable breeze, the city and its shipping soon glided from our sight. After passing near the elevated ground on which stands Pompey's Pillar, and then by a few country-seats of the nobles of Alexandria, we entered upon an open, dreary waste, and night began soon after to sink around us, and upon the still and melancholy scene; for, except our rushing boats, not a sight nor a sound met the senses, which soon became actually oppressed by the solitude. A dim moon threw a flickering and uncertain light upon the banks, and it required but little effort of the imagination, as we watched them flitting by, to make out shadowy forms, and cover the place with the phantoms of the many poor victims sacrificed and buried there.

But had they actually risen up, the whole 30,000,

and pointed their bony fingers and gibbered at us as we passed, they would scarcely have exceeded in numbers or terror the blood-thirsty tormentors that soon after this assailed us in the little cabins in our boats. We had extinguished our lights and laid down for repose, but repose there was none for us. The reader must excuse me if I draw such a nauseous picture; it is not fair that he should travel without sharing some of the pains of travelling, nor can he otherwise get a correct idea of the country. We soon found ourselves literally covered with vermin, whose bite, though dreadfully annoying, left us uncertain whether they were the animal that sometimes chooses our beds for their residence, or those that constituted the third plague of Egypt; and during the long night, while stung almost to madness, we were left to weigh the evidence in this agreeable query. The latter insects are, at certain seasons, common in every part of Egypt; and Sir Sidney Smith, having removed his tent to the desert, in order to escape from them, found them even among its sands. It was really quite a relief to us, when morning came, to find that our clothes were thickly sprinkled over with only the former less terrible insect. It was a long and wearisome night. I climbed the mast once or twice to cool my blood and seek for relief by gazing around; but only a flat, and utterly deserted country met the sight, and the ear could not detect a single sound; the hooting of an owl would have been a pleasant relief.

Morning did come at last; and as the sun began

to throw its welcome beams over the landscape, if landscape it may be called, the banks of mud bordering the canal grew higher, and receded on either side, until presently we found ourselves in a kind of basin, and soon after amid a multitude of boats. We had arrived at its termination. Casting our eyes on the left bank, where there seemed to be something in motion, we were able, by and by, to detect a village stuck into its side; the houses, or rather the single small chamber forming each house, being made partly by digging into the bank, and partly by building up a low wall of mud, with an opening in its front for a door. They were covered with reeds, and these again with mud. Creeping in and out, were a swarm of natives, in soiled habiliments, as dark looking as the houses themselves. This, together with some store-houses of the Pasha at the gate of the canal, and a few more decent dwellings on the banks of the river, form the village of Atf. On the right bank of the canal was a well paved quay, lined with boats, and covered with heaps of grain.

We ascended the steep, high banks on the right of this quay,— and had before us the Nile.

I believe we shall not soon forget the impression it made on us; for it is, there, a beautiful river, and its effect was heigthened by contrast with the dull, monotonous scene presented by the black sides of the canal and the deserted country around. The Nile is about as wide as the Connecticut at Hartford or the Ohio at Cincinnati; it flowed here at our feet in graceful and beautiful curves. In front of us was an island, low and flat, but covered with millet, and with shrubs and plants of the most intense verdure. A little higher up, on the opposite bank, from amid a mass of houses, towered the domes and picturesque minarets of Atfour, a city of 40,000 inhabitants, with a large building like a palace at its upper edge. Just above this was another island covered with trees, which were dipping their foliage into the waters, and behind which the river was lost to our sight. On our own side the view was less interesting. Only a few trees dotted the banks, and in the interior, the dreary stretch of flat, waste land was interrupted only by the deceitful *mirage* or imitation of water.

While some of the party were looking down on the river in high admiration of its modern beauties, or lost in meditations on its ancient fame, old Catalina, the Mahonese woman who attended on the Commodore's family, approached. Catalina had never seen any thing larger than the rivulet which flows near her native city, and is much frequented by the Mahonese washerwomen. The company watched her in order to enjoy her surprise. She was, indeed, surprised. When she had a little recovered from her astonishment, one of the party said to her, "Well, Catalina, what do you think of the Nile?" "Oh," she replied, with sincerity and earnestness, "it is very grand—if it was only at Mahon, what a fine place it would be to wash clothes in!"

EGYPT.

CHAPTER II.

Boats on the Nile. Our enjoyments on the river. Water of the Nile. Villages. Ovens for hatching chickens. Egyptian bricks and case of the Israelites. Singular costume of the females. Thievish boatmen. First view of the Pyramids. Stupendous undertaking of Mohammed Ali at the Barage. Approach to Cairo. Moonlight scene.

THE boats of the canal are confined exclusively to its waters, and we here found it necessary to look out for other conveyances, a necessity to which our last night's experience made us very gladly submit; nor had we at any time occasion to find fault with the comfort or cleanliness of the boats on the Nile. Those which we engaged had about three fourths of the length of one of our canal boats, and about twice the breadth, and drew from three to four feet water; near the stern were a forward and an after cabin, the former of sufficient height to allow us to stand upright. In front of it we spread awnings above, and at the sides, so as to make a cool verandah or vestibule for eating and sitting during the day; and, with the aid of curtains, a pleasant sleeping apartment for the night. Towards the bow the deck ceased, and gave place to an open area filled with sand, where our excellent cook erected his throne, and chopped off as many heads as might have satisfied even Mohammed Ali himself.

Our party, consisting of twenty-six persons exclusive of attendants, engaged three of these boats. The Commodore and his family, and, by invitation, ——, and the writer of this, occupied one of them; a second was engaged by a party principally of lieutenants; and a third by midshipmen from the two ships. We had on board of each boat a person called a Cavass, an officer appointed by government to attend on travellers; he goes well armed, and bears in addition, as a badge of office, a long cane capped with silver or gold, to which dangle chains of the same material. His presence places the party under the protection of government, and gives it access to all public places to which he may choose to lead.

We were all a happy party on that river. Our steward had laid in abundantly, and provisions along the Nile were plentiful and cheap; we had books and musical instruments, and chessmen and society. We changed back and forward among the boats, and sometimes gave tea-parties; and often landed for a stroll along the river banks, or among the palm-groves of the villages. The officers unanimously voted that it was far preferable to keeping watch on shipboard. Nor must I forget another source of real and actual pleasure, in drinking the Nile water. It is a delicious fluid, and the natives have a saying handed down from father to son, "that if Mahomet had ever tasted the waters of the Nile, he would have placed his Paradise along its banks." An earthern vessel, that would hold twenty or twenty-five gallons, was lashed at the stern of our boat, and kept filled, so as to allow the sediment to subside. The river, when we were ascending, was about one fourth advanced in the yearly flood, and the waters were of a light yellow color; on being allowed to rest in the jar, they took the color of lemonade, and were the most agreeable we had ever tasted. We drank prodigious quantities, but without having our health at all affected by them. The wind at this season blows constantly up stream during the day, but subsides a little after sunset, when we were obliged to come to and secure ourselves to the shore for the night. Descending boats take advantage of this interval of calm to drop down with the current.

We stopped first at Atfour, the city noticed above, where we found that what had seemed to us a palace was a large manufactory of Egyptian caps belonging to the Pasha. Thence we glided up the stream, the American ensign at the peak of each of our high lateen yards, fluttering, and seeming to rejoice as much as we at being on the Egyptian river. The banks, villages, islands, and groves, slipped along by our sides, presenting views sometimes highly picturesque, and always of a strikingly oriental character. The country, however, is generally at this season of the year tame and monotonous. The crops had been gathered in, and the open plains (for there are no enclosures, except occasionally to a garden) were burnt to a cinder by the fierce raging sun; the earth was gaping, and seemed to pant under its fury; and, except the neighborhood of the villages, and now and then a garden watered by artificial means, there was not a speck of verdure to be seen. The villages also, when we came to inspect them, we found to be miserable in the extreme. They consist of one or two hundred houses, made of bricks hardened in the sun and covered with domes of the same material. The bricks retain the original color of the muddy deposite, and the villages have a dull, gloomy appearance. Whitewash is never used within; but on the outside a mottled appearance is sometimes given to the houses by the custom of sticking cakes of camels' ordure against their front and sides to dry; this being the only fuel used in the country. It is said to burn very well, and when thus prepared, to have no disagreeable odour. If the reader will imagine a collection of houses thus daubed on the outside, with earthern floors and bare walls of mud, a small hole for a window, excessively filthy within, and abounding in vermin; he will have an idea of an Egyptian village. He must add also now and then a large, well-filled granary of the Pasha in the neighborhood of the villages; and in the villages themselves a number of dwellings in ruins; for the bricks often yield to the operation of the weather, and the badly constructed domes tumble in. As we sailed along, our attention was very often drawn to the houses for hatching chickens, one or more of which may be seen in each of their villages. They are formed by taking a number of pots, of the capacity of about a gallon, contracted at the neck, which is turned towards the exterior. About fifty or sixty of these are built up with bricks and mud into an edifice like an elongated bee-hive, twelve or fifteen feet in height. The eggs are small and the fowls diminutive, but of a very pleasant flavor.

I examined the Egyptian bricks with reference to the complaint of the Hebrews, that straw was not allowed them in the manufacture. A few here have straw mixed up with them, and it will doubtless check the process of disintegration to which they are exposed, but it does not seem at present to be considered a necessary ingredient. But it is universally employed in the process of manufacturing, or rather in drying the bricks. They are in size like our bricks, and are cut with a spade from the earth when moistened by the yearly floods. Fine straw is then scattered on the adjoining grounds, and the bricks are spread over this to dry; and were this precaution not used, the bricks in drying would adhere to the earth and be spoiled. I conclude, then, that here was occasioned the dilemma in which the Israelites soon found themselves; they could make the tale of bricks, but when they came to remove them at the close of their labors, they found them attached to the soil and their labors lost. I frequently saw

3*

bricks exposed for drying, but never without a layer of fine straw beneath.

Their villages occur at intervals of five or six miles; generally they are on the river bank, but are often scattered over the interior, and with the groves of the graceful palm-tree often formed pretty groupings in the landscape. The natives are of a light ash color; and the men, though rather slender, are remarkably well-formed, light, and active, and capable of enduring fatigue. Their dress is sometimes like that of the Turks, but often simply a long piece of white cloth, like the Roman toga, wrapped around the body, with the ends thrown across the shoulders or supported under the arm; it is a graceful, but not very modest dress. But the women! How strange are the caprices of fashion, and often how extravagant and silly! In Turkey a woman is not allowed to show her face at all; a handkerchief drawn across the forehead, and another just below this, so as to cover all the face, and leave room only for the eyes to fall bashfully on the ground and pick out the lady's way, secures their modesty. In Egypt a lady may expose all her face except the nose and mouth: these it would be the height of indelicacy to exhibit, and she protects them by a strip of black cotton stuff (black, think you!) about three feet in length and four inches wide. One end of this is fastened by a string passing across her forehead and tied at the back of her head; the cloth falls down over her nose and mouth, and the lady's modesty is secure. It would be well for them to cover all the face, for a more ugly set of ladies I have never met with in any country. The Turkish costume has at least the advantage of making us *imagine* beauty; and many a stranger is put in raptures of love by a pair of flashing eyes glancing on him from beneath the jealous muslins, when, if the covering was removed from the face, he would be ungallant enough to turn with disgust from both face and eyes. The Egyptian ladies show a want of taste in not adopting the Turkish fashion.

At one of the villages, called Negila, we saw some of the dancing girls of the country. They were dressed in the national costume, but were decked off with beads and a great variety of tawdry ornaments, and were disgusting objects. Here is a large granary belonging to the Pasha, with vast stores of every kind; in our way to and from it we were beset with beggars, whose appearance exhibited the utmost wretchedness.

The breeze was fresh and our boats were comfortable, and the banks and the hours glided swiftly along. We had music, we played chess, we read, we chatted, we dozed when we preferred doing so. When meal-time came we slipped the leather trunks together for a table, and brought good appetites to the repast. Cleopatra herself had not a more cheerful party than ours.

Our boatmen often amused us by their agility. The sand banks at the bends of the river are planted with water-melons, and as the flood was beginning to reach the fruit, the inhabitants were busy gathering it in, though it was not yet fully ripe. The Arabs of our boat would often make a dash at these melons, and would have just time to select the best when the owners would rush with cries to the scene of plunder. Down they would all go together into the river, flouncing and tugging; the one for revenge, the other, amid so many witnesses of his exploit, struggling for fame as well as for the water-melon, and pushing it before him with all his might. Sometimes they would grapple, and in the consequent struggle of fierce passions the melon would escape from both, and glide quietly down the river: but generally the boatman succeeded in depositing it safely under the wing of the Cavass.

Towards evening of the 17th we came to a range of sand hills stretching along on our right; they are the commencement of the chain that higher up assists in forming the valley of the Nile. Up to this point our view on either side took in an unbroken level as far as the eye could reach.

The Pyramids.—It was with a thrill of joy that, on the morning of the 18th, as we sat at breakfast, at an exclamation from one of our party, we looked up, and saw before us the Pyramids. We were then twenty-four miles distant, but, though thin and airy-like, they were very distinct. These monuments are most impressive when the spectator is either close beneath them or at a distance like this. On the present occasion they produced a very powerful effect. Their regularity of outline kept their impression clear on the mind as works of art; their shadowy appearance showed them to be very distant, while their great elevation at so remote a point affected the mind strongly with their astonishing vastness. They were in sight, with brief intervals, during the whole day, and to the last were grand and sublime objects.

About noon we found ourselves approaching a spot, in which, from the representations of our Cavass, we had become highly interested. We were near the head of the Delta, a place which Mohammed Ali has selected for a work, which, if successful, will place him far above the constructors of the Pyramids, and make him one of the greatest benefactors that Egypt has ever known. The place opened upon us at length, but on looking up our first impression was one of deep and unqualified disgust. Before us was a busy scene. On the high bank at our left men were appearing in great numbers, with baskets of earth in their hands, and after discharging it down the bank, were retiring to give place for others; but as they stood out in strong relief against the sky, we could see others with whips, which they were using freely upon the poor wretches, whose writhings and accelerated movements gave proof of the smart.

We stopped on this occasion only to take a glance at the *Barage*, for so this place is called; but on our return from Cairo gave it a careful examination, and, by the politeness of the chief engineer, M. Lenon, were furnished with plans and explanations.

The traveller along the Nile is everywhere struck with the great value of irrigation to these lands. Water is frequently raised from the river by wheels turned by oxen or camels, and sometimes by buckets swung at the end of a pole and worked by men; and wherever this is done, we found, even at midsummer, gardens of the most intense verdure and of extreme luxuriance. It may be doubted, indeed, whether the annual floods do not benefit the country quite as much by the irrigation as by their muddy deposites. The object of the Pasha is, by means of dams, to raise the waters of the river to the surface of the adjoining country, and enable the cultivators to carry it by canals to any part, and to irrigate the whole region freely, wherever they may choose, and the place we were now at is the one which he has selected for this great undertaking. The idea of this is not quite a novel one, but was first grasped by the capacious mind of Buonaparte, between whose character and that of the Egyptian monarch, there is, by the way, quite a strong resemblance.

The reader will remember, that of the seven mouths by which the Nile formerly discharged itself, only two remain; one, the eastern, passing into the sea at Damietta; while the other, or western, discharges itself in a similar way near Rosetta. The Delta, lying between them, is of extreme fertility. Should he succeed, not only will the productions of this be greatly increased, but, by leading the waters off east and west of it, he will be able to redeem from the encroaching deserts an immense extent of country now quite abandoned. But difficulties of an alarming kind present themselves. The bottom of the river is loose and unstable; and the shores are so friable, that if an attempt is made to build a dam across it at once, the water will, in the mean time, be working out for itself new channels along the sides. Minds like that of Mohammed Ali, however, are only stimulated, not discouraged, by serious obstacles. He has employed M. Lenon, a French gentleman, and self-taught, but an engineer of superior abilities; and trusting the whole matter to him, has given him, as a nominal superior, Mahmoud Bey, the late governor of Cairo, one of the most wealthy men of the country, and apparently an agreeable coadjutor in this great undertaking. The subjoined plan is copied from one drawn for us by M. Lenon, and the measurements were also furnished by him.

In this *A* represents the river before branching, *B B* the Rosetta, and *C C* the Damietta branch. It is proposed to build a dam across at *E* and *e*, sufficiently high to elevate the waters nearly to the level of the banks, which are here about thirty feet above the usual surface of the river. The engineer commences with cutting the canals *F F* and *f f*, each thirteen hundred feet wide and thirty-two in depth, leaving cross strips at *L* and *l*, until the canal is

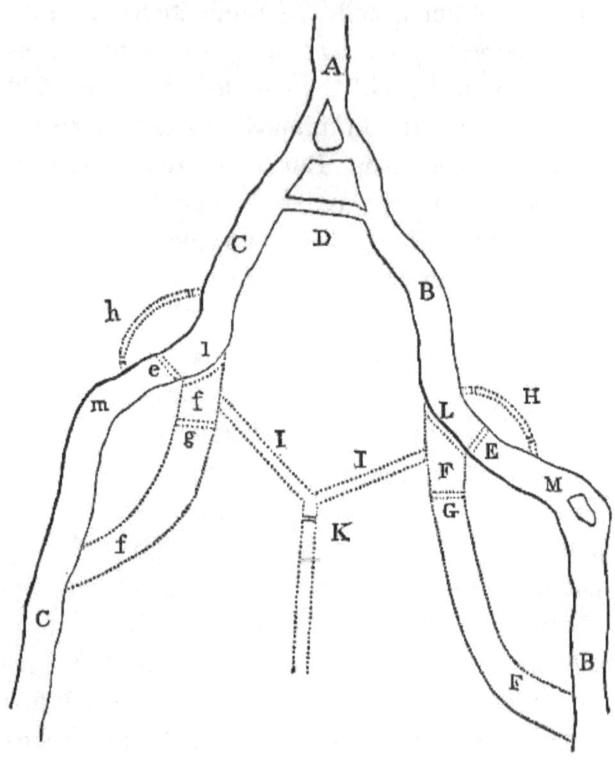

ready for use. Across these canals at *G* and *g* dams are to be constructed forty-one feet in height, including the foundation, and a hundred and twenty-eight in thickness; and in them are to be left sluices of sufficient capacity to allow the passage of the entire river. When these are completed, the sluices are left open, and the cross slips at *L* and *l* being cut away, the river seeks the more direct passage, and leaves the old channels *M* and *m* nearly dry.

Piles are now to be driven into the bottom of the river, and in these the dams *E* and *e* are to be constructed; the former one thousand, and the latter eight hundred and twenty feet in length, each thirty-four feet in height. These being completed, the sluices are to be closed, and the water is thus carried to the required height. By means of the canals *I*, *I* and *K*, it is to be carried over the Delta, and in a similar manner is also led off to the east and west, as far as they may desire. In this latter operation they will be assisted by the nature of the ground; for here, as along the Mississippi and the Ganges, the ground immediately adjoining the stream is higher than at places more remote. At *K* will be a gate for checking the flow of water, and at *H* and *h* small canals, with locks, for boats passing up and down the river. An immense water power will be thus created at the Barage; and it is in contemplation to erect there mills and manufactories of every species; and also to lay out a city after the European plan. Cairo will probably find here a formidable rival.

This is a great undertaking, whether we consider the advantages which it promises or the startling boldness of the design; for in our country we can scarcely form an idea of the difficulties that beset it on every side. Every thing, even the most trifling kind of tool necessary in the operation, has first to be made. Mons. Lenon informed us that he could not have found things less prepared for his hands, if he had commenced operations in the midst of the

4

African deserts. And, in addition, both he and the sovereign have to encounter the ignorance and the prejudices of the jealous officers of the court. They came once to Mohammed Ali, complaining that the engineer was going to needless expense in importing wood for piles when they had trees enough at home, which, if spliced, would answer just as well. "Say you so," replied the Pasha, "the experiment shall be made forthwith;" and looking out into his garden, he ordered trees at once to be cut down, and sent the complainants to see them spliced and arranged to their own satisfaction. This was done; the pile-driver was applied to them, and at the first stroke they flew into shivers. Since that time they have been more cautious in making complaints.

We found 10,000 men at work digging the canals; 6,000 on the Rosetta side and the balance on the Darietta branch. Mons. Lenon says, that if he can get men enough, he will finish it in three years: but at the present mode of working, it will require six or seven. They broke ground three months previous to our visit. One hundred great dredging machines are to be employed, thirty of which are already on the ground. These, as well as most of the tools, have tó be imported from Europe. In the latter they are yet very badly provided. The ground is broken by hoes, and worked into baskets with shovels or fingers, as the case may be: these are carried on the head to the side of the river, and there emptied down its banks. The men are divided into companies of from thirty to fifty each, with one or two drivers, who hasten their operations by a free use of whips.

This inhumanity must not be laid to the charge of the engineer, who has in several ways endeavored to soften the hardships of their condition. We found him erecting hospitals, and conveniences for grinding corn and cooking; and he has prevailed on the Pasha to allow them wages, a thing heretofore quite unknown. They receive each thirty-six paras, or four and a half cents per day, from which six paras are deducted for their board. This in Egypt may be considered pretty handsome wages.

At our second visit we stopped at the tent of Mahmoud Bey, whom we found to be a fine specimen of the Turkish gentleman. He is a venerable looking man, with a splendid white beard falling over his breast. The tent was of mammoth dimensions, carpeted, and ornamented within with stripes of cotton or silken stuffs of gay colors, producing a rich and pleasing effect. His attendants brought fruits, coffee, and pipes with mouth-pieces set in diamonds. At Mons. Lenon's tent we found the chief of the St. Simonians, who had lately been banished from France, and had taken refuge in this country.

Before dismissing the Barage, I should add a fact mentioned to us by Mons. Lenon, that in digging here they have come to bricks at the depth of sixty feet from the present surface of the ground.

But our boat is once more out upon the stream, and we are gazing upward, expecting each moment to see Cairo open to our view. Instead of the city however, came a hurricane, sweeping across from the western desert, and filling the air with a blood-red color and our eyes with sand. We took refuge under one of the high banks, and hugged the shore closely till it had passed. Again a little after sunset we gained the channel, and by the light of a dim moon glided onward towards the city. On our left soon appeared a mass of white houses, forming the the Pasha's summer palace of Shubra: it is surrounded by a garden forming a perfect fairy scene, and is connected with Cairo, three miles distant, by an avenue of noble trees. Of all this on the present occasion we got but an imperfect view; soon after several other large white edifices came in sight, and our imaginations, excited by the glimpses of splendor which we had caught, by the time, and the country, worked each into a scene of eastern enchantment, and we pictured in each of them fair captives from other countries, gazing through the lattice, and sighing for their distant native hills. The boat glided on, and presently our sympathies were interrupted by the glancing lights of the busy little town of Boulac, the port of Cairo. This city, as the reader is perhaps aware, is not situated on the river, but about a mile and a half from it on the west, and has at Boulac a landing-place and store-houses for all goods coming from the north; Old Cairo, a few miles higher up, answering a similar purpose for all vessels coming from up the river.

As it was too late to proceed to the city, we ran our boats across to the shore opposite Boulac, and made fast for the night near a summer palace and gardens. After tea we climbed the high bank over our boats to get once more a view of the Pyramids, now about eight miles distant on the west, but in the moonlight quite distinct.

There was something pleasing in being made to get our first impressions of this ancient region by moonlight. We were now amid the scenes of the earliest grandeur of Egypt. On one side of us, and but a few miles distant, had once stood the great city of Heleopolis; and on the other Memphis. Dim land of shadows and mystery, the pall of death hath been laid upon thee; but instead of concealing, it only makes thy features more sōlemn and more awful.

What a scene of life and bustle was once upon this now silent plain.

Ye buried ages, whose monuments stand yonder in the glimmering light, I have received the wizard's spell, by which the entombed are brought to life once more; and lo, I spread it over you. Arise!

Ha, this is Memphis! And see how it stretches across, and covers all the plain. Towering aloft, is many a grave but magnificent temple; there stretches the deep shadowed and interminable colonade; here frowns the massive tower for defence; and there lies concealed the luxurious bower of the gay. Dwellings of the simple and the astute, the noble and

4*

the lowly serf stretch around, far as the eye can reach, and countless multitudes flock along thy streets; while here, closer to us, in the city of mummies, lie an equally countless number in the searments of the grave. City of many centuries and of stately grandeur, we yield thee the reverence—but what noise is that? the buzz of the multitude has suddenly changed, and now comes the sound of wailing on the ear; and mark, how it increases in intensity, and spreads; and now all the land is filled with woe. The cause—I have it now—their god Apis is dead. A white bull, fed solemnly and reverently in their temples, and to which all the land bowed down in worship, has suddenly expired, and the houses are all filled with alarm and woe.—And here comes a long procession, sweeping onward from one of the gates; these, too, are mourners, and they seem to be touched with even deeper grief. They are carrying a dozen singed cats to the place for solemn embalming, previous to interment, with sacred rites. These animals had been their peculiar household gods, and were kept in a sacred edifice, well fed and carefully tended; but the building took fire, on which the alarmed worshippers rushed into the flames, regardless of themselves, and desirous only of extricating their gods. But the bewildered animals in their fright escaped back to the fire, and numbers were burnt to death; and the procession is now carrying their bodies to be embalmed. And there is another procession passing onward along the streets; they carry in solemn state a dog, their god, now dead, and which they are transporting to the place for sacred washing, preparatory to its removal in state to the city of Busiris for interment. Here, from out the water gate, comes another crowd in the habiliments of woe, and with sounds of grief. They are transporting, perhaps, a great benefactor to their city, some one whose bounties have flowed largely upon the poor, for such the mourners seem to be? No—these are two companies, one carrying a dead shrew-mouse, and the other a dead hawk, to the place of sacred burial. But see, here comes a couple of hogs, hooted at and bewildered; and mark the alarm of the mourners as the animals become entangled among their ranks; and see how they rush to the river, and with their clothes on, plunge in to cleanse their souls from the pollution caused by the swinish contact.*

Ancient Memphis! our spell has been too potent, and wrought too effectually for the safety of our enthusiasm; and so we bid thee good night. Thou art well where thou art—laid low in the dust and almost forgotten.

* That this is not an overdrawn picture of Egyptian superstitions, see the proof in Herodotus, Euterpe.

CHAPTER III.

Cross to Boulac. Splendid hospitality of the government. Our cavalcade. Kindness of Mr. Gliddon. Description of his house. The Baldac.

On the morning of the 20th, the U. S. Consul at Cairo, Mr. Gliddon, Jun., came over, and our boats were soon after removed to the opposite side of the river. And here commenced a series of hospitable attentions on the part of the government, which contributed most materially to our comfort during the time that we remained at Cairo. On the bank we found waiting a European-built carriage, with four white horses, for the ladies ; and for each of the officers a superb horse, with saddles of purple or black silk velvet, richly embroidered in gold, and with housings to correspond. Each horse had a groom, who kept constantly in attendance. These were all furnished from the Pasha's stables in obedience to orders from Alexandria, and each morning, during our stay in the city, were brought to our house, and also during the day whenever we required them. The Commodore's horse was a spirited charger from Tyre, the saddle and housings of purple velvet embroidered in gold, and stirrups of massive silver. About thirty of these were paraded on the bank at our landing; we looked at their flashing eyes and their powerful frame as they pawed the earth, with certain misgivings with regard to ourselves; but concealing these as well as we could, with the help of the grooms we soon found ourselves in the saddles; and then, having for a while measured with our eyes the distance between us and the ground, we turned to look at our cavalcade. It was a very pretty sight; and as we rode on, the natives stopped to gaze at us with that look of wonder and admiration which is so agreeable to a good horseman. The horses, after all, though spirited, were easily managed; and, except a bad habit of using their hinder legs against their neighbor's legs or bodies, were generally peaceable enough. They are taught a singular gait when in rapid motion, which to the natives may seem admirable, but to us was any thing but agreeable; it is as if the animal were to leap up with the whole four feet at once.

Preceded by a Master of Horse, and accompanied by two Chaouishes and five Cavasses, with the grooms, each in the fanciful eastern costume, we wound onward through the streets of Boulac, and, on looking around, felt pleased each with himself, with his horse, and with the world. The suburbs of Boulac and Cairo straggle off so near to each other as to leave but a short interval between; but there is little of note on the way, except the garden where Kleber was basely assassinated. It is elevated above, and faces an open area or parade ground, which we crossed just before entering the gates of the city.

After winding through a great labyrinth of streets, we drew up at length before the house of Mr. Gliddon, Jun. How greatly are we all indebted to the hospitality and the very kind attentions of this gentleman. As soon as he had learnt we were coming, he sent down his large boat for the Commodore and family, and it had reached Atf only an hour after our departure: he now had broken up his bachelor establishment, and threw open his house to us. He planned our visits so that each day brought with it some object of pleasing and useful curiosity; and when our excursions were distant, took upon himself all the trouble of preparation for them. We thanked him warmly at parting, but our hearts continue to thank him more warmly than words can do.

We entered his mansion, and freely took possession of what had been so freely and kindly offered, and then prevailed on Mr. Gliddon to become our guest.

While resting here, I will briefly describe the mansion, as it is a good specimen of the better kind of houses in Cairo. Entering from the street, we found ourselves in a passage with seats on either side, a stopping-place for attendants, porter, or servants, who may come on business. This opened into one angle of a court, enclosed on three sides by the house; and on the fourth by a wall separating it from an outer yard or garden. Turning here to the left, we came presently to a stairway leading to the second story of the edifice. The lower part is occupied by servants, and as store rooms or for similar purposes. At the head of the stairs on the right was a chamber opening into the kitchen and its offices, and on the left a vestibule conducting to the dining-room, a lofty and very airy apartment. The walls and ceiling were ornamented with a variety of carved work in wood, and for windows were lattices in a great variety of handsome patterns: at one side of the room were two large recesses, adjoining projecting lattices; the floors in these were raised about two feet, and furnished with carpets and cushions. And here, after dinner, our company retired to enjoy their Turkish pipes. Ascending to the third story, and turning to the end of the building opposite the dining-room, we came first to a vestibule, the most striking object in which is several mammoth jars of earthenware, filled with Nile water. Through this vestibule we are admitted into the principal apartment of the house. It is about fifty feet in length, and airy and lofty; and raising our eyes to the ceiling, we have here explained to us an object which is apt to puzzle a traveller on his first approach to an Egyptian city. He sees on each of the flat roofs of the town before him something like a low shed, closed at the sides but open in front, and with a very long slanting roof. Here we discover its use, for the elevated ceiling of this room, instead of being flat throughout, towards one end begins to ascend, and rising high above the roof of the house, a large opening is thus made for the admission of air from above. This opening is covered with fanciful lattice-work.

Its utility must be evident in a city where the houses are three or four stories high, and the streets usually not more than four feet in width. Entering this long room, the visitor finds each end of it occupied by a platform about a foot in height, covered with Turkey carpets, and lined with broad, luxurious ottomans. These platforms are separated at the centre of the room by a strip of marble pavement about twelve feet wide; at one end of which, opposite to us as we enter, is a recess with marble shelves for confectionary, pipes, and for supporting the priceless and most tempting Baldac. The Baldac, the reader, after this encomium, will be surprised to hear is only an earthen drinking vessel, in shape of a Florence flask, though about three times as large; it is unglazed, and the water oozing through its thin sides, evaporates, and produces a delicious coolness. I do not know any piece of furniture that, if taken from the inhabitants, would be so much regretted as the Baldac. Each one, as he needs, drinks at once from the Baldac, five or six of them being always kept ready for use. Water for the whole city is brought from the Nile on the backs of camels or mules.

We return to our description of the house, which, however, is nearly completed. The remainder of the third tier is appropriated to sleeping apartments, and a fourth range over them is devoted to a similar purpose. The roof is flat, but irregular. Nearly all the windows in this building look into the court: but in most of the buildings there are latticed windows looking into the narrow streets ; sometimes they project a little, so as to give the fair inmates an opportunity of seeing all that is passing below, without being seen themselves. Occasionally we catch a glimpse of a dark eye or a jewelled hand, through the openings of the fanciful but jealous lattice.

CHAPTER IV.

Visit to the Governor of Cairo. Court of the Mamelukes. Their massacre. Schools in the Citadel. Court of Justice. Pala[illegible] o the Pasha. View from it. The "City of Tombs." A human monster. Plain of Memphis. Heliopolis. Mosque of the bloody baptism. Joseph's Well. Mint. Manufactory of Arms. The Citadel. "The Lions."

EA[illegible]LY in the morning of the 21st we found the grooms with our horses in the court below, and after breakfast mounted for a visit of ceremony to the Abdi Effendi, the governor of the city. The carriage was waiting in an adjoining bazaar, where it [illegible]ad been compelled to stop by the narrowness o[illegible] the streets; and here our cavalc[illegible]e was formed in the following order: 1. Two Cavasses; 2. The carriage; 3. Eight Cavasses; 4. Two Chaouishes; 5. A Master of the Horse; 6. Dragoman; next the Commodore and Consul, and after them the remaining officers of the party. Having traversed the whole length of the city, we began, near its southern outskirts, to ascend, and presently found ourselves before the frowning walls of the citadel of Cairo. Here, in this strong eyrie, well guarded both by nature and art, the Pasha of Egypt has built his palace, and gathered his treasures, and formed his arsenal for arms. The citadel stands on a spur from the range of Kebel Mokattam, the mountains that, stretching along on the East, help to form the valley of the Nile. Here they [illegible]ake a bend and stretch off far to the eastward; and at the angle, on an irregular platform thrown off from it, the citadel was built, or at least enlarged to its present dimensions, in the 12th century, by the famous Saladin. It is a place of great strength, and may be considered as the key of all the upper parts of Egypt. On passing the heavy exterior gateway, we found ourselves in the court, where, twenty-five years ago, by order of Mohammed Ali, was perpetrated the bloody massacre of the Mamelukes. It is of irregular shape, with high walls on one side, and on the others steep ascents or precipices, surmounted by ramparts, above which again are heavy buildings, and among them the ruins of Saladin's palace. It was a place well chosen for such a butchery, and the whole plan of operations was strikingly characteristic of the man.

It will, perhaps, be recollected by the reader that the Mamelukes, as a distinct body, owed their origin to Saladin, who, distrusting his native troops, formed a body-guard of slaves, procured by purchase or capture from the countries bordering on the Caspian. They rose gradually under successive sultans, and all the fortresses at length being trusted to them, they concluded to turn the power to their own use, and through their Beys became the governors of Egypt. Various, after this, were their changes of fortune; the hardy soldiers, being generally successful in the field, but circumvented by their cunning adversaries in the council-room. The French found in them most obstinate and determined opposers; and when, at the close of this war, the British arms were triumphant, Lord Hutchinson demanded of the Sultan of Constantinople, to whom the country was yielded, the restitution of the Mamelukes to their former privileges. He promised compliance, but had determined on the extinction of this race of dangerous subjects. The Turkish admiral, who was sent for this purpose, first enticed a great number of them to a pleasure excursion in boats off Aboukir, and his ships opening fire upon them, the greater portion were destroyed. War with their race being thus declared, Mohammed Ali, then first rising into notice, was sent with a force against them, but was defeated and compelled to retreat. This was the origin of the inveteracy of Mohammed Ali towards the Mamelukes.

On the invasion of Egypt by the English in 1807, the Beys united with the rising Pasha; but it was only a momentary truce; and the defeat of the English, giving him secure possession of Egypt, sealed at the same time the fate of his too trustful allies. He immediately formed a plan for the total destruction of the Mamelukes. His son Tousson was about this time preparing to lead an army against the Wahabees, and as this was a religious war, it was determined to invest him with the command under circumstances of unusual splendor. The Mameluke Beys were invited to the ceremony, which was to commence in the citadel. They came, led by their chief, Chahyn Bey; and a more splendid cavalcade never filed in through the portals of this fortress. They amounted to 470 men, on horseback, together with about an equal number of attendants of the same race on foot. Their reception was flattering. The Pasha addressed them individually, and with a bland aspect and smiles, welcomed them to the festivities. At length it was necessary to form a procession, and the Mamelukes were honored by being put in a body near the head of it: they filed down and entered this rocky court; but when their whole body had gained it, the gates were suddenly shut both in front and rear, and they found themselves cruelly entrapped. The heights above were in a moment covered with the Pasha's soldiers, and a deadly fire was poured down on them. Rage and execration were in vain: they were coolly shot down till not an individual remained alive. One of the Beys escaped by spurring his horse up the steep outer wall; in the descent the animal was dashed to pieces, but the rider was unhurt.

This was the end of the Mamelukes. On the following day the soldiers rushed into the city, and under pretext of searching for more victims, plundered a large part of it before the Pasha and his son durst venture out to repress their fury.

Our horses, on reaching this bloody court, seemed themselves to be seized with the very spirit of violence; for pricking their ears, they rushed up the

5*

steep ascent with headlong speed, and, whirling through Saladin's court, and then through a larger one, brought us up at length in front of the governor's palace. It is a long building and spacious, but is otherwise by no means remarkable. Abdi Effendi has been in England and France, and speaks the language of the latter country fluently. He received us with great politeness, and entertained us with the usual eastern hospitalities. His questions with regard to our own country were pertinent, and evinced a good knowledge of its laws and institutions. He spoke in terms of high admiration of his own sovereign; and indeed Mohammed Ali seems to have the faculty of creating a strong attachment for himself in all his officers. The governor said that if the Pasha could live twenty years longer, he would make Egypt more civilized and more prosperous than it has ever yet been; but added, that he stood all alone, and greatly needed some one who could be a second self to him.

From the audience-hall we were taken to visit a number of schools in the same building; they occupy a number of rooms, and contained altogether four hundred youths, preparing for public employments in the country. As far as I could judge, they seemed to be awkwardly conducted. At the extreme end of the building we came to the Hall of Justice, where, on an ottoman and all alone, sat the judge, a man of prodigious corporeal dimensions. He was at this time unemployed, but our attention was drawn to a new mat with which the floor was covered. It had just been put down in place of one that, a few days before, had been worn through by the writhings of a poor wretch, who had been bastinadoed here; the punishment having followed close on the heels, if not of justice, at least of the culprit.

The adjoining side of the court into which this palace looks, is formed by a large palace of Mohammed Ali, to which, in the course of sight-seeing, we were next conducted. It is quite new, and in some parts not quite finished; and is more remarkable for the airy and spacious character of the rooms than for any beauties of architecture. Indeed, all the palaces which we visited in Egypt, though cool and spacious, are marked by great simplicity. A hall of great width passes across at the centre of the building, and is intersected by another of somewhat narrower dimensions, running lengthwise; and thus at each angle a chamber is formed. These chambers are carpeted, and have the most luxurious ottomans passing quite around. These, with sometimes a glass lustre suspended from the lofty ceiling, constitute the only furniture. In the palace, which we were now visiting, the ottomans were covered with the richest French silks, with raised figures in beautiful patterns worked on them. In front of the seats hung down an impenetrable veil of silken tassels.

And now let us rest ourselves for a while on these

tempting seats, here by these lofty windows, from which we may look down over all the wide-spread landscape. The ladies of the Commodore's family have gone to visit the Sultana, and it will be some time before they return; and a better place for a view over all the city and the country beyond, we could not desire. The palace is built on the highest part of the citadel, and enjoys, indeed, a very extensive prospect, and even at this sultry hour we are here fanned by a delightful breeze.

There, look below where the mountains of Mokattam turn off towards the east, you see between them and the city a great number of buildings of remarkable and light Saracenic architecture, standing alone on the sandy waste. This is "The city of Tombs;" the burying-place of the nobles of modern Cairo. Many of these edifices, consisting, as you perceive, of domes supported by tall slender columns, are the tombs of the Mamelukes when their race was in power; but there you observe one larger than all the rest, surmounted by three domes, and remarkable for its light but rich style of architecture; that is the Mausoleum belonging to the family of Mohammed Ali. Its three chambers are enriched with tombs of Italian marble, and their marble floors are covered with Persian or Turkey carpets. Some of his wives and two of his children are buried here; and every Friday (the Moslem sabbath) their tombs are covered with Cashmere shawls. Here lies also buried the infant daughter of Ibrahim Pasha, taken off in innocent childhood; and close by is the recently interred body of Defterden Bey, a very tiger in cruelty, and as vile a monster as has ever lived. He was sent to this country when it was still subject to the Sultan, to watch the Pasha and collect the revenue of his master at Constantinople: but it is supposed that a 'arge part of it went no further than his own pockets; for in a short time he grew immensely rich. He was, indeed, at length inferior in wealth only to the Pasha himself. He owned the garden in which the brave Kleber was assassinated. He was often in power; and his favorite mode of punishment was to bury the criminal up to his neck in quick-lime, and thus leave him to perish. On one occasion, his farrier having neglecte to shoe a favorite horse according to his directions, he ordered the shoes to be nailed to the feet of the smith himself. The man died in a few hours in the greatest agonies.

On another occasion, when the Pasha's son Ishmael had been treacherously burnt in his tent in upper Egypt, Defterden Bey was sent to examine into the affair and punish the culprits. He called the inhabitants of the district together, to the number of 10,000, and in revenge burnt them all to death, including women and children; and then plundered the country.

He kept a pet lion, which by some means or other he had attached or awed into gentleness to himself; and one of his amusements consisted in throwing meat to the animal, and then ordering his attendants to take it away; on which the animal often flew at them and tore them to pieces.

This is only a portion of the inhuman acts of which he was guilty; but the earth at last grew weary of the monster, and his royal master seems to have grown weary of him also; for one day, after drinking coffee with the Pasha, he went home, was immediately taken sick, and died. Mohammed Ali seized on his immense property, and then honored the body by a burial place in his own tomb.

But observe now that river, how peacefully it glides along, unceasing in its flow, and ever distributing comfort and happiness to the dense population along its banks. Such are Heaven's dealings to us. What a contrast to this has ever been presented here in men's dealings towards each other. Say, is man still in the image of his maker?

Our eyes glance on the other side of the river, over the site of Memphis. The western mountains there recede about eight miles from the stream, and it is supposed that the whole of this was covered by its magnificent temples and its dwellings; now the very site of it is disputed by some persons; at all events its ruin is so complete, that objects can no longer be distinguished. Just below it is the Plain of Mummies, still tenanted, as it has been for ages, by forms of human beings that move not and speak not. Men there are at peace with each other. Over this well-peopled but silent city of the dead, we see the small Pyramids of Sakhara; and further down, at a distance of six or eight miles, arise the stupendous structures, the Pyramids of Ghizeh. I have never looked at them without a feeling of awe.

Between us and them, on the western bank of the river, is the little village of Ghizeh, from which they take their modern name; and still nearer to us, on the eastern bank, is the village of Old Cairo, now worthy of note only as the port for boats from upper Egypt. Between it and the larger city of its name you are noticing some hillocks, that seem remarkable objects on this level plain. They are composed of pottery and other rubbish from the city; and your memory will supply you with another example of such hillocks in the neighborhood of Rome. In the latter city the merchants have dug into the base, and formed wine-cellars, which are said to answer admirably well. Near these of old Cairo is also an ancient aqueduct, a fine looking object on the landscape, but useless, as it is now in ruins.

And now look directly north, about eight miles, and you see—no, you cannot see a solitary pillar standing on the open and deserted plain. There is not even a vestige of a ruin near it; and yet there stood in ancient times the great and the learned, as well as the splendid, city of Heliopolis, or "The City of the Sun." It was of vast extent, and had many large temples; among them one dedicated to the sun, with a mirror so disposed as, during the whole day, to reflect the rays of that luminary into the body of the edifice. Thither came the scholars of ancient times to drink from the streams of knowledge; there Herodotus acquired his lore; and, above all, there Plato studied; and there, too, it is supposed that Moses "was taught in all the learning of the Egyptians." But neither grandeur nor knowledge itself could avail to save it; and of its many splendid structures, but a single column remains to mark its site.

But here at our feet is Cairo, teeming with life, and with the human passions all at work; and yet it seems like a city of the dead. We hear no sound, no cry; life seems to be stagnant there; but it is not. The surface is not greatly ruffled, but beneath it the passions are fermenting: who shall follow them in their various changes and their devious windings? But we will not philosophise. Here, just below us, is the mosque of Sultan Hassan; and, as our time is short, we will hasten to occupy ourselves with its singular history; a history that has a strong dash of the Arabian Nights, and yet is solemn truth, that may be told in open day. This is the largest, and in its architecture the most imposing mosque in Cairo. It is massy, and ornamented with heavy mouldings; and though of the Saracenic style, is a solid and substantial building. And now for its history.

About two centuries ago lived Sultan Hassan, a sovereign prosperous and beloved, but withal somewhat eccentric. He had every thing to make him contented, but there rose up in him, by and by, a strong desire to travel. He longed to see foreign lands; to study the living world; to hear the sages of other climes; and, if possible, to turn philosopher himself. The royalty that acted as a barrier to the gratification of his wishes, became at length odious to him, and he determined for a while to lay it aside, and to travel as a private individual. He sent, therefore, for his prime minister or Vizier, and after a confidential interview, delivered to him in trust, during the sovereign's absence, the sceptre of honor and th. throne of state. He himself left the kingdom, and all traces of him were speedily lost. He now assumed the appearance of a merchant, and under this character travelled through many and far distant lands. He went wherever curiosity enticed him, toiling on from place to place, in hopes that at each it would still its unquiet yearnings and be satisfied; he studied man in every variety of character; he conversed with the wise men of every country, and at length he became a wise man himself, which was evinced by a resolution to return forthwith and be contented at home. Curiosity, he found, only gathered strength by each gratification; the world and its notions were a greater puzzle to him than at the beginning; and what little he knew of them, made him afraid to examine further; and as to wisdom itself, he found it every where less valued than money, and was astonished to see even himself, by and by, deserting the pursuit of it for the pursuit of wealth. He was rapidly successful in his dealings, and grew very rich; and now, ending where he had begun in his boyhood, with believing that Egypt was the best and happiest country in the world, he set out forthwith on his return.

But a disappointment awaited him. His faithless Vizier, concluding that the power which he found so agreeable for a short time, would be agreeable through life, had established himself firmly on the throne; and the old Sultan, on reaching the confines of his country, found that the very name of Hassan had been interdicted to his people, and that he was apparently forgotten. He kept his disguise, and, safe in the changes which time and exposure, and a long beard had wrought on his face, he travelled on, and found himself at length once more in Cairo. The wealthy merchant soon had many friends, and his business continuing to prosper, he applied by and by for permission to erect a mosque, as an act of thanksgiving to Allah for his numerous favors. The request was granted, and the foundations of this mosque, closely adjoining the citadel, were laid with the usual ceremonies. Under pretext of strengthening the edifice in so unstable a soil, he laid the groundwork strong and deep, and secured it moreover with numerous arches or vaults. The building rose, and the populace came in multitudes to look at the huge edifice and praise the piety of the liberal-handed merchant, who before long found that he had established a throne, at least in the hearts of the people. He was aiming, however, at a more substantial throne. He had by this time filled the deep vaults with men, whom by liberal pay he had engaged to wait there for his bidding, and whom he daily practised with the scimitar, till there was not one among them who could not at a blow sever without disarranging the light tuft of down, the acme of a Turkish swordsman's ambition. The edifice was finished, and a grand building, as you perceive, it really is; and the new courtiers, in their way back and forth between the palace and the city, stopped to applaud the zeal of the pious merchant; nor dreamed for a moment of the pandemonium beneath. It is customary when a mosque is consecrated to give it also a name; and this having now been finished, a day was appointed for these ceremonies; and as the edifice was so highly ornamental to the city, the Sultan himself consented to grace the occasion with his presence. He came with a great retinue of courtiers and a line of guards; and splendid indeed was the scene within the proud and stately edifice. The merchant himself was placed in a conspicuous and an honorable station. The ceremony commenced, and the prayers were said; and the Mufti at length, turning to the merchant, bade him pronounce the name by which his pious offering to Allah should be known. He rose from his seat, and while all leaned forward to catch the sound, he replied, "Call it Sultan Hassan." The multitude started as if each had been bitten by a serpent, and the Mufti grew pale; but recovering himself, demanded if he had heard him aright. "Yes," he cried, as a curtain rose at one end and disclosed the name in large letters of gold: "call it by my name, by that of your sovereign, Sultan Hassan;" and at the words, his myrmidons, who had been led up from the vaults and distributed through the church, falling on the astonished usurper and his train, put them all to the sword. From thence they rushed to the citadel, of which they got possession; and before the sun went down, Sultan Hassan was once more proclaimed sovereign of Egypt.

Such was the history of this building, as it was narrated to us on the spot. One of the Cavasses offered to show me the interior if I would disguise myself like a Turk; but as I felt no disposition to put my own neck to hazard in this mosque of the bloody baptism, I satisfied myself with looking at the outer walls.

Close adjoining it are some lions, however, which are worthy of a visit. They are just from the deserts, and are very different from the abused and broken-spirited animals exhibited in our country and in Europe. They are confined in a room of no great dimensions, and are fastened only by a chain attached to the wall; and if any man, who calls himself one of the lords of creation, would meditate on the justice of his vaunted title, I would advise him to go and do it in this den of lions.

The ladies of our party returned, after an absence of about an hour, greatly delighted with their visit;

they were, I believe, the first foreign ladies ever permitted to enter this part of the palace, and were allowed to depart only on the promise of a longer visit as soon as circumstances would admit.

From the Pasha's palace we proceeded to visit "Joseph's Well," a deep pit for supplying the citadel with water, dug, however, not by the Joseph of our Scriptures, but by Saladin, whose name, I believe, was also Yousef or Joseph. It consists of two shafts, the upper about 150 feet in depth and 45 in diameter, with a winding gallery around, separated from the shaft by a wall pierced with openings for the admission of light. This is all cut out of the solid rock. The lower shaft is about 120 feet in depth, making altogether 270 feet. The water is raised to the top of the first shaft by means of oxen, and poured into a reservoir, whence it is carried up in a similar manner to a reservoir in the citadel; but it is brackish, and used for drinking only in times of siege.

Mounting our horses once more, we returned through the court of the Mamelukes, and at its further extremity, within the citadel, alighted to examine an extensive manufactory of fire-arms. They first took us to a foundry of brass cannon in active operation, and thence to a suite of rooms where some hundreds of native workmen were employed manufacturing muskets, pistols, swords, and gun-carriages, &c., in rolling sheet copper for the navy, and in making bolts and sheathing nails. They manufacture here 36,000 muskets annually, with pistols and sabres to correspond. The various parts of the musket are made exactly of the same size, so that if any part is injured, it can be immediately replaced. The different branches are superintended by foreigners, mostly from France; but the master workmen are all natives of the country, many of them having been sent abroad to qualify them for these stations.

The mint is also kept in the citadel, and on a subsequent visit they took us over every part, explaining the whole process of money-making, and striking for us impressions on paper of all their coins. The machinery is old and clumsy, but they had just imported a new set made of cast iron from England, which they were about putting into operation. We found the superintendant of the mint, an old man with a superb white beard, poring over a great atlas just printed at Constantinople, and sadly puzzled with its labyrinths. He seemed quite grateful for a little assistance we were able to give him in comprehending them.

CHAPTER V.

Visit to the Cotton factories. Iron founderies. Palace of Ibrahim Pasha. English garden on an island in the Nile. Stables of Ibrahim Pasha. Arabian horses. Bazaars. Slave market. Madhouse. The maniac butcher.

THE Egyptian monarch is fond of having his improvements inspected by foreigners, and our own inclinations being in no wise averse to this, we gave the 22d to an examination of a variety of objects of this kind bordering on the Nile. Leaving the city by the Boulac gate, we turned soon after down the avenue leading to Shubra, and, after pursuing it for a mile and a half, crossed some open gardens, and were then shown into a large inclosure containing the summer palace and grounds of a nephew of Mohammed Ali, and one of the officers of his court. It is a pretty place, and as the day was growing hot, we particularly enjoyed a marble kiosk, with fountains tossing their delicious waters into the air. From this we proceeded to one of those large edifices that in our moonlight sail up the river had fixed themselves so strongly on our fancy ; but in the broad daylight, instead of a magnificent palace, with a scene of Eastern enchantment spread all around it, we found a steam cotton factory, puffing and blowing, and sending jets of smoke from every one of its numerous tall chimnies. But as we all called ourselves philanthropists, we considered it, or tried to consider it, a very pleasing sight; and our gratification was really great, as we proceeded through the establishment and inspected its very extensive operations. The principal building is for spinning and weaving, and I counted here more than one hundred looms of cast iron, just imported from England; in this they were just putting into operation a steam engine of twenty horse power, also of English manufacture; the floor of the second story in this edifice is supported by cast iron columns, and every part is not only neat and convenient, but also substantial. It is superintended by a Scottish gentleman, Mr. Galloway. Attached to this is a yard for bleaching, a machine manufactory, and a long building for printing the cottons. The printing is all done by blocks, both made and worked by the natives, who in this business, we were informed, show great aptitude and skill. The patterns, copied mostly from the French, are handsome; and the colors are said to be enduring. The price of labor here is almost nothing, and the Egyptian Pasha has only to persevere, in order to succeed in all the Eastern markets. A difficulty presented itself in the expense of fuel for his steam engines, but his enterprise seems to be in a fair way to surmount even this. Some explorations on Mount Lebanon, conducted by his orders, have lately resulted in the discovery of a mine of bituminous coal, at a place called Carnayl, on the western side of the mountain, about four miles from the sea, and twelve northward from Beirout. Where the stratum first presented itself, it was three feet three inches in thickness, and the coal was too much mixed with impurities to be fit for steam power; but when we left Beirout, there were indications that it would increase both in quantity and purity. Mr. Brattell, an English gentleman employed by the Pasha in these investigations, thinks there is coal also on the eastern side of Mount Lebanon, and is sanguine also in expectations of discovering lead and iron ores. There can be no doubt that the latter is very abundant in that mountain.

From the manufactory we returned to rest ourselves in the cool kiosk, where we were hospitably served also with fruits and other refreshments.

Returning from this along the banks of the river, we were conducted, near the outskirts of Boulac, to a large foundery for iron cannon and other castings; it contains, I believe, three furnaces; but t midday on the 22d of July, in Egypt, we felt little disposition to be sticking our heads among iron furnaces; and instead of this useful curiosity, hastened to put all the Baldacs we could find in requisition, declaring unanimously that we had never met with any fluid so delicious as the water of the Nile. At Boulac are also manufactories for cotton handkerchiefs, and for clothing for the army and navy, as well as store-houses filled with their productions, which we were invited to visit; but the heat had become so oppressive, as to leave little disposition to bodily effort, and, mounting our steeds, we passed through Boulac, and hastened to deposite our persons in the large and cool palace of Ibrahim Pasha.

This palace, quite a new building, is situated on the outskirts of Old Cairo, about two miles above Boulac, and a few hundred yards from the banks of the river, from which it is separated by well-shaded pleasure-grounds. The halls or passages by which it is crossed in the manner already described, are here unusually spacious; and the stairway being also wide, it has an air not only of magnificence, but of delicious coolness. In the Audience hall a fountain gushes out of the wall, about six feet above the pavement, and forming a succession of small cascades, at length reaches the floor, where it is received into a large marble basin; from this it meanders in a marble channel to the centre of the hall, and spreads out into a small lake about three feet in depth. Along the channel are numerous fish, sculptured in marble, in various attitudes.

The usual hospitable refreshment of sherbet, pipes, and coffee, was presented us here, and, seated on the luxurious ottomans at the end of the longitudinal hall, enveloped in odorous fumes, and listening to the waterfall, or watching the natives, who, in their picturesque costumes, were passing back or forward, we spent the time till the heat of the day had passed.

About two hundred yards from this is the island at the head of which, in an edifice erected for it, is situated the celebrated Nilometer, or graduated column, for measuring the depth of the river, and from which report is made when the river has attained an elevation sufficient to ensure a favorable season. When this is done, the banks which restrain the water from flowing into the canal leading to Cairo, are cut down, the water flows in, floods the squares ot the city, and then ensues a season of hilarity and merry-making throughout the whole city.

The island contains about seven or eight acres, and, until lately, presented nothing remarkable; but it is now a very fascinating spot. About four years since, Mohammed Ali employed an English horticulturist, Mr. Trail, to put it in order. He built a stone wall around it, reaching from below low water-mark, to a height above the greatest elevation of the floods, and had machinery constructed for irrigating it by means of canals, at all seasons of the year. It is laid out partly in regular plots, but chiefly in the English garden style, with winding walks, serpentine streams, lakes, grottoes, rustic bridges, glades, and lawns; and, what in Egypt is rather curious, in one place is ornamented with *artificial* ruins of temples and similar objects. The size of the trees here are a proof of the astonishing fecundity of the soil when irrigation is well supplied; for, although the time has been so short, the ground is covered with trees thirty and forty feet in height; the shrubbery is luxuriant, and embosoms many delicious retreats from the sultry sun. They have collected here all the plants natural to the country, together with many of foreign origin. Egypt, however, does not produce a great variety of flowers or useful shrubs. Mr. Trail has a house at one side of the garden, in which we were hospitably entertained.

On returning to the palace some of our party returned home, while the rest of us proceeded to visit the stables of Ibrahim Pasha. Th's warrior chief is a great lover of horses; and in the course of his expeditions into Syria and Arabia, has had the best opportunities of making a collection; and he appears to have profited by them.

The Master of Horse, who came to receive us, informed us that the whole collection amounts to eight hundred, among which are many of pure Arabian blood; but that the best were either out at pasture, or with the Pasha's army in Syria. At our visit there were about four hundred animals of various breeds in the stables; and on entering we were presented with a spectacle of ferocity bordering on the terribly sublime. Whether it is a matter of instinct or education I cannot say, but they no sooner caught sight of our foreign dress, and heard our language, than each animal seemed changed into a fury; their eyes flashed, their manes seemed to rise, they kicked, and writhed, and tried every means to break loose; snorting, and showing in every part of their distorted features the most savage rage. Their keepers went among them, and succeeded in establishing a little more quiet; but it was really curious to see the malice which they seemed to bear towards us to the last.

Among them were eight full blooded Arabs of a superior breed; and I suppose I shall suffer in the opinion of all amateurs of horses, when I say that I was disappointed in them. Their limbs are well formed for activity, but their necks appeared to me too short and heavy for the highest kind of beauty; but I will add that I am no great judge of such matters, and ought to offer an opinion with diffidence. We saw here the horse that had carried Ibrahim in all his wars with the Wahabees; it is a gray, and is a handsome animal; but is now thirty years old, and, though well fed and kindly treated, is never used. There were one or two others in the collection similarly situated; one I noticed, so old as to be scarcely able to stand, and the picture of decrepitude. Some horses from Dongola, in Upper Egypt, were striking animals; they were large and very powerful, with glossy coats of pure jet black. The Arabians were of various colors: white, bay, and brown. Among them were numerous colts and some mules; we saw also a donkey, of a white color, for which the Pasha had been offered $600. It was the largest animal of this description that I have ever seen. A mule by an Arab mare was also a beautiful object; it had legs like those of an antelope, and an eye of fire. They informed us that two strong men were required to manage it.

July 23d. Most of this day was spent in loung-

7

ing among the bazaars. Some of these are wide, and the roof or covering being elevated to a height of forty or fifty feet, they are not only airy, but the effect on the eye is good; but most of them are not at all remarkable, while the generality of the streets in Cairo are, I think, narrower than usual, even in Turkish cities. Provisions are abundant in them, and very cheap. Passing one day along the bazaars, we turned into a court adjoining them to take a look at the depository and market for slaves. The court is not large, but is surrounded with houses of irregular shape, swarming with slaves, tier back of tier, as far as our eyes could reach. They were all of a jet black, with smooth glossy skins; and the hair of the females was worked up by a greasy substance into long ringlets, which fell on either side of the head. Their cheeks were in some instances marked by scars in regular figures, evidently designed to be an addition to their charms. As we passed among them, they put on their best looks, and by smiles and gestures invited us to become their purchasers; to which, I believe, we felt not the least inclined, though their price was extremely low.

Taking a Cavass on another occasion, I went off to visit the madhouse, of which I had heard some singular accounts. After threading a great labyrinth of streets, he told me that we were approaching it, and that it would be necessary for him to take them some provisions as a kind of admittance fee. So I furnished him with money, and he filled his arms with the cakes, somewhat like a thick pancake, which are the common food of the lower classes in Cairo. On this introduction the keeper admitted us, and I found myself in an open square or court, surrounded by a stone edifice in which were the cells of the maniacs. It was a sight not only mortifying to the pride of man, but adapted to harrow up all his feelings of sympathy. The cells were not more than seven or eight feet square, with uneven floors of stone or earth, and were grated on the side towards the court. Their inmates were sometimes fastened with chains, but sometimes at liberty to make the most of the narrow precincts of their cells. They were quite in a state of nature, filthy, and often covered with sores; and seemed, poor creatures, to be badly fed. On seeing the cakes, their countenances brightened; they stretched out their emaciated arms between the iron bars, and on being supplied, began to devour rather than eat, till in a short time our supply was exhausted. I turned, saddened and sickened, from the sight.

A short time before our visit, a butcher was brought and shut up here in a state of complete and dangerous madness. After some time he grew more gentle, and by and by was sometimes permitted by the keeper to leave his cell, and to go at large through the court. One morning the latter, on returning to his duty, was met at the gate by this man, with an expression of joy on his face, and invited to come in and make a purchase of his meat, which he said he could highly recommend. The keeper, on entering, found, to his surprise, in one corner of the court a rude imitation of shambles, well furnished with meat cut up in a variety of forms. He gazed with astonishment, and a horrible idea now suddenly crossing his mind, he began a hasty examination of the cells. He was right. The half-starved wretch had murdered one of the other maniacs, and dragged the body piecemeal through the bars; and it was the dismembered carcass of his comrade that was suspended on the shambles.

CHAPTER VI.

Preparations to visit the Pyramids. Audience of leave with the Governor of Cairo. Visit of the ladies of our party to the Sultana. Description of the Harem.

THE 24th was a day of bustle, a large portion of it being spent at home, superintending the storing of wines and fruits, the cooking of fowls and eggs, and the preparation of all the *et ceteras* that would be required by a few days' residence on the desert.

The plan, as formed by our good friend, Mr. Gliddon, was to make an early start on the morrow, to the great Pyramids of Ghizeh, thence proceed to the Pyramids of Sakhara, sleep in tents in their neighborhood; on the following morning examine the site of Memphis, and then going on board his boat, which would be directed to meet us there, to drop down the river, stopping by the way at the military and naval school at Toura.

As it was the Commodore's intention, after this excursion, to start immediately on his return to the ship, he had sent on the 23d, to the governor of Cairo, to say that he would this day have an audience of leave; and the ladies of his family also had despatched a messenger to the Sultana, stating that they would make the visit which, on the previous occasion, they had promised her.

7*

Accordingly, at 9 A. M. the party proceeded to the citadel in the same order as before, where the officers were received by the governor in a larger and more magnificent hall than at the former visit. While the usual compliments of pipes, coffee, and sherbet were offered, the Commodore made the governor his acknowledgments "for the honor and great attention shown him as an American officer, and to the officers with him; stating that their civilities had left us nothing to desire, and that, individually, he felt under great obligations to his Excellency the Pasha, a lively remembrance of whose kindness he should ever retain." To this the governor replied, that he acted only according to his instructions, and was happy in being the instrument of carrying them into effect; the American commander was considered the guest of the Pasha, who, if he had been present, would have been able to do more, and would doubtless have ordered a palace for our accommodation. To this there was added much on both sides that was complimentary, if that can be called compliment on our part, which proceeded from real admiration and truly grateful feeling.

From the governor's hall, the party retired to the palace of Mohammed Ali, and were again served with coffee, &c.; the mouth-pieces of the pipes served on this occasion being richly set with diamonds; the coffee cups were set in fillagree work of gold, enriched also with the same precious stones. Some hours were spent in smoking, and in visiting the interesting objects in and about the citadel not seen before; while, in the mean time, the ladies of the Commodore's family were making their visit to those of the Harem.

I am allowed to insert here an account of this visit from a letter, written without the least idea of publication, but which places before us, in graphic language, scenes which strangers were never before allowed to witness. Our interest in reading it takes a melancholy character from the reflection that the accomplished youthful writer is now an inmate of the tomb.

* * * * * *

"We are the only Christians who have ever been admitted into the Pasha's Harem. We were there twice. The first time was a mere visit, but the second was to spend the day. I must endeavor to describe it for you. At the gate we were received by a dozen male attendants, who led us to the garden gate, where we found three girls playing upon different Arab instruments, while two others were singing and two dancing, magnificently dressed in crimson and blue cloth, embroidered in gold—the full pantaloons hanging over the foot, just allowing an embroidered slipper to be seen—a jacket, tight to the shape, without sleeves, open a little upon the chest, where appeared a chemise of blue or white gauze, closely spangled, sleeves of the same, hanging large and full to the elbow, and down behind in a dozen plaits; and on the side and top of the head, large sprigs of diamonds. A sash of gold tissue, with a deep gold fringe, finished the dress. These pretty creatures preceded us to the palace door, where we were met like old friends by the Sultana, her maids of honor and attendants, to the number of a hundred at least. The great hall of state into which we were ushered, was an immense one, lined and floored with white marble; in the centre a basin fifteen feet square, and a large fountain, from which the clearest water was playing; the ceiling richly painted and gilt; one side of the hall lined with ottomans of white silk, embroidered in gold, and a beautiful Persian carpet spread in front of them. As soon as we were seated, coffee and pipes were handed to us. The Sultana is about 35 years old, with a fine face, though the eye is stern—dignified and affable in her manners. Her dress was a chali, made in Turkish style, only more closed over the neck. On the head was a sort of skull cap, formed entirely of diamonds. Around this was twisted an embroidered kerchief, and on the left side, down near the ear, was placed a sprig of flowers, made of enormous diamonds: earrings, a single pair, shaped like a drop, as large as the end of my little finger, and on her little finger was a most superb diamond ring. Around us stood the hundred attendants, dressed in colored silks; and every one, even of the lowest rank, with heads covered with diamonds. The pipe stems and sockets of the coffee cups were also covered with these precious stones. Such a glitter I never saw before. An

Armenian woman, who spoke Italian, was there as our interpretess. Our gloves and buckles excited their admiration, indeed our whole dress. I don't know that I was ever so hauled and pulled about as I was that day.

"We were taken all over the palace, and it vied throughout in elegance with the great hall. At half past 12, we were led by the Sultana down to the reception room to dinner. As we entered, girls bearing silver basins approached; others with pitchers poured water over our hands; others again presented us towels. On the centre of the Persian carpet was placed a small table, about a foot square, covered with a cloth of gold tissue. On that was a circular glass waiter, about three feet in diameter. In the centre was a dish of roast mutton. The Sultana sat down, with my mother and self on either side of her; then E——, and G——, and a lady of the court, formerly a slave of the Pasha's, now married to a colonel. The interpretess stood and carved for us. The china was French and handsome—silver knives and forks, &c., which the Sultana knew not how to use. She punched at the meat in the most unmerciful manner. When we sat down, a napkin was placed on each of our laps; another, embroidered in gold, laid over the right shoulder; and a third, and a finer one, laid upon the lap, to wipe the mouth with. Some of the slaves fanned us—some held the different dishes—others salvers of knives, and others again silver pitchers, and so on. What with the beautiful dresses, the glitter of gold and diamonds, the divan, the spacious hall and fountain, it seemed that the scenes of the Arabian Nights were realized before me. I wish you could have seen it. Our only regret was that this beautiful scene could not be enjoyed by some of our friends.

It is said there is no pleasure without pain. Truly it was so in this case. The dinner was almost too much for us. We counted thirty-nine different dishes, served one at a time, and of each we were obliged to eat a little. And so strangely served as they were! The first five dishes were of mutton, rice, &c.,—then a sweet dish—then fried fish and fried lemons—then meat—then another sweet dish—next fried fish and nuts—and so on till the thirty-ninth, which was stewed rice and bonny-clabber. The glass salver was then taken away, and a silver one, with melons, peaches, grapes, &c., replaced it. When we rose from the table, the girls with the basins knelt before us, and hands were washed as before, when pipes and coffee were given us to finish off with. While we smoked, the Sultana retired to prayers, which she does five times a day. Then if you could have witnessed the scene, you would have imagined us amongst a parcel of great children. Oh! how we were dragged about, patted and pulled; each woman declaring we belonged to her, and should not speak to the others. At 3 o'clock we were sent for to depart, as the gentlemen were satiated with smoking, and could wait no longer. They had been with the

Governor all this time. The Sultana held us tight, and said the Capidan Pasha had no business to send for us; and it was 4 o'clock before we could get away. We made a great procession through the garden. First went the musical, dancing, and singing girls; then the Sultana and ourselves, slaves bearing fans of peacock's feathers over our heads; and then came the attendants. At the garden gate, sherbet was handed, when we took a kind farewell of our hospitable Sultana, and were consigned to the care of the male attendants, and at the carriage found the gentlemen impatient to hear all about what we had seen."

CHAPTER VII.

Visit to the Pyramids. Their diminutive appearance as we approached. Effect when we reached the base. Pyramid of Cheops. Visit to the interior. Pyramid of Cephrenes. Belzoni's forced passage. His successful researches. Large stone enclosure east of this Pyramid. Tombs adjoining on the west. Dine in one of them.

Earliest dawn on the 25th found us up, and our court filled with animals of all shapes and sizes, from the towering dromedary to the wee bit of a donkey; and each one was allowed to choose his mode of travelling for himself. In the end, I believe, the largest of us were found on the donkeys, and the smallest perched on the backs of dromedaries; and as I was among the former, I amused myself along the streets with watching my more ambitious companions, in danger of being caught up, as was Absalom, if not by their hair at least by the clothes, and left dangling at the end of the beams that every where project from the sides of a Turkish bazaar. The gait of the dromedary is also extremely uncomfortable; the rider, unless accustomed to it, being tossed from side to side at each of the long steps of the animal. I believe when we reached the Pyramids every one of our ambitious comrades selected some more humble animal for the rest of the journey.

And here I may be allowed to give a tribute of just praise to the Egyptian donkeys. They are extremely small, but beautifully formed, and are of a mouse color, with a streak of black running along the back, and intersected by another crossing it at right angles, and passing down the fore shoulders. These black lines are believed, by the superstitious of the Eastern countries, to be copied from the cross, and to be here in consequence of our Saviour's having selected this animal for his entry into Jerusalem. The Egyptian donkey is very gentle and tractable; and for riding, is the most agreeable of the donkey tribe that I have ever seen.

Thanks to the tact of Mr. Gliddon, and of our caterer, Lieut. S., the preparations for our excursion were admirably made, and we got off without confusion; although, as we had provisions for two days, tents, &c., our train consisted of seventy animals; and our company, amounting to about as many persons, comprised a singular variety of nations and languages. Preceded by torches, we marshalled ourselves in the dark and narrow streets, and the word being given, at length we put ourselves in motion.

"Get out of my way, there," cries an aspirant after high places to one of more humble elevation; and the way being cleared, on sweeps the dromedary at a rapid pace, the saucy occupant of his back now beginning to bob up and down, and trying in vain to find something by which he may steady himself

8

and in his efforts to check his beast, only making it go the faster. "Which is the way?" cry at once half a dozen travellers, lost in the mazes of the streets, and each, advising a different course, only heightening the embarrassment; till at last they yield the reins to their more sensible mules, which in a brief space succeed in extricating them. "Johnny Turk, here, lengthen this stirrup for me," says another; when the Arab groom, understanding only the gesture, and his eyes already offended by its unwonted and ungraceful length, draws it up still higher, till he brings the rider in the graceful attitude of the Turkish horseman, with the knees up almost to the chin. "What an unsightly attitude," the Arab murmurs to himself, "with the legs sprawling about, when he can bring them close up to the breast." To our great satisfaction we emerged at length from the narrow streets, and had the pleasure of riding on without incessant danger of scaling our ancles and knees.

Arriving at Old Cairo, we were ferried across the river, passing in our course the head of the island already noticed, and by the edifice with the famous Nilometer. Opposite to Old Cairo, as I have elsewhere remarked, is the village of Ghizeh, from which the largest Pyramids, which we were now about to visit, take their distinctive name; Ghizeh is celebrated also for its ovens for hatching chickens.

Passing this, we had now the Pyramids in full view before us, nine miles distant, but separated from us only by the level plain. The morning air was cool and pleasant, our animals travelled well, and we left the ground rapidly behind us. But as we journeyed on, disappointment took possession of every one of us. The fabrics of which we had been reading with wonder and admiration from our childhood, were before us; there were the Pyramids; but how diminutive!

Still, as we approached them, we watched to see whether they would not at last appear in that magnitude and grandeur which we had always connected with them; but it was all in vain. Each one indulged in some epithet of dissatisfaction, and even of contempt; and thus we reached the bottom of the eminence on which they stand. But when we had wound up its sides, and reached the piece of table land on which they are erected; when we checked our animals at the foot of the first of them, the Pyramid of Cheops, and looked up; there, they were again the Pyramids, and grander far than our fancy had ever pictured them. The effect, indeed, is almost overpowering. Their simplicity contributes to this as well as their vastness. There is nothing to break up and confuse the attention. The mind, without effort, embraces the whole object; one single idea occupies the attention; a single impression is made, but it is astounding; and we feel all the sublimity of the object, because by this single impression so great an effect is produced. We cast our eyes upward; we look again at ourselves, and we wonder that we are so diminutive; we who just now were passing sentence of condemnation, and looking with contempt on this mighty work! We sink into nothingness beside it, and wish to dismount and get yet lower, and from an humbler place yield it the deep homage that the mind willingly pays to greatness. "This is great, this is very grand," was the language from the lips of many, and I believe from the hearts of all, as we passed along the base of these stupendous monuments.

There are three of them at this place, called, after their reputed founders, the Pyramids of Cheops, Cephrenes, and Mycerinus. They stand on a natural platform, or piece of table land, one hundred and fifty feet in height, projected from the adjoining range of mountains. That of Cheops is the largest, and has been repeatedly measured; but on account of the rubbish that has accumulated along the sides, it is difficult to do this correctly; and there is great discrepancy in the results.

	English feet.		Feet.
Herodotus makes its height	800,	and length of each side	800.
Strabo	625,		600.
Le Brun	616,		704.
Thevenot	520,		612.
Davison	461,		746.
French Sçavans	470,		704.

As the angles are exposed to view quite down to the foundation, there is less difficulty in ascertaining the number of layers, which is said to be two hundred and six; each layer being of smaller dimensions than the next lower. A series of steps is thus formed, each about thirty inches in height and twenty in width. The Pyramid of Cheops is truncated, terminating above in a platform of about twenty feet square; that of Cephrenes is continued up to a sharp point, and is coated from this about one fifth of the way down, with triangular blocks, so as to present, at this part, a perfectly smooth surface. It is supposed that the whole of this Pyramid was originally coated in this manner; and that it was covered with hieroglyphics. I ascended to the smooth portion of its surface, but could discover no traces of such inscriptions. The three Pyramids stand nearly in a straight line, running north and south, and face exactly the four cardinal points. Belzoni measured that of Cephrenes, and found it to be six hundred and eighty-four feet on each side at the base, and four hundred and fifty-six in height; that of Mycerinus is much smaller, and has been mutilated so as to be rather an unsightly object. They are composed chiefly of secondary limestone taken from the adjoining mountains. As the angles of the Pyramids have suffered from the weather, and probably also from human violence, and have thus been broken into smaller steps, we were able, without much difficulty, to ascend to the summit of that of Cheops. The natives, many of whom had been attracted from a neighboring village by the sight of strangers, when seen from this elevation appeared dwindled into the merest pigmies. A visit into the interior was a matter of greater difficulty. I had been over to examine the Pyramid of Cephrenes, and on returning to that of Cheops, found that the party had entered, carrying with them all the candles; so that I had to choose between remaining without or groping my way along in the dark. Taking a couple of Arabs, who professed to know the way, I clambered over a quantity of rubbish, rolled down from the upper portions of the Pyramid, and reaching to the entrance. This is on the northern side, about thirty feet above the base, and at an equal distance from each of the angles. We here entered a square passage, three and a half feet on each side; and inclining at an angle of 26°, which, it is worthy of remark, is the inclination of the entrance passage in each of the Pyramids yet explored. This passage was lined quite around with polished granite; and the descent would have been dangerous, but for rude steps or holes for the feet, cut in the lower flags in more modern times. This passage is about one hundred feet in length; and by the time we reached its extremity, daylight had quite deserted us. I found myself now in a place where I could stand upright; and after stumbling over some rocks, was brought to a stand by a rough wall, where the hand of violence had been at work, probably endeavoring to force a passage into some of the chambers. Here an Arab got before to drag, and another behind to push me, and by their good help I soon found myself swinging in mid air, in the blackness of darkness; but presently reached a ledge about eighteen inches wide, regularly formed, and ascending at the angle already noticed. Following this up, I at length began to hear voices, and soon after, to my great satisfaction, found myself in a lighted chamber, and once more among my companions. This was what is called the King's chamber; a name given to it on account of a sarcophagus of red granite, seven feet six inches in length, and of proportionate width and depth, highly polished, but entirely plain. This apartment is thirty-seven feet long, seventeen wide, and about twenty in height; and is cased in every part with polished Egyptian granite.

Leaving this chamber, and returning part of the way, I found that the ledge on which I had ascended, had at its side a passage to another apartment lower down than the King's chamber; this is seventeen feet long, fourteen wide, and twelve feet in height; and is also cased with polished granite. There are other chambers in this Pyramid, but of irregular shape; and it is uncertain whether they were part of the original design, or are accidental; a pit, descending, with several offsets, to a depth of one hundred and fifty-five feet, or to a level with the Nile, with which it probably had a communication, has also been explored. It is probable that there are several other passages not yet discovered, and among them one by which there was a subterranean entrance to the Pyramid, a passage, apparently of this character, having been recently discovered in the Pyramid of Cephrenes.

For what we know of the interior of this latter Pyramid, which stands within one hundred yards of that of Cheops, we are indebted to the most enterprising of all modern travellers, the patient and yet acute Belzoni. Herodotus had declared that there were no chambers in this Pyramid; and, except a few lazy efforts of the Sçavans of the French invading army, no attempt had been made to ascertain whether this writer was correct or not. The ambition of Belzoni having been fired by his success amid the monuments of Thebes, he determined to make an effort upon this Pyramid; and he began first by attempting to force a passage into the northern side. This still remains as when he abandoned it; and on examining it, I was struck with astonishment at the perseverance and determined resolution of the operator. He has cut a large passage (in many places nine or ten feet square), for a distance of one hundred feet, into the heart of the Pyramid; the whole being through a solid mass of stones, often of prodigious size. The danger, as well as the expense of this mode of operating, compelled him at length to abandon it; but his resolution was not to be overcome. He examined again the Pyramid of Cheops, and, after careful admeasurements, discovering that in this of Cephrenes, at a point corresponding exactly with the entrance into the former, the surface of the Pyramid was sunk a little, he commenced here anew, the native workmen looking on in wonder, and calling him *magnoon*, or fool. Having removed a quantity of rubbish and cut through the outer rocks, he at length found his toils rewarded; slabs of granite, like those lining the entrance into the other Pyramid, began to appear; and to his joy he found at length a similar passage open here before him. It is four feet in height, and three feet six inches in width. Having removed the rubbish which had fallen into it, he reached, at the bottom, a portcullis of stone, "which," he says, "stared me in the face, and said *ne plus ultra;* putting an end to all my projects." With great labor this was raised at length sufficiently to allow him to creep under; and "after thirty days," he adds, "I had the pleasure of finding myself in the way to the central chamber of one of the two great Pyramids of Egypt, which have long been the admiration of beholders." A passage cut out of the solid rock, brought him from this to the entrance of a large chamber.

"I walked," he says, "slowly two or three paces, and then stood still to contemplate the place where I was. Whatever it might be, I certainly considered myself in the centre of that Pyramid, which, from time immemorial, had been the subject of obscure conjectures of many hundred travellers, both ancient and modern. My torch, formed of a few wax candles, gave but a glimmering light; I could, however, clearly distinguish the principal objects. I naturally turned my eyes to the west end of the chamber, looking for the sarcophagus, which I strongly expected to see in the same situation as that in the first Pyramid; but I was disappointed when I saw nothing there. The chamber has a pointed or sloping ceiling, and many of the stones had been removed from their places, evidently by some one in search of treasure. On my advancing towards the west end, I was agreeably surprised to find that there was a sarcophagus buried on a level with the floor." A closer examination led him to the discovery of bones in this sarcophagus, which, on being sent to London, were pronounced to be those of a bull, or of that species of animal; a fact which strengthens the opinion that the Pyramids were erected by the Egyptians, not for the burial of their kings, but for religious purposes. The enterprising traveller, however, found that he was not the first that had penetrated these mysterious recesses. The covering of the sarcophagus had been partly removed; and on going further, he discovered both Roman and Arabic inscriptions; the latter stating that "the Master Mohammed Achmed had opened them." This chamber is hewn out of the solid rock, and is forty-six by sixteen feet at the sides, and twenty-three feet six inches in height. He discovered some other chambers, and numerous passages, together with a well, as in the other Pyramid.

Adjoining the Pyramid of Cephrenes on the south, are the ruins of a large enclosure, formed of huge stones; while on the north and west are scattered a great number of tombs, of heavy and solemn architecture, forming entire streets. In these the stones are also large; they had flat roofs, above which rose a parapet with heavy mouldings; some are in good preservation, but most have suffered greatly from the hand of time, or, more probably, of human violence; the roofs having fallen in, and the sands of the desert having entered and filled them up. Their inner walls are covered with stucco, on which are painted numerous figures of men and beasts, in procession or engaged in religious sacrifices, or in agriculture. We opened a passage into one of them, and were glad to find in it a refuge from the fierce sun, which now seemed to be shedding fire upon us and upon the glowing sands all around. The tomb consisted of three chambers—two in good preservation, and one uncovered; all of them ornamented in the manner just described; it was large enough for all our party, except the Arabs, who seemed to care little for the sun. Our hampers being dragged in, we enjoyed here a comfortable meal; after which, retiring to the outer chamber and making a pillow of the sand, I gazed on the dim figures traced on the wall, and indulged in antiquarian reveries.

CHAPTER VIII.

Some interesting facts in our own country in connexion with these Pyramids. Pyramids of Micocatl in Mexico, and of Quanhuahuac and Cholula. Their history. Notices of a deluge, and confusion of languages, in the picture writing of Mexico. Pyramids in the Polynesian islands. "High Places" of Scripture. Temple of Belus. Universality of this kind of structure explained. Our western mounds. View from the Pyramids of Ghizeh. The Sphinx. Visit to the plain of Memphis, and the Military and Naval School at Toura.

WE are stretched on the sand in a tomb at Ghizeh, gazing on the solemn and dreamy figures every where painted on its walls. They carry our thoughts back to the ancient days, and a spirit of musing steals gently over us. What is the origin of the Pyramids? Nay, start not, kind reader, for I am not going to enter into a disquisition on this worn-out subject, or to rake up old theories, but to mention a few circumstances connecting it with our own country, which have always appeared to me to be extremely interesting, and which do not seem to have received the attention that they deserve. It would be somewhat strange if the obscurity which has hung over these monuments from the earliest times should be cleared away by discoveries in this new country of ours.

About twenty-four miles east of the city of Mexico, in a plain, called by the aborigines, *Micocatl*, or *the*

Path of the Dead, are two Pyramids, one 180, the other 144 feet in height, the former being 676 feet on each side, at the base. They are constructed of clay mixed with small stones, which was encrusted on the outside with a thick coating of porous amygdaloid. They presented four stories or platforms, each considerably narrower than the one next below; and on the top were originally two colossal statues of stone, covered with plates of gold, designed to represent the sun and moon. They are surrounded by several borders of smaller pyramids, about thirty feet in height, forming streets, which run exactly in the direction of the four cardinal points.

Eastward from these, as we descend the Cordilleras, towards the gulf of Mexico, is the Pyramid of Papantla. It had seven stories, and was higher in proportion to its width than any other in the country, being 59 feet in elevation, and 82 feet on each side at the base. It was built entirely of hewn stones, of extraordinary size, regularly shaped and neatly fitted together. It had three staircases, each leading to the summit; and the stairs were ornamented with hieroglyphics, and small niches symmetrically arranged.

South-eastward from the ancient city of Quanhuahuac, on the western declivity of the Cordillera of Anahuac, rises an isolated mass of rock, 358 feet in height, shaped by human labor into a regular conic form. It has five stories or terraces, the sides of which incline inward as they ascend, each being

9

covered above with masonry; the uppermost of these is 236 feet from north to south, and 315 from east to west; and is encircled by a wall of hewn stone six feet and a half in height. The base of the hill is also surrounded by a deep and very wide ditch, whose outer circumference measures nearly two miles and a half. In the centre of the upper natural platform was a Pyramid of five stories, of which only one now remains. It faces exactly the four cardinal points, and is on one side 67, and on the other 57 feet in extent. The stones of which it is composed are regular in shape, fitted neatly together, and are covered with hieroglyphics, each figure occupying several stones; among them we discovered heads of crocodiles spouting water, and men sitting cross legged, as is the custom in Eastern nations.

But the greatest, and perhaps the most ancient of the Pyramids of this country, is one on the plain of Cholula, which is separated from the valley of Mexico by a chain of volcanic mountains, extending from Popocatepetl towards Rio Frio and the peak of Telapor. This Pyramid was also so constructed as to face exactly the four cardinal points, and had a base of 1449 feet on each side; it rose by four terraces, and had an elevation of 164 feet. It was built of unbaked bricks, three inches thick by fifteen in length, alternating with layers of clay. In some places it has been penetrated, and chambers have been laid open, in one of which were found two skeletons, idols of basalt, and a great variety of vases, polished and varnished. On the summit of this Pyramid was an altar dedicated to Quatzee, the god of the air.

These Pyramids of Mexico were in existence when this region was conquered by the Aztecks, in the year 1190 of our era; and were attributed by the conquerors to their predecessors, the Toltecks, a powerful and highly civilized nation, who had obtained possession of the country about the year A. D. 648. But whether they were not built by another people long anterior to the Toltecks, it is now impossible to say, though it appears probable that they were.

Of the origin of the last of these Pyramids there is preserved, in the Mexican picture writing,* a clear and distinct account, which appears to throw light, not only on the Pyramids of Mexico, but on those of Egypt, and on the Pyramidal form so common among the temples of Hindostan.† It is as follows:

* Of this picture writing, there are several originals preserved; one at Vienna, three or four in the great library at Mexico, two in the Vatican at Rome, and one in the royal library at Paris. I was allowed to see that at Vienna. It is on deer-skin, and is about fifty feet in length by nine inches in width, folding like a Chinese book; the writing occupies both sides. The translation of it, which I have given here, is by Baron Humboldt.

† At Benares is a Pyramid like those of Egypt, formed of earth, and covered with bricks. The Brahmins of India, when they heard the Egyptian Pyramids described by Mr. Wilford, declared at once that they were religious structures; and inquired whether they had not a subterraneous communication with the Nile. He described the well in that of Cheops to them, when they affirmed that it was for supplying the priests with water in their ceremonies, and that the sarcophagus in the great chamber was on such occasions filled with water and lotus-flowers. At Medun in Egypt is a Pyramid, with broad off-setts like those of Mexico; and similar ones are stated to exist on the banks of the Indus and Ganges.

"Before the great inundation, which took place 4800 years after the creation of the world, the country of Anahuac* was inhabited by giants. All those who did not perish, were transformed into fishes, save seven,† who fled into caverns. When the waters had subsided, one of these giants, Xalhua, surnamed the builder, went to Chohollan, where, as a memorial of the mountain Haloc, which had served for an asylum for himself and his six brethren, he built an artificial hill in form of a Pyramid. He ordered bricks to be made in the provinces of Tlamanalco, at the foot of the mountain range of Cocotl; and to convey them to Cholula, he placed a file of men, who passed them from hand to hand. The gods beheld with wrath this edifice, the top of which was to reach the clouds. Irritated at the daring attempt of Xalhua, they hurled fire on the Pyramid. Numbers of the workmen perished; the work was discontinued, and the monument was afterwards dedicated to Quetzalcoatl, the god of the air."‡

To this Humboldt adds,

"Of the different nations that inhabited Mexico, (at the time of the conquest,) paintings representing the deluge of Coxcox are found among the Aztecks, the Miztecks, the Zapotecks, the Tlascalans, and the Mechoacanese. The Noah, Xisuthrus or Menou of

* A region embracing Cholula. Au.

† The reader will notice the coincidence with the number of Noah's family. Au.

‡ Humboldt's researches, English translation, v. 1. 95—6.

these nations is called Coxcox, Teo-Cipactli, or Tezpi. He saved himself conjointly with his wife Xochiquetzal in a bark; or, according to other traditions, on a raft of *ahue huete* (cupressus disticha.) The painting represents Coxcox in the midst of the water, lying in a bark. The mountain, the summit of which, crowned by a tree, rises above the waters, is the peak of Colhuacan,* the Ararat of the Mexicans. The horn which is represented on the left, is the phonetic hieroglyphic of Colhuacan. At the foot of the mountain appear the heads of Coxcox and his wife. The latter of these is known by the two tresses in the form of horns, which, as we have observed, denote the female sex. The men born after the deluge were dumb; a dove from the top of a tree distributes among them tongues, represented under the form of small commas. We must not confound this dove with the bird which brings Coxcox tidings that the waters were dried up. The people of Machoacan preserved a tradition, according to which, Coxcox, whom they call Tezpi, embarked in a spacious *acalli* with his wife, his children, several animals, and grain, the preservation of which was of importance to mankind. When the Great Spirit, Tetcatlipoca, ordered the waters to withdraw, Tezpi sent out from his bark a vulture, the Zohilote (vultur aura). This bird, which feeds on dead flesh, did not return on account of the great number of carcasses with which

* A peak of the Cordilleras of Mexico.

the earth, recently dried up, was strewed. Tezpi sent out other birds, one of which, the humming-bird, alone returned, holding in his beak a branch covered with leaves. Tezpi, seeing that fresh verdure began to clothe the soil, quitted his bark near the fountain of Colhuacan. * * * * The tongues which the dove distributed to the nations of America, being infinitely varied, these nations disperse; and fifteen heads of families only, who spoke the same tongue, and from whom the Toltecks, the Aztecks, and the Acolhuans descended, unite, and arrive at Aztlan." Ib. II. p. 63.

"The group, No. 2,* represents the celebrated *Serpent Woman*, Cihuacohuatl, called also Quiliztli or Tonacacihua, *woman of our flesh;* she is the companion of Tonacateuctli. The Mexicans considered her as the mother of the human race; and after the god of the *Celestial Paradise*, Ometeuctli, she held the first rank among the divinities of Anahuac. We see her always represented with a great serpent. Other paintings exhibit to us a feather-headed snake, cut in pieces by the great spirit Tercatlipoca, or by the sun personified, the god Tonatiuh. * * * *

"Behind the serpent, who appears to be speaking to the goddess Cihuacohuatl, are two naked figures; they are of a different color, and seem to be in the

* This picture represents a woman standing on the left; in front of her a serpent is erect, and looking towards her, with projecting tongue; beneath them, towards the right, are two figures struggling; and towards the left, two small objects, that may be vessels, though it is difficult exactly to determine their character.

attitude of contending with each other. We might be led to suppose that the two vases, which we see at the bottom of the picture, one of which is overturned, is the cause of this contention. The Serpent woman was considered in Mexico as the mother of two twin children; these naked figures are perhaps the children of Cihuacohuatl; they remind us of the Cain and Abel of the Hebrew tradition." Ib. I. p. 195.

Pyramidal structures are also found scattered over the islands of the Pacific. "The natural temples (in the Polynesian islands) consisted of a number of distinct Maraes, altars, and sacred dormitories, appropriated to the chief pagan divinities, and included in one large stone enclosure of considerable extent. Several of the distinct temples contained smaller inner-courts, within which the gods were kept. The form of the interior or area of the temples was frequently that of a square or a parallelogram, the sides of which extended forty or fifty feet. Two sides of this were enclosed by a high stone wall; the front was protected by a low fence; and opposite, *a solid Pyramidal structure* was raised, in front of which the images were kept, and the altars fixed. These piles were often immense. That which formed one side of the square of the large temple in Atehura, according to Mr. Wilson, by whom it was visited when in a state of preservation, was 270 feet long, 94 feet wide at the base, and 50 feet high; being at the summit 180 feet long and 6 wide. A flight of steps led to its summit; the bottom step was six feet high. The outer stories of the Pyramid, composed of coral and basalt, were laid with great care, and hewn or squared with immense labor, especially the *trava*, or corner stones." Ellis's Polynesian Researches, vol. I. p. 339, 340.

"The most remarkable objects in Easter Island, are its monuments of stone-work and sculpture, which, though rude and imperfect, are superior to any found among the more numerous and civilized tribes of the South Sea islands. These monuments consist of a number of terraces or platforms, built with stairs, cut and fixed with great exactness and skill, forming, though destitute of cement, a strong durable pile. On these terraces are fixed colossal statues or busts."* Ib. vol. III. p. 325.

* Query, were not the "High Places," mentioned in Scripture, also Pyramidal edifices. They were not natural hills, for the Hebrew term for the latter being גבעה, while for the high places the word במה is universally employed. See 2 Kings xvi. 4., where the distinction is clearly made. They were in use among the Philistines, when the country was taken by the Hebrews. Numbers xxxiii. 51, 2. 2 Kings xvii. 9—11., and were,

1. Artificial structures. 1 Kings xiv. 23. 2 Kings xxi. 3. Ib. xi. 7.

2. Capable of being removed, but not so easily as the groves, altars, &c.—1 Kings xv. 14. 2 Kings xxiii. 13.

3. Were erected in their cities. 2 Chron. xxviii. 25. 2 Kings xvii. 29.

4. And in the country. 2 Chron. xxi. 11. 1 Kings xiv. 23.

5. Had small chapels on the summit. 2 Kings xvii. 29. 1 Kings xiii. 32.

6. And altars for offering sacrifice. 1 Kings iii. 4. Numbers xxii. 36, to end.

7. Also human victims probably. Jer. xix. 5.

Last among the Pyramids that I will notice here, though the first in date, is the celebrated tower of Babel, or, as it was afterwards called, the temple of Belus. This temple was square, measuring at its base 660 feet on each side; and consisted of eight successive layers or towers, formed of huge unburnt bricks, each layer 75 feet high, and each smaller than the next below. It was thus altogether 600 in height, and had on the summit a chapel for the golden statue of their god. According to Diodorus Siculus, the gold of this statue, and the decorations of the temple, were equal in value to ten millions of dollars; while the worth of the utensils employed, and the treasure deposited here, amounted to an equal sum.

We have thus, throughout Hindoostan, on the banks of the Euphrates, through Egypt, in the remote region of Mexico, and among the Pacific islands, structures in shape exactly alike, and often of stupendous magnitude. For an effect so general we must find a cause as extensive, and it must be one operating with powerful effect. It appears to me that we are supplied with this in the hints given by the picture writing of Mexico.

8. Seem to have been connected with the worship of the sun. 2 Kings xxi. 3.

9. And with purification by fire. Jer. xxxii. 5.

10. Perhaps also used as places of burial. 2 Kings xxiii. 16. In Isaiah liii. 9. במה is used to signify a grave.

11. Sometimes used as fortifications. Judges v. 18 and 19.

12. They appear sometimes to have been of earth or stone. 1 Kings xv. 14. 2 Kings xxiii. 8.

13. Sometimes of wood. 2 Kings xxii. 15. xxiii. 8.

After the confusion of languages at the tower of Babel, the stricken and confounded families of the plain of Shinar, as they were gradually scattered over different, and often far distant regions, carried with them, each, not only a deep impression of the event, but also a feeling of awe connected with the edifice where had been such a wonderful display of supernatural power. And they afterwards adopted this structure, as the model for temples for the worship of the mysterious divinities that their superstitious fears gradually wrought out for them, the god of fire, the god of the sun, or the god of the palpable but invisible air.

We have here a case sufficiently extensive in its operation, and also sufficiently powerful. When looking at the huge structures in Egypt, I can hardly imagine any other cause than that of religion to be able to produce such a stupendous effect.

Only one of the Pyramids of Ghizeh is truncated, or adapted for a chapel on its summit; that of Cephrenes might have had its altar in the huge stone enclosure already noticed as directly adjoining it on the east; but it is probable that in this land of mystery, the solemnities, whatever they were, were performed chiefly in the hidden chambers of the Pyramids, to which the priests had access by subterranean passages.

The idea that they were places for worship, is perhaps strengthened by the presence of the colossal Sphinx, which lies about two hundred yards east from them, and on the side of the eminence on which they stand. Avenues of sphinxes leading to their temples were common in the ancient Egyptian cities; and in Memphis, if my memory is correct, was one of great extent, formed by colossal sphinxes, which have all disappeared. May we not suppose that this, which now stands alone, was, or was intended to be,* one of a great number, forming a most imposing avenue, leading upward from the plain to these stupendous temples? Its face is towards the east, and it adjoins what was evidently the ancient way of ascent to the Pyramids.

The dimensions of this Sphinx, as given by Pococke, are, height of the head and neck, twenty-seven feet; breast, thirty-three feet wide; whole length of the figure, one hundred and thirty feet. Pliny states its height to be equal to sixty-three English feet. It is now covered with sand, except the head and shoulders. Some years since the whole figure was laid bare by the persevering efforts of Mr. Caviglia; but the light sands of the desert speedily resumed their place, and have left no traces of his labors.

In conclusion, I would throw out the query, (and it is only a query,) whether the mounds in our western country, which are often of prodigious size, had not the same origin and a similar purpose, the circular form being only a slight change in conse-

* For it is doubtful whether the Pyramids were ever completed.

quence of the material here employed. The Pyramid of Quanhuahuac, in Mexico, was built on a hill wrought into shape of a cone; and at Ruapua, in Hawaii, (or Owhyhee,) Mr. Ellis visited a *heiau*, or open temple, in which "the place where the altar had been erected could be distinctly traced; it was a *mound of earth*, paved with smooth stones, and surrounded by a firm curb of lava." Polyne. Researches, v. iv., 116.

But up! up! and let us get out once more into the pure and open air. The fiery sun is throwing his rays slantingly, and the Pyramids are casting long shadows across the plain; and, though over yon sandy mountains and the panting deserts beyond, the sky is still in a glow, the fury of the heat is past. Turn here to the eastward. In this clear and pure atmosphere, how distinct are distant objects. From our elevated ground we trace the courses of the numerous canals, intersecting the wide plain beneath; yonder is Cairo, a white house here and there giving a mottled appearance to the reddish mass of edifices; there goes the silvery river, in gentle and graceful curves; and here, on our left, stretches off towards it a low ridge or causeway, supposed by some to have been made for transporting stone for the Pyramids from the river, but which was more probably formed when this region was robbed to supply Cairo with building materials.*

* The Caliph Melec-Alaziz-Othman-ben-Yusouf (quite worthy of his name) sent a large number of workmen here with orders to

How calm now and quiet is all this scene; but over this plain only a few years ago swept the wild and destructive hurricane of war. There, a few miles from where we stand, advanced the legions of France, led by him who was himself a host; and there wheeled the squadrons of the fierce Mamelukes; and here both rushed on to the bloody encounter. What spot on earth is there that man has not marked with deeds of violence, or from which the voice of his brother's blood, shed by him, hath not cried to heaven from the ground?

Looking southward from our present position, the Pyramids of Sakhara were striking objects in the plain of Memphis, distant seven or eight miles. They are on the level plain, and are, I think, six in number, but are small compared with those of Ghizeh. One of them was remarkable, even at this distance, for the ruggedness of its outline; the successive layers of stones in this receding very much, and making it resemble considerably the Pyramids of Mexico.

Towards evening the party, once more resuming their various means of conveyance, proceeded on by

destroy the Pyramids. They spent eight months, with pickaxes, ropes, &c., and put him to an enormous expense; but after all were able only to disfigure one front of one, that of Mycerinus, the smallest one. Even Saladin bade his workmen consider Memphis and the Pyramids as quarries, from which to procure materials for building the walls and the citadel of Cairo. Recent accounts from Egypt state that Mohammed Ali is taking from the Pyramid of Mycerinus materials for his great work at the Barage.

the Pyramids of Sakhara; and on the plains of Memphis found, through the foresight of Mr. Gliddon, a comfortable supper and commodious tents prepared for them. This plain is covered with ruins, often of great size, but too unsatisfactory at the present time to detain a traveller long; and the company embarked at an early hour on the following day on board Mr. Gliddon's boat.

On the right bank of the Nile, about seven miles from Cairo, is the military and naval school of Toura, an admirably conducted institution, under the superintendence of a Spanish gentleman, General Seguira. He was a high officer in the constitutional government of Spain, and having been exiled in consequence, has been protected by Mohammed Ali, who had sense enough to see and appreciate his merit. He has his family with him at Cairo, holds the rank of Bey, and receives the liberal salary of $11,000 per annum. The college edifice consists of a quadrangle, inclosing a court planted with shade trees for the recreation of the pupils. Each lad has for himself an iron bedstead, mattress, &c., a bureau, secretary, and a chair. The sleeping rooms are large enough to accommodate thirty-seven of them in each, together with a teacher; in the school-room they have also every comfort, and a hospital is also proivded for the sick.

The party landing here, were received with great politeness by Gen. Seguira, who, after conducting them through the buildings, and calling on the lads to exhibit their proficiency in geometry, trigonometry, and drawing, ordered those destined to be artillerists to bring their cannon on the ground for practice. The young cadets (about twelve or fourteen years of age) wheeled their guns to the spot, and went through a variety of evolutions with great rapidity, firing at the targets with admirable success. Their improvement in the school for drawing is also wonderful, if we consider the short time which they have been able to allot to this branch. The young naval heroes did not appear to be so well trained; there are two armed brigs anchored in the river opposite the school, on board of which they are examined in loosing and furling sails, lowering yards, splicing and knotting, unmooring and mooring, and in practising the guns; but the evolutions which they attempted on this occasion, were pronounced by our tars to be sufficiently awkward. We had, however, frequent opportunity of seeing the Pasha's ships manoeuvring at sea, and saw no occasion for finding fault. The school at Toura contains about four hundred lads, and considering the short time which it has been in operation, reflects great credit, both on the Pasha, and its polite superintendent Gen. Seguira.

CHAPTER IX.

Rest on the Sabbath. Visit to the Pasha's summer residence at Shubra. Exceeding beauty of the ground. Lake, and sports of the Pasha. Pic-nic in one of the Kiosks. Pear tree from the Pasha's place of nativity. Brief history of Mohammed Ali. Departure from Cairo. Regret at parting with Mr. Gliddon.

SUNDAY, 27th, was a day of rest, which our previous severe exercise made unusually refreshing. In the afternoon Gen. Seguira and family, Mr. Taylor, an English gentleman, and his lady, and the French consul, called to pay their respects to the Commodore and family.

The next morning our baggage was again transferred to the boats, which were sent down the river with orders to wait for us at the palace of Shubra; and towards noon, mounting our gallant steeds for the last time, we wheeled out into the avenue leading to that magnificent summer residence of the Pasha. Our company was augmented by Mrs. Seguira, her two daughters and son, who had accepted an invitation to a pic-nic, by which the day, and with it, our visit to Cairo, was to be concluded. The members of this family all speak English fluently, and we found them a delightful acquisition to our party.

The gardens at Shubra are under the care of a native horticulturist, who had been sent by the Pasha to France, and had spent six years on an experimental farm near Marseilles. He received us politely at the gate, and ushering us in, we found ourselves in a scene more like the creation of a wild and luxurious fancy, revelling in joyous freedom and without restraint, than a thing of real life. The first walk into which we turned was lined thickly on either side with oleanders in full bloom, mingled with roses and jessamine; they grew to the height of ten or twelve feet, and bending over the path, suspended over us a canopy of flowers, from which the richest odors were distilled. The vista was terminated by some striking and beautiful object, which I do not recollect, for the mind was too intoxicated to make careful observations, and I desired to look and drink in the rich pleasure rather than to note. The grounds, we were informed, contain one hundred and fifty acres; we rambled over a portion of them, and found every where something to admire. By and by our course was arrested by a lake embowered amid lofty and spreading trees; it is of a quadrangular form, and is surrounded by an arcade of marble, at each angle of which is a kiosk or summer-house richly furnished. In the middle of each of the four sides is a portico, formed of Italian marbles; and here, as well as in the kiosks, are marble figures spouting out water, which is carried around in marble troughs, and made to descend by cascades into the lake. In the centre is an island with a marble edifice, to which is an ascent by a flight of steps of the same material. It is apparently sup-

10*

ported by four crocodiles in marble, also spouting water. The water is about four feet in depth, and is also paved below with marble. This is a favorite resort of the Pasha, and we saw a boat in which it is said he sometimes carries out his wives; when well off from the shore, he upsets the boat, and amuses himself with seeing them flounder in the water. At the time of our visit the place was undergoing some improvements.

There is also a menagerie in the gardens, but the most valuable animals had just been given away, and at this time it did not contain any thing very remarkable. The palace itself, into which we were admitted, and where we were shown over the ladies' apartments, is richly furnished, but not equal to the one in the citadel.

After rambling about till our curiosity was satisfied, we retired to a large kiosk, whose soft ottomans invited to repose; and our hampers of claret and champagne having been brought in, the corks were made to fly in the very penetralia of the Moslem Pasha; nor were his officers loth to pledge their impudent guests. To our feast the superintendent of the grounds added an abundance of choice fruit from the gardens. The Misses Seguiras had brought their guitars, and music was also made to lend its charms; they sing sweetly, and accompanied the instruments in some of the airs of their distant father-land.

This name of father-land reminds us of a tree which we passed at the early part of our saunterings through this garden. We had come to a spot where a covered walk, bordered by flowers, suddenly expands into a little open area, paved with pebbles from Rhodes, which, being of different colors, are arranged so as to form a tasteful mosaic work. In the centre is a kind of canopied throne, and the whole spot bears the marks of unusual attention. The superintendent directed our attention to a pear tree growing at one side of the opening; it was slender, but healthful looking, and bearing fruit. "That tree," he said, "was brought by his excellency the Pasha from his native town, and was planted here by his own hand, and he seems to take particular care in nourishing it."

The fact discloses to us a vein of sentiment in that extraordinary man which we should scarcely have expected to exist. He is said, however, to be very kind in his domestic relations. His eldest children have all been carried off by disease, or (as in the case of Youssoun) by violence; those still living, three in number, are quite young, and he often amuses himself in playing with them in this garden.

Mohammed Ali is a native of Cavalla, a small town in Albanie, and owes his present exalted station entirely to his own intrepidity. He began his public career as a subordinate collector of taxes in his native district; and, on one occasion, having distinguished himself in putting down some refractory inhabitants who had refused to pay their part of the contributions, was rewarded by the governor of the place with a rich wife and the rank of Boulouk Bashi. Soon after this he became a dealer in tobacco, without however forgetting his profession of arms; he was successful in trade, but in a short time the invasion of Egypt by the French, called his talents into a higher sphere of operation. He was raised to the rank of Bimbashi or captain, and sent to Egypt with 300 men, the quota of soldiers furnished by Cavalla on this occasion. His bravery in this country soon drew the attention of his superior officers, and led to his advancement to higher rank; and at length, after the massacre of the Mamelukes by the Turkish admiral at Aboukir, as already noticed, Mohammed Ali was placed in command of one division of the forces destined to march against the remainder in Upper Egypt, and effect their extermination. The Mamelukes, however, fought with desperation, and their enemies were defeated; and Yousef Bey, who had the supreme command in this expedition, in order to shield himself from trouble, charged Mohammed Ali with treachery. The latter was near losing his head; but he managed affairs with skill, and gained a kingdom. The army had been badly paid, and was disaffected towards their rulers; he had ingratiated himself with the soldiers, and seizing the occasion, he first rid himself of the Turkish viceroy, and then of the leading Mameluke Beys, and soon after was entreated by the army to save Egypt from destruction by becoming himself the chief representative of the Porte. He yielded of course, and the Sultan being compelled to yield also, appointed him, though sorely against his will, the Viceroy of Egypt. I have related the manner in which he soon after exterminated the Mamelukes, and the reader is himself aware how he has since made himself, in effect, entirely independent of the Porte.

Our friends were compelled to leave us in time to get back to the city before sunset, when the gates are closed; and bidding them a reluctant farewell, we ourselves moved down to the river, and took once more possession of our boats, which were there awaiting us. Mr. Gliddon, we found, had lent his own comfortable boat for the use of the Commodore and his family.

So adieu to Cairo! Our attendants had been rewarded with "beckshishes," or presents, in return for their own services, and for the use of the horses; the Cavasses and Chaouishes had been paid; the city, I believe, was at peace with us, and we had received much pleasure in it; and now, stepping from the gardens into our boats, we began to drop down the stream. Mr. Gliddon and Mr. Trail were kind enough to accompany us as far as the Barage, where we came to for the night, and where, in the morning, they went with us to examine this stupendous undertaking. To both of these gentlemen we owe many thanks, and to the former in particular, though far off, we all bear grateful hearts. "Two weeks' residence in the same house," (I take the liberty of copying from the Commodore's private journal,) "and constant communication, with his amenity of manners, and his devotion to our comforts, and to render our visit pleasant, had greatly attached all to him; he planned our excursions, and took the trouble to provide the means to enable us to effect them; and to him we are indebted for having obtained views of every thing in and about Cairo worthy of attention. We shall never forget the very happy time we passed at Cairo under his hospitable roof. It was therefore with the deepest regret that we bid him adieu, and saw him leap to the shore, amid three hearty cheers from us all. May he prosper in all his undertakings, and be happy!"

CHAPTER X.

Return to Alexandria. Ruins about that city. Pompey's pillar. Cleopatra's needles. Modern improvements in Alexandria. Arsenal. Harbor of Alexandria. Rail road to Suez. New law for protecting his subjects. Presentation to the Pasha. Description of his person.

Our return to Atf occupied four days, one day more than our voyage up the stream; as the wind still blew strong from the northward during the day, our progress was chiefly during the night, when we took advantage of the lull, and dropped down with the current.

On our reaching Alexandria, an officer of the Pasha waited on Commodore Patterson, to offer him the use of one of his palaces, a large airy building on the edge of the harbor, and enjoying the sea-breeze during most of the day. The Pasha himself had returned from Syria, and on application for an audience, the morning of the 5th of August was appointed for this purpose. The interval was spent in making and returning visits of ceremony, in inspecting the arsenal, and in examining the ruins about Alexandria. Of the latter there is the greatest abundance, extending for miles from the present city; but in most places presenting only a confused mass, which can give little satisfaction to the visitor. The Catacombs are a succession of chambers extending to an unknown distance, and dangerous to visit, on account of the facility with which a person may be lost in their labyrinths. Pompey's Pillar, a Corinthian column, 9 feet in diameter, and of 90 feet elevation, to which is added a capital of ten feet in height, stands on a low eminence about two miles back of the present city ; a dedicatory inscription to the Emperor Dioclesian is to be seen on the pedestal, but it is difficult to say by whom the column was erected.

In an angle of the present city walls, on the eastern side, are the two obelisks which usually go under the name of Cleopatra's Needles. They were probably brought from Heliopolis or Thebes, to adorn an ancient gateway, or the entrance to a temple. They are eight feet on each side at the base, and are 64 feet in length; are of red granite, and covered with hieroglyphics. One is prostrate and broken ; but the other is still erect, and is in good preservation.

The modern city of Alexandria is more an European than a Turkish or Arab city ; it is full of Franks, and a large portion of it is laid out after the European fashion ; this is particularly the case with an open square, around which they have just finished some large edifices in the Grecian or Roman style of architecture. I cannot say that I consider this imitation of European cities in Eastern countries a great improvement. About a mile and a half from the city is a garden belonging to Ibrahim Pasha, but open to the public ; it is irrigated by water raised from the canal, and is full of thriving fruit or shade trees, under which is found a delightful retreat from the scorching sun.

While these improvements of a civil nature were going on in and about the city, the arsenals exhibited a very active scene. They were then forming a dry dock, and so deficient were they in tools, that the materials excavated were passed up and thrown out by hand; the number of the workmen, however, making amends for the want of instruments. They expected to complete it in two years, when they would immediately commence two others; the stone for them has all to be brought from Cairo. There were five building ways complete, and two in progress; on the stocks were three ships of 100 guns each, ready for planking; and the day after our arrival the keel of a sixty gun frigate was laid with religious ceremonies; the Pasha himself, and his officers of state, attending on the occasion. The timber is brought from Syria, where they procure both oak and pine in the greatest quantities, and of an excellent quality. Their ships are even more wall-sided than our own; but in all other respects they follow the French style of building; and according to a fashion now beginning to prevail in the navy of that country, keep all the decks for cannons clear of state-rooms and other encumbrances; the whole battery being quite clear, fore and aft, and at all times ready for action. The officers' rooms are all placed on the orlop, which is well supplied with air-ports. Their

11

largest ship carried 138 guns, and was constructed to meet one belonging to the Sultan, and carrying 144. Owing to a difficulty in getting her out of the harbor, they were, at the time of our visit, reducing her to one deck less. The harbor of Alexandria is spacious and of sufficient depth, but the entrance is winding and difficult, and the channel is obstructed with knowls of rock, over which there is but four fathoms' water. The Pasha had sent to England for steam machinery for breaking down these rocks, and as they are of sand-stone, he will probably succeed. In the arsenal are rope-walks, two stories in height, and large ranges of store-houses well supplied. The whole establishment exhibited a neatness, and order, and efficiency, that greatly pleased our officers. The seamen receive, first class $2, and the second class 1.50 per month, together with clothing and a ration. The officers are well paid, and on receiving their commission, receive with it an anchor, together with one, two, or three stars, made of diamonds, the number being according to their rank; these, worn on the breast, constitute their only distinctive uniform. The admiral, rear-admiral, and all officers of a lower grade, are natives; the vice-admiral is a Frenchman, and so also is the chief naval constructor.

However strongly we must condemn the iron despotism of the Pasha of Egypt as regards his subjects, in all public improvements there is very much that we may approve. In addition to the schools at

Toura, and in the citadel, each of four hundred lads supported at the public expense, there is one also at Castleaine, in Old Cairo, kept in a large palace, and containing 1000; another at Boulec containing 600; and another is to be got up in the same place, to contain also 1000; all of which are at the expense of the government. At Boulec is also a surgical and medical school, under the care of a German of great ability. In addition to the public improvements which I have noticed, it is in contemplation to construct a railway from Cairo to Suez, the route for which has already been surveyed. The day before we sailed, the Pasha directed his chief engineer, Mr. Galloway, to proceed to England, and make contracts for iron rails, cars, engines, &c.; the estimated expense of the whole work was 806,400 dollars; he intends, by and by, to extend this rail road to Alexandria.

With regard to his subjects, he has made an excellent law, by which no one is allowed to be punished capitally without his permission. A short time before our visit, a man of wealth, and high in rank, having put one of his slaves to death, was sent for, and ordered forthwith into the presence of the Pasha. The fact was admitted, but he pleaded that the man had been his own slave, and that therefore he had felt at liberty to do with him as he might choose. "No," was the reply from the Pasha; "though he was your slave, he was still *my subject*;" and to make the case an impressive one, he ordered the master himself immediately to be led to execution. There is a doubt, however, whether his object, in this instance, was so much to protect "his subjects," as to rid himself of a citizen who had several times given him some trouble, and whose wealth he coveted; the property of criminals, capitally punished in this country, always falling into the hands of the sovereign.

The city of Alexandria stands on a piece of land resembling the letter T, with a harbor on each side; and on the strip or point running westward, stands the palace of the Pasha. On the morning of the 5th, the Commodore, Captain Nicolson, and as many of the officers as could be spared from duty, took boats, and landed at a flight of stairs leading up to the inner court.

The building, in which is the audience hall, is large, but has nothing striking in its exterior; and the hall itself is in a style of plainness that seems to show a mind overlooking all artificial helps to greatness.

The Pasha was seated at one angle, and on our entering, put the Commodore at his left hand, which in these countries is the seat of honor; he received us sitting, but stood up when the Commodore rose to leave the room, which, I believe, is an unusual compliment. After the compliments usual on such occasions, coffee and sherbet were brought in by the attendants, but pipes were omitted. I was informed that, on the occasion of the recent introduction of an English traveller, some difficulty had arisen on this score; if I recollect right, the gentleman had declined the pipe, which was considered by the Pasha as an insult. At all events, since that time pipes have always been dispensed with at his interviews with foreigners.

The Commodore thanked him for the numerous instances of hospitality and kindness which we had experienced, and spoke in terms of admiration of his various improvements, to all which he made suitable answers; and expressing himself also in terms of strong friendship for our country, and hinting a desire for more intimate relations. He showed considerable knowledge of our institutions, and put many pertinent questions with regard to the productions of the country, our modes of cultivation, &c.; and expressed great surprise when the Commodore stated the size to which the coffee tree grows in the West Indies, it being in Egypt and Arabia only a shrub, which must be renewed every five or six years.

Mohammed Ali is about 60 or 65 years of age, about five feet eight inches in height, and heavy; though he can scarcely be called corpulent. His forehead is large and rough; the eyes gray and small, with a deep wrinkle running upward from the outer angle; they are very keen and restless; and I believe there was not one of our large party upon whom they were not repeatedly fixed during this interview. He converses with earnestness, and laughs frequently, but his laugh is discordant and unnatural.

11*

The nose is aquiline, the mouth depressed at the corners, and garnished with a superb silvery beard. The expression of his face when he smiles is rather pleasant; but at other times a person in his presence feels as he would do near an open barrel of gunpowder, with a shower of red-hot cinders falling around him.

SYRIA.

SYRIA.

CHAPTER XI.

First view of the coast of Judea. Anxieties as we approached. State of the Country. Recent Rebellion. Investment of Jerusalem. Character of the Natives. Earthquakes. Taking of the City. English and American Missionaries. Death of Mrs. Thompson. Defeat of Ibrahim Pasha. Re-capture of the City. Conscription.' Strange conduct of our Consul at Jaffa. He is dismissed from Office. Jaffa. Large clusters of Grapes. Eastern Story-tellers. Gardens and Watermelons of Jaffa. The Cactus.

We left the coast of Egypt on the 10th of August. Early on the morning of the 12th we had the pleasure of seeing the hills of Palestine emerging from the waters. What a thrill was occasioned by the sight!

The birth-place of a wide-spread and wonderful religion—the land of a thousand miracles—the original home of a people now spread every where, and every where a miracle; and every where, from Lapland to India, still yearning towards their father-land—the mountains, the plains of Judea were before us. In our earliest infancy we had tried to picture them—they were mingled with the deepest and warmest feelings of our maturer years; in imagination how often had we wandered over the hallowed ground, and here before us was now the reality itself.

A stretch of low and whitish coast gradually developed itself; and beyond this, at the distance of several miles, rose a chain of hills, as our glasses informed us, under pretty good cultivation, and sprinkled with villages. By and by the sun was reflected from a mass of white houses on the shore, encircled with walls and towers; this was Jaffa—the Joppa of the Scriptures, and the ancient as well as the present seaport of Jerusalem. I believe I may say there was a very strong sensation excited universally throughout the ship by the scene before us; for the religion of Judea had at least been that of our childhood, and there was probably scarcely an individual among us, in whose mind it was not connected with the tenderness of a good parent, or the kindness of some early friend still dear to our memory.

Our noble ship glided on, and began to approach the coast. She was the first American vessel that had ever entered these waters; and in her joyous motion, as she pushed the ripples aside, and threw back the morning rays from a cloud of canvass, we could almost imagine a participation in the feelings of her inmates. The stripes and stars were presently replied to by a similar ensign over the house of our consul at Jaffa; and the other consuls following suite, there was presently a display of nearly all the European flags in that ancient city.

The city of Jaffa is built on the side of a hill that rises immediately from the water's edge; the houses are white, rising tier above tier; many are covered with whitewashed domes; and the white being now relieved by the consular flags, it had quite a pleasing appearance; its walls and towers, and a castle at the upper extremity, gave it also a show of strength; and had we found time for it, this proud array of pennon and battlement, assisted as it was by an encampment of soldiers in the neighborhood, might easily have carried the mind back to the days of chivalry and romance.

But we were occupied chiefly with ourselves; for with our pleasure at seeing the Holy Land was mingled an apprehension that, after all, we should not be permitted to set foot on shore. At Alexandria we had dire accounts of earthquake and war; and, what alarmed us more, of the plague; for although not one of us but would have been willing to meet this disease in his own individual case for the sake of seeing Jerusalem, yet the risk of introducing it into the ship was not to be thought of, and we knew that if there was any danger of this, the commodore would at once decide to have no communication. With these anxieties we approached the coast; and as the ship speeds onward, it may be well to state to the reader what was the state of Palestine at this time.

The ever-restless Pasha of Egypt had, about two years previous, without any warning to his master the Sultan, marched a large army into the country; and, on pretence of settling some difficulties among the natives, had seized on its strong places; after which he set the Turkish power at defiance. The Egyptian soldiers are almost universally men of light, but active and well-knit frames; and are capable of enduring fatigue, and fitted for any kind of warfare. The restlessness of their sovereign keeps them also in a state of constant activity; and many of them, though young, are already veterans in the field. The Turkish soldiers, on the other hand, are unused to motion—are mostly without experience, and lack confidence both in themselves and in their new system, which they but imperfectly understand. They have no particular attachment to their officers; while the Egyptians, though at first disliking military service, are said in a short time to become so fond of it, as to have and to desire no other home than their tent; they feel also, universally, a strong attachment both to Ibrahim Pasha and to Mahomet Ali.

We may find in all this the secret of their success whenever brought into contact with the Turkish soldiery; and there can be little doubt, that if foreign powers had not interfered, Mahomet Ali, if he had chosen, might have seated himself on the throne of Constantinople. Some of the Turkish soldiers taken in the recent expedition toward the Turkish capital, were sent to Egypt as prisoners; and we were informed, excited universal ridicule in their passage through Syria by their sluggish and awkward movement. But I have wandered a little from my subject.

On getting possession of Syria, Mahomet Ali began there the same system that he had been pursuing in Egypt, but without having properly weighed the difference in the native character. He first laid heavy exactions on the purses of the inhabitants, who indeed had little to spare, the country producing scarcely more than enough for their own support. This they bore, though with grumbling: tax after tax was laid, and with difficulty raised; and a general dissatisfaction was the consequence. At length he demanded their sons for his army and navy, and at once, the whole infuriated populace rose into rebellion. "Take our purses," they cried, "if it must be so; we can part with them; but our children we will not give." Jerusalem, where the Egyptian garrison was strongest, was in a few days invested by a force of 20,000 men, fierce and lawless people, and now maddened into phrenzy. This was eleven weeks previous to our visit. The rebels were badly provided with ammunition, and had no cannon, but spread themselves over the hills around, hoping, perhaps, to starve the garrison into terms, or succeed by stratagem; or more probably, scarcely knowing themselves what they wanted, or whither to direct their efforts. It seems to have been a sudden and universal outburst of indignant feeling, almost without aim and without hope. The reader, to form a conception of the scene, must fancy a people, in color, costume, and disposition, very much like the Indian tribes bordering on our white settlements; for such, in a striking degree, are the appearance and character of the country population of Palestine.

I have selected for this comparison the Indians dwelling on our borders, as their debased character

12

and squalid appearance bring them nearer to the Arabs of Palestine than are their brethren further back; and except that the Arab lacks the broad face and high cheek bone of the Indian, I could almost have fancied the wild looking beings whom I have seen stalking into Jerusalem, to be a portion of the same wretched people we often meet in the streets of our frontier towns. Their dress consists of a *hyck*, a species of long blanket wrapped around them, in the manner that the blanket is used by our Indians; and, as with them, under garments are sometimes employed, and sometimes the *hyck* is the only garment; over the head a handkerchief is thrown so as to leave the face exposed, and falls over the neck and shoulders, and this is kept in its place by a small fillet drawn tight over the temples. From beneath the handkerchief peep out dark elfin locks and black uneasy eyes, while the expression of the face is any thing but gentle or attractive. A large part of them are indeed robbers by profession, and plunder without scruple whenever any one more helpless than themselves may happen to fall in their way.

The condition of the inhabitants of Jerusalem, when they found themselves encircled by this wild and lawless host, was, as may be imagined, a very uncomfortable one; but another horror was immediately added, one of a more frightful, because more mysterious character. It seemed as if heaven itself was about to fight for their enemies. During the very night which succeeded the investment of the city, it was shaken by an earthquake—the shocks were repeated during the next day and night—many of the houses in the city were shaken down, and the massive walls of the convent at Bethlehem were split from top to bottom. The affrighted inhabitants took refuge in the yards of their falling tenements, and in the open places of the city; and thus, while the hills were rocking to and fro, and wailing was going up from every part of Jerusalem, some of the enemy found admittance one night, it is said, by subterranean passages, and these throwing open the gates, the hordes rushed in, and the place was given up to pillage and outrage. There were, at that time, an American, and also an English missionary family, living in the city. Mrs. Thompson, the wife of the American missionary, was in feeble health, and had an infant but a few months old to increase her anxieties; her husband was absent, and after repeated but unsuccessful attempts to join her during the siege, had been compelled to return and wait the issue at Jaffa. She took refuge with their English missionary friends, Mr. and Mrs. Nicholayson; and they had all, at the early part of the war, shut themselves up in Mr. Nicholayson's house, subsisting in a rude way on some grain and dried fruits, which he had providentially on hand. Mrs. Thompson, in a letter to her husband, has touchingly described their situation, the horrors of the earthquake, and their greater horror when the cries of terror and triumph arose on the taking of the city; and when, on the following morning, they heard the Arabs forcing their own doors, and soon after met them peering among the chambers below. Mr. Nicholayson, who speaks the native language, and understands their habits well, immediately bribed some of the intruders, and, by paying them well, engaged a dozen of them to act as guardians of his house and premises, and thus saved the families and his effects from injury, except a few articles which the guardians themselves took a fancy to and carried off in their subsequent hasty retreat. Mr. Thompson's house was stripped, not a single article escaping their hands. The Egyptian soldiers who had formed the garrison of the city took refuge in a strong castle at the Jaffa gate, which is near Mr. Nicholayson's dwelling, and the invaders seizing on all the neighboring houses, a fire was kept up between the two parties, which I believe did little injury, except to the houses, some of which were riddled by the balls from the castle; among them was that of Mr. Nicholayson, and his family were once more compelled to take refuge in the yard. Mrs. Thompson about this time began to sink under the effects of such repeated alarms, and of the fatigues and exposure operating on her feeble health; a violent attack of ophthalmia succeeded, by which she lost her sight, and was reduced to extreme feebleness; at length, after much suffering, borne with meekness, she yielded her spirit with soothing hope into the hands of Him who gave it.

Just previous to her death she was heard to say, "native, native, native land." She was a lady of superior endowments and great excellence of character; but doubtless, in the hands of a wise Providence, from this seeming evil good will yet arise.

Ibrahim Pasha, on the first news of this rebellion, had hastened from Jaffa for the relief of the city; but he seems to have underrated his enemy, and to have acted without his usual prudence. The rebels took post in a narrow pass about seven miles from the city, and starting suddenly up from amid the steep and broken ground, poured upon his troops such a deadly fire, that they broke; and it was only by hard fighting, and a masterly retreat, that he saved his army from entire destruction. He retired to Jaffa, and having, as soon as possible, provided himself with sufficient force, once more advanced upon the city. But he found no enemy there. The natives, the excitement of their first fury now past, and probably despairing of success against a foe of such formidable resources, dropped gradually away from the city, and, with their plunder, retired to the distant fastnesses of their mountains. They were, however, not allowed to rest. The Egyptian leader, binding his field pieces to the backs of camels, crossed the Jordan in pursuit, and, at the time of our visit, was ferreting them out, though not without great risk to himself. He advanced so far that the communication between him and Jerusalem was for some time cut off, and serious fears were entertained

12*

for his safety; but he at last succeeded, not only in subduing, but what was a matter of greater hazard, in disarming the people. Camel loads of guns and attaghans or swords were sent to Jerusalem and Jaffa; and, relentless to the last, he forced from them the conscripts whom he judged necessary for his wide and ambitious military schemes. I saw some of the latter marched into Jaffa one day, between files of soldiers, and forced into the boats waiting to convey them on board his fleet, then lying off to receive them. Poor fellows! they looked heart-broken, and probably a large portion of them were destined never again to visit their native hills. A more melancholy company I think I have never seen; they dragged themselves along mechanically, without noticing any one, and some were able to keep on only by clinging to the garments of those before, or by being supported by a companion on either side. After traversing the city they came to the water-gate, which is a narrow passage between two towers, and is terminated by a wooden platform six or eight feet square, and projecting about five feet above the water. This is the only landing place; the boats were lying below; and forced along the platform, they were driven by the point of the bayonet, or caught by the shoulders and tumbled unceremoniously into a heap at the bottom of the boat, to extricate themselves and find a better place as well as they might be able. In spite of my commiseration, I could scarcely help smiling at their horror, when, in turning the angle of the gate-way, they found themselves in such proximity to the salt water. Some of them shrank back with all their might; but it availed them nothing; the boats were successively filled, and pulling off, presently reached a sand-bar crossing the road-stead, where they began to plunge in the breakers;—then each sought its separate vessel, and the mountain recruits were swallowed up in the vortex caused by Mohammed Ali's wild ambition.

I must now carry the reader back to our own ship, which he will recollect we left, only yet approaching the coast. When within a few miles of it, our motions became cautious, for we knew nothing of the sea from experience, and our charts and books gave but little information. The schooner Shark was, by and by, ordered to approach, and directed to run in and inquire about the health of the city and the country adjoining. I got permission, and availed myself of a boat sent with the flag-lieutenant to her, determined if I should not be permitted to touch the Holy Land, at least to have a better view, and to get as near to it as possible. As we approached the shore, we saw a boat putting off with our national ensign, and concluding that it contained the consul, laid to till it came sufficiently near for parley. His answer to the first question, "What is the health of Jaffa and Jerusalem?" produced a sensation of thrilling joy. "Both enjoyed good health," he replied, "and the country was in a state of tolerable quiet." So we invited him on board, and right glad he seemed to be, to get out of his small vessel and find himself on board of a larger one. But alas for our new-fledged joy! The Shark presently got out to sea, and began to roll and pitch among the waves; our consul got sea-sick, and we thought frightened too; and now alarmed us with news that they had the plague in Jerusalem, and more than half suspected it to be in Jaffa; that a Frank of distinction had just died of it in the former place—that the monasteries had put themselves in quarantine, and that for us to venture there, would be highly dangerous and imprudent. We did not know what to make of this, but carried him on board the Delaware; and now, in that large ship, as quiet and as firm as the solid land, he came to himself, and declared once more that the country was safe, and the cities healthy. As night was approaching, we ran out to sea to avoid the dangerous proximity of the shore; and though in the morning we were some distance off, the consul, who had remained on board, still adhered, I believe, to his last opinion; but the Commodore, not knowing what to make of him, turned for information to another source. The Egyptian fleet cruising here in aid of Ibrahim Pasha, had come down and anchored in the evening about a mile from Jaffa, and the schooner was sent to the Admiral with Commodore Patterson's respects, and with inquiries respecting the health of the cities and the country between. The result was gratifying; the Admiral said he had not heard of the plague having been at all at Jerusalem—that it certainly was not there now, nor did he know of any other sickness in the country. The reply was accompanied with the compliments and offers of service usual in such intercourse of men of war. He advised us also to run in till within a mile or a mile and a half of the shore, and there anchor, as there is a strong current setting to the northward, and we might be in danger of getting entangled in some shoals lying eight or ten miles in that direction. This we accordingly did; and then, forthwith, began to make preparations for our long-talked of visit. A word more, however, about our consul, before he is dismissed. He accompanied us to Jerusalem, and was a great annoyance from first to last. The Commodore had reason from other sources to suppose him unworthy of his office, and took measures immediately to have him removed, and another person, one of merit, to be put in his place; and before long we had the pleasure of being informed that all this was done; and Americans who may hereafter visit Jaffa, will doubtless meet with courteous and gentlemanly treatment.

Jaffa, to which we made several visits while preparing for the journey, proved, on closer inspection, to be a filthy and wretched-looking place. The streets were of course narrow, that is common in all eastern towns; in addition, however, those of Jaffa go straight up a hill so steep as to require steps cut in the rock, and as these steps are worn, and often slippery and covered with filth, a walk through the town is one of some labor, and we did not often attempt it. Indeed there is little to tempt a person to do so, as the city is not large, and has not a single building of any importance. I ought to mention one street as an exception to the general character. It starts at the water-gate, and stretching along by the city wall, on the sea shore, is sufficiently level; on the land side of this are ranges of small warehouses, which were nearly empty at the time of our visit, and in no wise abstracted from the dull monotony of the place. By and by, this street turns into the city, and beginning to ascend a low eminence, becomes the principal bazaar, or, I believe I should say, *the* bazaar, of the place. The shops which line it on either side were poorly furnished, and I found nothing to interest me in the whole bazaar, except some bunches of grapes. But these *did* interest me. One of them I am certain was two feet in length, not, however, with grapes thickly clustering along, but scattered at intervals; it was thus not so remarkable for the quantity of fruit, but for its length; and I can easily imagine that where such clusters are common, some of similar length, and fully charged with fruit, may easily be found. On my speaking of this cluster to some of the officers, they told me that they had seen others in the market still larger.

Along this bazaar I witnessed a scene, the evening of my return from Jerusalem, which caused the place, with all its previous dulness, to leave a pleasing impression on my mind. Darkness had, on this occasion, gathered round us, while yet some distance from the city, and I had been riding on, engaged in sad musings about the country and its melancholy history; we crossed at length the open waste between the gardens and the city, and then passing beneath the dark archway of the gate, and over its pavement of loose and slippery stones, I found myself suddenly amid a group, which conjured up at once all that I had read in the Arabian Nights. Just inside this gate is a coffee house, in front of which the street spreads out into two or three times its usual width. The place was now all lighted up with lamps, hung upon pillars, or amid the trellis work supporting a large grape vine, or to the overhanging vines themselves; mats were strewed around, and thickly occupied with groups in the rich and striking costume of the east; some were sipping coffee or sherbet, and others engaged with their pipes; but all were gazing with kindling eyes and animated features on a man who stood in the midst, with outstretched arms and great volubility of tongue. He was an oriental story-teller, and, to judge from the deep and unusual interest stamped on the features of his audience, must have been one of quick sagacity and considerable eloquence. Further on I passed another company similarly employed.

But though Jaffa may have but little to attract a stranger, its gardens will have much, particularly if he happen to be there in the season for its watermelons, as was the case with us. We had heard a great deal about the Jaffa watermelons, and our expectations were so highly raised, that any thing short of the highest perfection would have disappointed us. But we were not disappointed. The melons are not unusually large, but of a richness and delicacy which, I believe, is no where surpassed, if it can be equalled. Some of our officers thought they had sometimes met with as good melons at home, but most of them were decided in the preference for those from the Jaffa gardens.* These gardens commence a few hundred yards from the walls of the city, and are from a quarter to half a mile in length; the soil is almost a pure sand, and seems incapable of producing any thing at all; but wherever watered, rewards the labor of the operator with abundance of fruits and vegetables of the greatest variety. Pomegranates here are in the highest perfection, and the cactus, or prickly pear, grows to the height of twelve or fifteen feet; along the road to Jerusalem it forms a hedge for the gardens, and a most effectual one it is. Its fruit grows on the edge of the leaf, and in these countries is oval in shape, and about three

* A very large number of the seeds were sent home by us that autumn, and were planted by our friends last summer. They produced vines in abundance, and fruit; but I have heard of but one melon that came to maturity; this one was spoken of as very delicious. The failure of the others was perhaps owing to the shortness and coldness of the season.

inches in length; it is full of seeds, but is cooling and refreshing, and has, to me, an agreeable taste. Back of the gardens of Jaffa, the country is generally open and deserted; but in spots it is cultivated, and appears to be sufficiently productive.

CHAPTER XII.

Start for Jerusalem. Appearance of our Cavalcade. Djerid play near Jaffa. Plain of Sharon. Night ride. Ramla. The Cadi's theory about Earthquakes. Beth-Horon. Entrance to the Hill-Country. Aboo Ghoosh. David's Brook. First view of Jerusalem. Difficulty in getting accommodations. Greek Monastery. Distressful night.

Our joy at finding all obstacles removed, and that we were actually going to visit Jerusalem, was great indeed. The visit had been a subject of pleasing anticipation from the beginning of the cruise, and a disappointment here would have cast a damp upon all our other pleasures. But here we were at last, ashore at Jaffa, mounted and ready to be off; every face cheerful, and our hearts swelling with expected enjoyment. We wound through the low bazaar, and then slipping and stumbling over the execrable pavement of the gateway, found ourselves out in the country, and fairly on our way. And here we turned to look at each other, and enjoy the oddity and grotesqueness of the scene. We were, indeed, a curious looking set of pilgrims. As we arrived ashore, there was a general scrambling for the animals, which, by orders of the governor of Jaffa, had been brought in from the country for the occasion; and as these included every variety, and there was little time for choosing, it was amusing to see the mal-agreement which often occurred between man and beast. A stout and heavy man might be seen sweating and toiling along on the back of one of the most diminutive of donkeys; a graceful cavalier, who prided himself on his horsemanship, and had selected what appeared to be a fine-looking Arab, found himself on an asthmatic animal, which neither whip nor the pins stuck into his boots for lack of spurs, could force from a sluggish walk. Then came along a young midshipman, on a streak of lightning, clinging to the mane or saddle, and agape to find himself in a situation where his superior officers, and even the Commodore, were glad to yield the deck to him. His horse, brought up on the wild hills, is unconscious how sadly he is violating naval etiquette; and away they go, till a turn in the road hides them from our sight. "Give my Jack a punch," cries one, "the nasty beast, I can't get him to move;" while at the act, Jack suddenly finds the use of his hinder quarters, and the puncher, from being a grave-looking personage, suddenly takes to hopping and singing, and working his features into the oddest grimace. Some of our company had no animals at all, and others were debating whether they had not better leave those they had; while the animals themselves stood straight up to second the motion. My friend M——, thinking perhaps that necessity hath no law, stepped up coolly to a horse fastened to a bit of shrubbery, and having loosed him, and thrown his Turkey rug over the saddle, seated himself on the top of it; concluding, with good reason, that the owner would soon be after him, and that he could then, perhaps, make a bargain for the beast. It turned out that the horse belonged to a soldier going our way, and who, on promise of a *bakshish*, or present, agreed to this impudent arrangement; but the next morning horse and soldier were missing, and with them the fine large Turkey rug,—showing how universally we may apply the counsel, "set a rogue to catch a rogue."

Amid this scene of confusion, the general attention was directed to the family group at the head of the party, a group respected and beloved by all of us; and it was gratifying, in the cheerful looks of the ladies, to find that they were rather amused than dismayed by the necessary discomforts of this new kind of travelling. We got, by and by, into pretty good order, and moved cheerily on. Our company consisted of the Commodore, lady, and three daughters, the consul and lady, thirty-six lieutenants, midshipmen, &c., twelve petty officers and servants; and muleteers in addition sufficient to make a party in all, of more than seventy persons.

Nearly every individual was armed, and our warlike accoutrements, as well as the rest of our fitting out, had a broad dash of the picturesque.

While we were getting ready for a move, an old seaman came up to me, and begged hard that I would get him permission to accompany us. "Why, W——," I replied, "I don't see what reason I can give for it that fifty others might not urge, and besides, you have no donkey you see every thing with four legs to it is already taken up." "Oh," he replied, "ask to allow me to walk by —— and take care of the sedan; and as to a donkey, I don't need one, I am willing to walk all the way." I succeeded in the application, and had forgotten the circumstance, till one day, eighteen months after, when the crew had been discharged, W—— came up to me on the wharf at Norfolk, and, taking my hand, said I had conferred a favor on him which he would remember to the last day of his life. I asked him what it was: "Oh," he replied, "you got me permission to go to Jerusalem."

When I returned from the Holy City, I brought back a quantity of olive root from the Mount of Olives, and giving it to the carpenter on board ship to saw it up, on going to the bench, I found the seamen around, catching the sawdust, and picking the earth from the holes among the roots. So strong was the feeling of interest with which the proximity of the city had inspired us.

It may be supposed, then, that we wound along among the gardens of Jaffa with cheerful alacrity. The road is sandy and toilsome, but is bordered with shrubbery interwoven with the huge cactus, and gay flowers were pendant on every side. We had left the city at 4 P. M.; and the sun, now throwing its rays slantingly among the blossoms and foliage, gave them their richest effect. About a mile from the walls we came to a Turkish fountain, about twenty feet in height, and highly ornamented. The road bends at this place, and soon after ascends a range of low hills, where cultivation ceases, and the traveller finds himself in the open country, without enclosure or habitation in sight.

A number of the European consuls, and other gentlemen resident in Jaffa, had done us the honor to accompany us thus far. They were mounted on fine spirited Arabs, and now driving the shovel-shaped stirrup into their horses' sides, flew up the hill side, and at length, brought at the summit in bold relief against the sky, they formed a picture such as is seen only in these glowing eastern countries. They wore the native costume, presenting a variety of brilliant and fanciful colors ; and in this case the dress was perfectly clean, and evidently put on with careful and studied effect. Having presently reached a level piece of ground, they scattered, and commenced the djerid, a play in which the Arabs greatly delight, and which is adapted to bring out the powers both of horse and rider, and show them to fine advantage. Each horseman is furnished with a stick of some tough material, four or five feet in length, and of the thickness of the middle finger ; they divide about equally, and each selecting an opponent, the effort is to strike the adversary with the rod. In doing this they pursue each other at the top of the horse's speed, often bring him to a halt so suddenly as to throw him on his haunches, whirl at an instant's warning, hang by the leg and arm so as to avoid the whizzing rod, catch it in the air, or, while the horse is at full speed, snatch it from the ground, and turning, become the pursuer till the rod is discharged, or the adversary has again recovered one in his turn. It is an exciting and highly animated sport, and was kept up on the large plain, now on our right, now on the left, till one or two of the company became provoked by some well-dealt blows, and the play began to look serious; while a few showed by their soiled dresses that they had come in closer contact with the ground than was pleasant. Kind feeling was, however, soon restored by some smart hits in return, and the play wound up in good-humor; after which, our Arab guide, with his long, slender spear, once more putting himself at the head of our party, our friends wheeled their steeds, and having made a graceful salaam, darted over the hill on their return to Jaffa, and were soon out of sight.

We were now fairly on the celebrated *Plain of Sharon;* but times have sadly changed, and we might have looked in vain for roses or any other shrub. The road laid through a country not absolutely flat, and yet scarcely undulating; with scarcely a tree, and no where presenting any sign of cultivation. Towards sunset, however, we found ourselves approaching an olive grove, beyond which, on our left, was a wretched looking village of ten or a dozen houses; also a ruin of large dimensions, which we had not time to examine. Beyond this the country assumed the same open and deserted appearance; and, except a fountain which we passed a few miles onward, there was nothing to show that it was the habitation of men. Darkness, by and by, began to fall around us, we drew our company into a more compact form, and having examined our arms, passed on in silence; a spirit of sadness and musing, excited probably by the melancholy nature of the country, having apparently seized on the whole of our party.

We were now in what was formerly the territory of the tribe of Dan, their possessions, I believe, having extended from the sea inward to a distance of thirty miles, and about twelve from north to south. Of Dan, it was said by his father Jacob, that he was "a serpent by the way, an adder in the path, that biteth the horse-heels, so that his rider shall fall back." And the position which long afterwards fell by lot to this tribe, appears to have been adapted to produce or to cherish such a trait of character.

Two thirds of the great highway from Jerusalem to its sea-port Joppa, laid through their territory; and the long winding ravine by which this road ascends from the plain of Sharon into the mountainous region that encircles Jerusalem, affords admirable facilities for plundering. Until very recently, the upper extremity of this ravine was occupied by Aboo Ghoosh, at the head of a set of daring fellows, who regularly laid contributions on travellers; while a village near the other extremity bore no better reputation. Dr. Clarke's baggage was seized upon and carried to the latter town, where he had great difficulty in recovering it; and, more recently, the French traveller, De la Martine, found it prudent by judicious means to secure in season the good favor of Aboo Ghoosh. This robber-chief, whose power extended over a large tract of country, and was well systematized, has recently been appointed by the Pasha of Egypt to a high office in Jerusalem; and we saw him on our visit enthroned in his new state, where he seems ill at ease. Mohammed Ali has thus removed a nuisance and secured a powerful friend; but it is not probable that his robber-propensities will be greatly checked by these new dignities.

When shall this desert region rejoice and blossom as the rose, and when shall we be able to speak of "the excellency of Carmel and Sharon?"—"The highways" now "lie waste, and the wayfaring man ceaseth; Lebanon is ashamed and hewn down, and Sharon is like a wilderness."—Though it is sad to look at a plain like this of Sharon, about eighty miles in length by twenty in width, and of extensive fertility, and bordering also on the sea, yet now little more than a desert waste; though sad, there is nothing very remarkable in it, for it is the character of many such plains in Asia; but there is something very remarkable when we think of this country in connexion with the strange people whose fatherland it is, a people who are over the whole face of our globe, an astonishment, a proverb, and a by-word; turning ever with warm desires towards the home of their fathers; yet still "scattered among all people, from one end of the earth to the other," and among them finding no ease nor rest, but distressed "with a trembling heart and failing of eyes, and sorrow of mind"—outcasts every where, the "heaven over their head is brass, and the earth under their feet is iron." I do not see how a man can read the 28th chapter of Deuteronomy, and be satisfied that it was written at the time it purports to be, and yet remain an infidel; and that it was written at that time, is a matter capable of very easy proof. I have seen the Jews in a great many countries; and if we were to sit down to describe their condition, we could not find terms to express it more accurately than is done in that chapter, penned 3287 years ago.

About nine o'clock we discovered lights ahead, and heard the barking of dogs, and soon after entered Ramla, the ancient Arimathea, which was to be our stopping-place for the night. Here, to our surprise, we found also an agent of our government, a vice-consul appointed by the consul at Jaffa, to whom, I believe, he had paid a consideration for the office. He was an Armenian gentleman, apparently wealthy, and certainly kind and hospitable. Our arrival had been expected, and every thing grateful to hungry and wearied pilgrims had been provided. Tables were loaded with fowls and mutton, and with the delicious water-melons of Jaffa, as well as abundance of other fruits, and with wine. When our large company had all been fed, such conveniences as the house afforded for sleeping were freely given up to us; our host all the while sitting unobtrusively at one side of the eating room, and seldom speaking, except to order additional supplies of refreshments. However, Mon. Damon, the consul at Jaffa, who with his lady had come with us, in order that the credit for the entertainment might not be lost, took it all to himself; bustling about, and telling us that the house was his own, that he had provided the feast, and bidding us welcome. I am happy to be able to add, that through the influence of Commodore Patterson, this gentleman, Mr. Marcus Abers, has since received an appointment independent of the consulate at Jaffa. We received, with the freedom of sailors, what was so freely and generously offered; and when, in the morning, our caterer, after some hesitation on the score of delicacy, offered remuneration, as the company was so large and miscellaneous, it was declined, and the party was cordially invited to repeat the visit on our return.

Ramla has at present little to detain a traveller, though it was formerly a city of considerable dimensions; its population now is about 3,000, principally Mahommedans and Christians of the Greek church. At the borders on the western side, thirty miles from Jerusalem, are some vast subterranean apartments belonging to the ancient times of the city. One is one hundred and fifty feet long by forty in width, and is twenty-five feet deep; the second and third are each seventy feet square, and of the same depth as the former. Adjoining the second, is a tower twenty-five feet square, and still one hundred feet in height, and a conspicuous object at a great distance on the plain. Our time did not admit of a visit to these ruins, and for the dimensions I am indebted to Mr. Thompson, by whom they have been described. Mr. Thompson was at Ramla during the recent earthquake, and heard a debate on its causes by the learned men of the city. The Cadi, or Judge, spoke at last, and with gravity suitable to his high station, gave his solution of the phenomenon. "The earth," he said, "has seven foundations; the first, water; second, air; third, a mountain; fourth, a cushion; fifth, (Mr. T. does not recollect;) sixth, a great rock; and seventh, the horn of the great ox. When the ox becomes fatigued, he changes the rock from one horn to the other, and that caused the shaking."

After some slight refreshment, at an early hour on the 16th we resumed our journey, and soon found ourselves once more breathing the country air. We passed some ruins on our right just after leaving the city, and also, soon after this, a company of about 200 cavalry at drill on the plain. Our road, I ought to have remarked before this, was not directly across the plain, but in a slanting direction, Jerusalem being situated a little to the south of east from Jaffa. The distance from Ramla is thirty miles. We descended two or three steep banks, separated from each other by intervals of several miles, and thus arrived, at length, at the lowest level of the plain, which appears to consist of this level, and, on the west of it, of a succession of terraces, each about forty feet in height, and three or four miles in width. The country, during our morning ride, was not of so melancholy a cast as on the day previous, patches of millet or indian corn occurring here and there, with other signs of cultivation; but the sun now beat upon us with scorching power. About ten o'clock we passed a miserable village close on our left, and an hour after, a cone-shaped eminence on our right, with some ruins, supposed to be the remains of Beth-Horon, noticed in 2 Chron. viii. 5. 1 Samuel, xiii. 18.*

The hill is about 400 feet in height, and in most parts is of difficult ascent; it was well adapted for defence, and the extensive and massive ruins on the top show that it was a place of considerable strength. This was probably the *upper* city: for the site of the "Nether-Beth-Horon," we must look among the broken ground that skirts the lower part of the eminence. This was a place of importance, as it commands the entrance of the winding ravine, along which the road ascends from the plain into the mountainous district, or what is called in the first chapter of John, the "hill country" of Judea.

The entrance into this ravine is about two miles east from Beth-Horon; and as it stood gaping before

* See also Josephus, Bell. Jud., Lib. II. chap. xix. § 2 and 8.

14

us, with the mountains on either side towering to a great height, while the representations of travellers had led us to expect beyond it only mountains, still darker and more dreary, we turned some reluctant looks backward towards the plain. The roads over these mountains we had been also informed by Mr. Damon, were the worst possible; but in this latter respect we were to meet with an agreeable disappointment. One of the consuls at Jaffa, a merchant, (I believe the Sardinian consul,) in order to divert the trade of the Mecca and Jerusalem caravans from Damascus to his own city, had lately put the road in excellent order. In many places he had blasted rocks, and at others had built up walls; the operation had been an expensive one, and the enterprise of the gentleman merits a better reward than I am afraid it will receive.

As we were entering the ravine, we met a company of Egyptian soldiers; and, further on, in a narrow part, encountered a much larger force, returning to the west. They had with them a great number of camels loaded with baggage and accoutrements, and often with field-pieces, some of the latter (brass six pounders) being lashed to spars which were fastened to the backs of two camels, one before the other. The soldiers, though the balance of power was greatly on their side, were very civil; and in no instance showed a disposition to offer annoyance, or give us unnecessary trouble. It was in this pass that the Roman army, under Cestius, were almost totally destroyed.

We found the ascent up to the ravine, though long, yet far from being toilsome. At the summit, at a spot commanding a view of all the plain of Sharon and the sea beyond, we stopped in an olive grove for dinner. This was near the village of the ex-robber, prince Aboo Ghoosh; but a change has come over the country under the sovereignty of Mohammed Ali, for the people did not even come to look at us.

Descending again, we passed, at the bottom of a valley, a village, on the borders of which is a large church belonging to the time of the crusades. A more desolate scene than presented itself as we wound up the hills beyond this village cannot be easily imagined. The rocks in all this region are secondary limestone, and the hills, consequently, are rounded, presenting few bold peaks or precipitous ridges; but all was gray rock from the bottom to the summit, and the senses became pained by the gloomy monotony of the scene, a wide and dreary waste of bare rocks. By and by, descending again, we found ourselves in a valley watered by a rivulet, and with some fields and a vineyard; but soon plunged again into the same succession of bare rocky hills, where not a tree nor shrub was to be seen, and not a living thing, except a bird now and then whirling in its solitary flight. A steep descent brought us at length into the narrow defile where occurred the battle between Ibrahim Pasha and the rebels already noticed; and skeletons of horses were still scattered by the road side. This pass is also a favorite haunt of robbers; particularly at a spot where a bridge crosses a dry channel which winds through the bottom of the valley.—*Siste viator*. This channel, now dry, but covered by a considerable stream in winter, is that from which David selected pebbles for his sling when going to meet Goliah; I believe, however, this event occurred some distance further down. We passed this bridge on our return an hour before daylight; and, as we approached, an officer of the Pasha's household who accompanied us, made the party halt and form into compact order; and then had the bridge reconnoitred before he allowed us to proceed. There was no one there, but further on, at the battle ground, a strange horseman rode up and passed us several times, as if scrutinizing our company, and others were seen on the other side of the glen; but apparently they did not like our equipment, as they gave us no further trouble.

Having crossed this bridge, we were now in constant expectation of getting sight of Jerusalem; and as we approached the summit of a long hill, our caterer, Lieutenant S——, made the officers in the van fall back, so that Mrs. Patterson might be the first to advance and catch a view of the sacred city. But we were to be disappointed; it was not in sight, and these disappointments occurred so often, that at length we grew less earnest in our look out ahead. Evening was fast approaching, and just as distant objects were beginning to grow indistinct, a sudden rise on the road brought to view some white buildings far off, and a little to our left. A sudden cry of "Jerusalem" burst from the foremost, and all hurried forward to enjoy the welcome sight; again, however, we were mistaken. But, a few minutes after this, while we were gazing at the objects just described, and debating whether they were the sacred city or not, a long white wall, with battlements and towers, presented itself suddenly right before us; and then arose a general cry of joyful surprise—*for this we knew to be Jerusalem.* I believe there was not one of us who was not affected with powerful emotions; and among these feelings was generally a sensation of pleasing surprise at the imposing appearance of the city; for whether it was owing to its contrast to the small group of houses we had been looking at, or to the manner in which it bursts upon us in a dreary desert, or whether there was sufficient cause for this in the city itself, I cannot say; but the first impression was certainly a very favorable one.

The city, as viewed from the west, presents a stretch of wall about two thirds of a mile in length, battlemented and strengthened with numerous towers, and, at the Jaffa gate, which is midway along, fortified with heavy castles. South of this gate, the walls stand on the edge of a ravine or valley sixty feet in depth and two hundred feet wide, and at this part, particularly, the effect is very bold and striking. As we ap-

14*

proached, battlement and turret were here thrown out into strong relief against the clear evening sky.

This was our first view and first impression of Jerusalem. To myself, however, little time was given for observation. The Commodore called for me; and telling me that as this was a city in the line of my profession, they must look to me to provide quarters for the company—said he wished me to ride forward rapidly, and see where we could find accommodations. So I changed my humble donkey for a spirited steed, and taking for interpreter a young Arab officer who had accompanied us from Jaffa, set forward at a pace that made us look more like crusading knights at a tilt than peaceable pilgrims. The gates, which are usually closed at sunset, we found were kept open in expectation of the arrival of our party, and a large number of citizens were standing in groups without. On our drawing up and inquiring the way to the house of Mr. Nicholayson, the missionary from England, he himself stept forward and gave us a hearty welcome. His house he immediately placed at our disposal, but on his inquiring how many there might be in the party, and receiving my answer, "I think about seventy," he stood aghast. A company of seven or a dozen, the number as he had supposed our company, he could readily accommodate, and his house was cordially at our service for as many as it would hold; but where to find accommodations for seventy he could not tell, some of the monasteries, the usual resort of pilgrims, being now, he said, in quarantine on account of the plague. We turned into the city, however, to make an effort; and crossing an irregular open area, and then winding down some dark narrow streets, stopped at length at a low gate in the face of a high massy wall. It admitted us into the chief Latin convent; but the Prior, on our being presented, said that nearly all the building was in quarantine, some of the monks having recently died of the plague, and that an adjacent establishment belonging to his order was in a similar situation. Foiled here, we proceeded on a little further, and on applying, though with reluctance, at the Greek convent, were successful; their large building, forming a hollow square with a court in the centre, being given up to us. We returned forthwith, and found that our company had already entered the city, and in attempting to follow us, had got jammed up in one of the narrow streets, where a scene of vexatious and yet amusing confusion was just commencing; the baggage mules with their broad panniers and projecting loads sticking fast between the opposite houses, and, in their efforts to extricate themselves, taking little note of rank or office; while torches glancing here and there upon pistol and cutlass, and the dusty, and jaded, and sometimes disconsolate looking features of our companions, mixed up with the wild and curious gaze of the natives, assisted in making up a singular scene. They had just learned the result of our application at the Latin convent;

and to a wearied man, the idea of passing the night in such rough and odoriferous streets as these, could not be a pleasing one. They were highly gratified to find that we had at length been able to procure quarters. The Commodore and his family were invited to the house of Mr. Nicholayson, where, among the kind and agreeable members of his family, they soon found themselves in a pleasant home; while the rest of us, passing through the low strong portal of the convent, and emerging by and by from the dark narrow passage, into the enclosed court, turned to see what species of accommodation we were to have. The prospect seemed melancholy enough. Around the court was a range of buildings, three fourths of which were given up to us, the remaining fourth being occupied by the Prior's rooms and offices of the church, and by the church itself. The lower part of our portion of the edifice was occupied as stables, kitchen, granary, &c.; and gave also accommodation to some of our party. Ascending from this by a large stairway, we entered on a platform passing around three sides of the court, with a parapet along its interior edge, while on its opposite border was a range of cells, which we found on inquiry were to be our dormitories. Tired as we were, we recoiled from the sight of them. They were usually about eight or nine feet square, and so low that a person could scarcely stand upright in them; a broken door, a hole for a window, a stone or mortar floor, and a thin reed mat, and dust in the greatest abundance—this was the sight that presented itself as we came to examine our domicils. Some joked, some took it all in quiet, and some said "it was really too bad." But uncomfortable as these abodes appeared to us, other creatures did not seem to think them so, for they were really well tenanted; and when our lights were extinguished, and we had wrapped ourselves each in his blanket, and had stretched ourselves on the stone floor, we soon discovered how far from solitary was the life of our friends the monks. Our chambers were alive with lilliputians, which immediately commenced an attack on us. As D., and S., and myself, were lying in our little room, we first heard some notes of distress on the outside, and occasionally an exclamation of "Hollo, are you out here too?" and then there was a general cry—"I can't bear this any longer;" and we rushed out to the platform to which we found every cell ejecting its inmates. We did not get asleep until nature, towards morning, was absolutely worn out, when the fleas, having worried us into utter exhaustion, were allowed to gorge themselves at their leisure. The reader may perhaps think that I might have spared him this scene, which is not a pleasant one, and must jar on the feelings of one who would come with other sensations, and be occupied with other thoughts, in this city of solemn and touching associations; but my impression is, that he would like to see the modern city as it is, and I wish also, as far as possible, to make him also a traveller, and carry him along with us; this is no exaggerated picture of our first night, and may be taken as a sample of the rest. Jerusalem, however, is not alone in this; but the whole of this region, from the cataracts of the Nile to Constantinople, is teeming with fleas. We thought, however, that this city was peculiarly infested with them, and were informed that in the most cleanly houses, no care could keep any part of the building free from them.

The night passed away at length, and ushered in a brilliant dawn, such as is not often seen except in these eastern countries, where the thin and scanty exhalations are just sufficient, without obscuring any portions of the landscape, to tinge all with roseate and purple hues.

CHAPTER XIII.

Morning view of the city. Glance at the localities. Question with regard to the place of the Crucifixion. Its practical nature. Scene usually sketched in the mind. The event probably more humiliating in its attendant circumstances. Traditions forced upon the visitor to Jerusalem. Their effect on the mind. Danger of such visits to those who will not separate truth from error. "El Devoto Peregrino." Dr. Clarke.

I AROSE early on the morning of the 16th; the sun was shining bright, and the atmosphere had a freshness and a balminess quite exhilarating. Having made a hasty toilet, I placed a ladder against our range of cells, and climbing to the flat roof, by which they were covered, gazed around; and now, for the first time, felt that I was really in Jerusalem.

Immediately east of the city, and separated from it by a narrow valley or ravine, was a mountain large enough to command our respect by its vastness, and yet not too large for gracefulness and beauty. I knew it at once to be the *Mount of Olives*. It has three summits, one in the centre and one at each extremity; they are of nearly equal height, and when viewed from the city present for their outline a gentle and beautiful curve. A large part of it is covered with olive trees, particularly the central and northern summits and declivities; and they still form so striking a feature, that if the mountain were now to be named, we should be apt to call it the Mount of Olives.

Nearer to me, and just within the city walls, on the east, was a large open place, and from the centre of this rose an octangular edifice of considerable beauty; I had seen pictures of it, and recognized it as the mosque of Omar, standing on the supposed site of the Temple of Solomon. There at least was undoubtedly Mount Moriah, and my own eyes were gazing upon it.

I turned from it soon, however, to look for a spot of still more absorbing interest. Where was Mount Calvary? Not far from me rose two domes, one somewhat peaked, the other one more obtuse, but very large. In all directions, however, were domes of various sizes, and the mind was puzzled, though still arrested by the position as well as the magnitude of these two. A couple of old and venerable looking monks were hanging over the parapet of a neighboring convent watching my motions, and turning to inquire of them, I found my surmise had been correct. This was the church of Mount Calvary and of the Holy Sepulchre.—"Put off thy shoes from off thy feet, for the place whereon thou standest is holy ground."—"At least," a voice seemed to say to me, "walk here with seriousness and humility; bow thy head, and cleanse thy heart, and tread with meekness the ground trod by Him who was here humbled for thee, and here bore thy sins upon the cross." It was the Sabbath also—this first day of our visit; and the quiet and healthful influence of that holy season was added to the power which Jerusalem would at any time have exercised upon the heart.

I am not ashamed of the gospel of Christ. Imagination in its highest flights has not pictured a scene that will compare in interest, or in deep and searching pathos, with the reality here displayed in the redemption of man. It partakes of the character of all the works of God, combining a simplicity that opens it to the comprehension of all men, with a grandeur and sublimity that must excite the admiration of the highest seraphim. I have seen it where I have seen man's proud philosophy quail and shrink into nothingness—in the sick room and by the dying bed; I have seen it come gently and quietly, and open the feeble lips in praise, and in utterance of joyful and triumphant hope. I have seen it sustain and cheer those whom the world, and the world's enjoyments and earthly hopes too, had all deserted, and who would otherwise have been left in maddening solitude and wretchedness; I have seen it sustain them; and while the body was tortured with pains, I have seen it raise the mind superior to bodily feeling, and while the cold sweat was breaking out upon the brow, keep that brow calm and serene. The tortured child of clay thought of his Saviour's humiliation and pains, and of the glory wrought out for him; and, in the boundless love that led to the sufferings of Calvary, found assurance that God was

15

even now a friend closer than a brother, and would not desert him to the last. "I am not ashamed of the gospel of Christ crucified, for it is the power of God unto salvation to every one that believeth;"—and the highest honor of my life was on that day, when I was permitted to walk amid scenes dignified and exalted by the great events of our redemption.

It was, indeed, a day of concentrated interest and gratification, such as I had never experienced before, and do not expect ever to feel again. After breakfast our large company broke up into smaller parties, and proceeded to visit the various localities. In company with Lieutenant F. I walked over to Mr. Nicholayson's, and, under the guidance of that gentleman, we went, with the Commodore and family, first to the church of Mount Calvary and of the Holy Sepulchre.

But is this church really on the site of the crucifixion, and of the sepulture of our Saviour? This is a question which it may be well to settle before proceeding further, so that we may know with what feelings to approach spots of such sacred and interesting titles. It is a subject on which my own mind is satisfied almost beyond a doubt, and if the reader will for a short time give me patient attention, in a somewhat dry and difficult examination of facts, I think he may find himself rewarded for his labor. It is true that the question with regard to the exact *locality* of these events is of little consequence, compared with the great subject of the redemption itself, and the query whether we have, by a living faith, made that salvation ours; but still it is one not without its practical consequences. The mind often tries to picture the scene of the Saviour's sufferings, the uplifted bloody cross, the hours of agony, the tumultuous crowds of scoffers below; and our feelings are touched, and the heart is benefitted, by contemplating the price that was paid for our salvation, the obligations under which we are placed by it, and the assurance it gives us of the surpassing love of Him who spared not his own Son, but gave him freely for us; the whole scene is often one of pious thought and of pulpit description, and has frequently enlisted the skill of painters, and is a matter of practical interest. My impression is, that the scene we sketch is very seldom correct, and that the event itself had a depth of humiliation that our thoughts do not reach; and in this I do not have reference to the condescension of the sufferer, but to circumstances connected with the locality of the suffering. Our thoughts, when they turn to this subject, I believe place before us an eminence of considerable elevation, sloping gradually upward, and crowned at the summit by the crosses of our Saviour and the malefactors, while the slopes are all crowded with the excited spectators. This, I believe, is the picture that is generally presented to our mind; and there is in it a degree of physical dignity, that the event itself, I am inclined to think, did not possess. On the other hand, if my apprehensions are correct, the crucifixion was attended with every physical circumstance that could make it humbling as well as painful; instead of being on the summit of a lofty eminence, it was on a rocky knoll at the bottom of a natural theatre of hills; on one side, at the distance of five hundred feet, was the city wall; on another, the low and wretched suburb of a suburb; it was in an open place, with dusty roads to various parts of the city passing near it; a thoroughfare, in short, where the spectacle of dust and confusion was broken only by a few gardens, the remains of a larger range of such enclosures, now nearly destroyed by the encroaching suburb.

Such is the scene which the result of my investigations, commenced there, and followed up since my return, places before me. I examined the ground in and about the city as carefully as my time would allow, and with the aid of Josephus, have constructed a map, which is here offered to the examination of the reader. In my younger days, I used to take great interest in maps of Jerusalem, till, finding that each differed from every other one, and that they were filled with the localities of public buildings, some of them evidently placed at random, I lost in a measure my confidence in all the plans, and as they furnished me with no means of judging for myself, I gave them up in despair; and this is probably the case with many other persons.

In this map I have laid down nothing for which we have not authority, and I have in every part quoted the authorities; so that, if the reader chooses, he can examine and form an opinion for himself. He will find that I have been guided chiefly by Josephus, whose descriptions of the ancient city are, undoubtedly, by far the most correct as well as the most minute that we possess.* If I have not rightly understood them, it has not been from the want of study. I have read him carefully, and compared one part with another, and have seized on every allusion to localities, and have again and again studied and compared, and did not stop till I had a map that would correspond to all such descriptions and allusions. He is, I think, deserving of our confidence; for he spent much time in and about the ancient city; his duties as an officer in Titus' army led him to examine, and as far as possible to get the admeasurements of its walls and towers; he must at this time have been preparing for his work on the Jewish nation, and probably made his records on the ground; and with a little allowance for the pride and prejudices of a Jew, as regards his country, seems to be a fair and candid narrator of events, a large part of which fell under his own observation. In some places he is obscure, and at times appears to contradict himself; but a little study will enable us to understand and

* I have been surprised as well as pleased to see the large number of copies of Josephus that are sold in this city [New-York.] I have attended the book auctions here quite frequently; and have observed that there is no book of its size that meets with such a ready sale, or brings so good a price. The work merits all this—Josephus has not received the praise from literary men that he deserves.

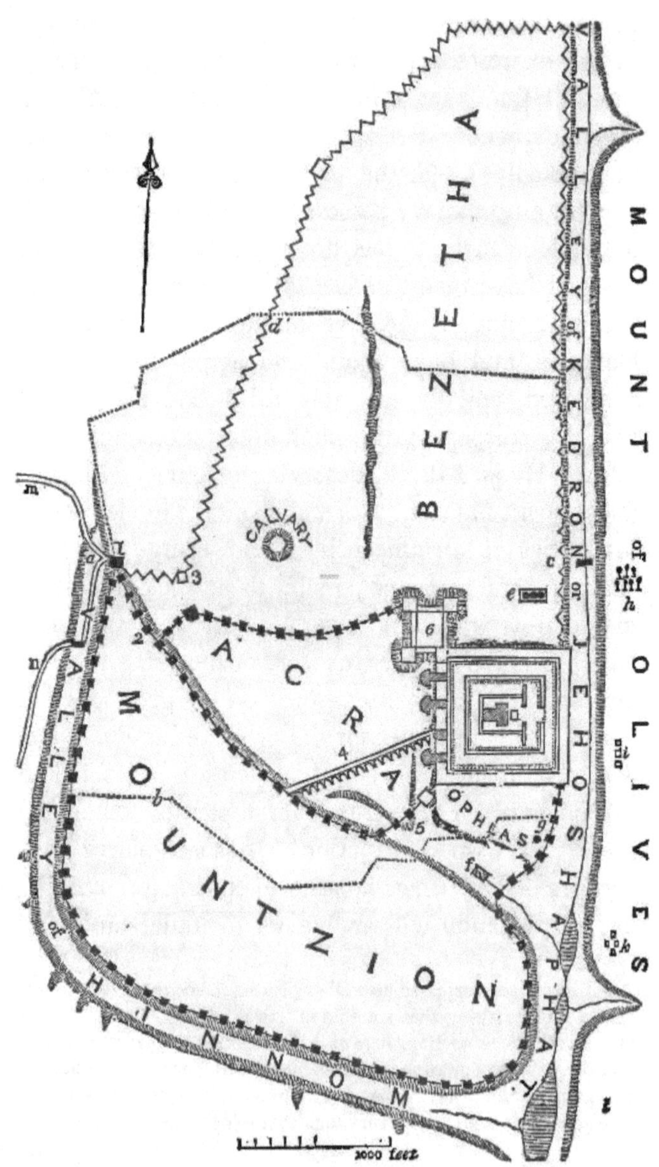
MOUNT of OLIVES
VALLEY of KEDRON or JEHOSHAPHAT
BEZETHA
CALVARY
ACRA
MOUNT ZION
OPHLAS
VALLEY of HINNOM
1000 feet

reconcile most of these passages; in many parts, particularly in scenes of pathos, there is a simplicity and yet a force, in his descriptions, that are really admirable.

In the map* just spoken of, I have sketched also the line of the present city walls, as I found it could be done without producing confusion, and I thought the reader would like to be able to see how much of the ground of the ancient city is occupied by the modern Jerusalem.

* PLAN OF THE ANCIENT AND MODERN CITY OF JERUSALEM.

The castellated lines represent the walls as they existed at the time of the crucifixion.

The zigzag lines mark the supposed course of Agrippa's wall, erected a few years after that event.

The dotted lines represent the walls of the present city of Jerusalem.

The square figure represents the court of the ancient temple, with the temple in the centre.

REFERENCES.

ANCIENT CITY.	MODERN CITY.
1. Castle of Hippicus.	*a*. Jaffa Gate.
2. Gate Gennath, or Gate of the Gardens.	*b*. Zion Gate.
3. Tomb of the High Priest John.	*c*. St. Stephen's Gate.
4. Bridge connecting the Temple with the upper city.	*d*. Damascus Gate.
5. Supposed site of the Xistus.	*e*. Reputed Pool of Bethesda.
6. Castle of Antonia.	*f*. Pool of Siloam.
	g. Fountain of the Virgin.
	h. Garden of Gethsemane.
	i. Monuments of Absalom and Zachariah.
	k. Village of Siloa.
	l. Supposed Mount of Corruption.
	m. Road to Jaffa.
	n. Road to Bethlehem.

The traveller to the present city, at least the Protestant traveller, is excessively annoyed at every step with traditions in which he cannot believe, and with having localities pointed out in which he can place no confidence whatever; and the effect is bad in a great many ways. It not only disturbs sadly the feelings with which he would wish to walk over the grounds of Jerusalem, but, sickened and disgusted, he is apt to run into the opposite extreme of incredulity, and reject even where there is proper grounds for belief. I have now before me large extracts which I made from a book called El Devoto Peregrino, or "The Devout Pilgrim," published at Madrid in 1654, by P. F. Antonio of Castile, Commissary General of Jerusalem for Spain, and Guardian of Bethlehem,* in the last of which places he had spent a number of years. It offers a good specimen of the accounts of places that are thrust on the visitor to Jerusalem, and as it is a book of high authority, I will by and by give some of the extracts at length. In this work he points out edifices, at present standing, and which it must be evident are comparatively modern structures, as the houses of Pilate, of Simon the Pharisee, where Mary Magdalen washed our Saviour's feet with her tears, of St. Ann, of the Rich Man, &c. &c.; and this in the face of authentic his-

* "El Devoto Peregrino, viage de tierra Santa, compuesto por el P. F. Antonio de Castillo, Predicador Apostolico Padre dela Provincia de S. Juan Baptiste y Comisario General de Jerusalem en los Reynos de Espana Guardian de Belem."

tory, which informs us that the city, when taken by Titus, was, with the exception of a few towers, levelled with the ground, and that a ploughshare was made to pass over it. There is scarcely an event of any description, mentioned in the New Testament as occurring in or about Jerusalem, of which they do not designate the exact locality; and to all this they have added traditions so absurd as to be beyond all belief, to say nothing of their childishness. All this is repeated to the visitor to Jerusalem, and produce a revulsion of feeling not only disagreeable but dangerous; and men whose faith is not previously settled, or who do not like the trouble of sifting the truth from error, I believe would be apt to be injured by such a visit. And it appears to me that most Protestant visitors, and our missionaries also, have been betrayed by these feelings into an excess of scepticism, which has led them to reject some things against sound and proper evidence. We must not reject all because some is false, any more than we would reject all species of coin because some is spurious; a wise man will be led by the fact that there is spurious money, to believe that there is good money some where; and therefore, these tales, instead of provoking utter scepticism, while they make us cautious, should at the same time lead us to suppose that there *is* ground for belief.

Dr. Clark is the boldest of these modern sceptics; for while others simply doubt, he goes further, and with a feeling bordering certainly on rashness, attempts at once to designate other sites for these distinguished events. His boldness is not more surprising than is the small amount of evidence he produces for his localities; and I believe he has had scarcely a single follower, among either readers at home, or travellers to these interesting spots. As he stands quite alone, the subject of wonder rather than of credence, we will not stop to examine his theories; but proceed to notice the old belief, and the doubts of more cautious and moderate men.

CHAPTER XIV.

Localities in Jerusalem that are certain. Valley of Kedron. Mount Moriah. Valley of the Cheesemongers. Mount Zion, its ancient limits. Present remains of its northern boundary. Line of the "Old wall." Acra. Gate of the Gardens. Limits of the city at the time of the crucifixion. Bezetha and the wall of Agrippa. Monument of John. Whither our judgment, unassisted by tradition, leads us as regards the place of the crucifixion. Rocky Knoll. Not called *Mount* Calvary in the Scriptures. Tradition. Conclusion to which all this leads us. Circumstances and scene of the crucifixion. The question with regard to the spot of our Saviour's burial

THERE are a few places in and about Jerusalem, in respect to which there can be no possible mistake. These are, the Mount of Olives; the Valley of Kedron, sometimes called the valley of Jehoshaphat; the brook Kedron; the Valley of Hinnom; Mount Moriah; Mount Zion; and the hill called Bezetha. The Mount of Olives speaks at once for itself, and has never been doubted by any one: it descends by a rapid slope down to the brook Kedron, in summer a dry water-course about nine feet wide, and in the wet season an irregular torrent: with regard to this brook, also, no one has ever had any doubt. This valley of Kedron formed the eastern boundary of the ancient,* as it does now also of the modern city. Immediately after crossing the brook Kedron towards

* Josephus, Bell. Jud. lib. v. cap. 4. § 5. Also, Antiq. lib. xiv. cap. 4. § 1.

the west, the ground at present commences ascending so rapidly, as to require a zigzag path: at the height of about eighty feet we come to the wall, and to the general level of the present city. This slope is made up of debris, or loose stuff, composed of earth mixed with pottery, fragments of bricks, &c.; and it seems probable that the ancient wall of Bezetha, standing on the line of the present rampart, had without it a much more precipitous descent.

Mount Moriah is at present a piece of level ground, of the same elevation as those portions of the city immediately adjoining it on the north and west, and is not in any way to be distinguished from them. It is occupied by an open court, about 1500 feet long and 1000 feet in width, surrounded by a wall and planted with trees. In the centre is a large oblong platform, paved, I believe, with marble, and reached by two or three steps running all around; on this platform stands the mosque of Omar, which is said by the Turks to occupy the exact site of the Temple of Solomon, and is considered by them to be next in sanctity to the venerated Caaba, or holy house at Mecca. So sacred is this place in their eyes, that no Christian is allowed to place his foot within even the large enclosure. There is thus no mountain at present here, and if any one should question whether this was the situation of Mount Moriah, I answer that it is the only place where we can look for it. Mount Moriah was on the eastern side of the city, and adjoining the valley of Kedron;[*] the valley of the Cheesemongers, which still remains, formed its boundary on the south;[†] and as the court of the temple, occupying the whole enlarged mountain, was 729 feet[‡] on each side, we thus get both the northern and the western boundaries, and thus have the exact position and limits of Mount Moriah. It is probable that the Turks are quite correct in saying that their mosque occupies the site of the ancient temple, except that the latter was at a much greater elevation; Mount Moriah having, by artificial means, been raised to a height of about 700 feet. This mountain was at first a rocky precipice, irregular both in shape and surface; it was inclosed by Solomon with a square wall of the dimensions just described, beginning at the bottom of the valleys that bounded it on three sides, and rising on the east and south to the stupendous elevation of 729[§] feet; on the west, from the nature of the ground below, its elevation was nearly 200 feet less; the interval within this was filled with earth, or formed into extensive suites of vaults; and the surface being brought nearly to a level, formed an area for the temple and its various courts.[‖] At the north-western[¶] angle of the temple was a tower or castle, commenced

* Josephus, passim.

† Jos. Antiq. lib. xv. cap. xi. § 5.

‡ Do. § 3.

§ These dimensions seem incredible; but this is a subject that will be noticed by and by.

‖ Jos. Antiq. lib. viii. cap. 3. § 9. lib. xv. cap. xi. § 3.

¶ Jos. de Bel. lib. v. cap. 5. § 8.

16

by the kings of the Asmonean race, but enlarged and strengthened by Herod, who gave it the name of Antonia, in honor of Mark Antony, his friend and patron. It was built on a lofty precipice 1450 feet in circuit, and consisted of a heavy castle in the centre, with a tower at each angle, that on the south-east being of sufficient height to overlook the courts of the temple.*

The opening or outlet of the valley of Tyropœon, or the Cheesemongers, still remains, and is very distinct. The ground begins to decline into it as soon as we leave the court of the mosque of Omar, advancing southward; and at the distance of about 400 feet we come to its lowest part, and the spot where it is lost in the valley of Kedron. This opening is opposite a mountain, called now the Mount of Offence, but styled by Josephus "that other hill," and described by him as just south of the Mount of Olives. A short distance up this valley we come to an oblong pool sunk partly in the ground, and walled on three sides, the fourth being broken down; it is called the Pool of Siloam, and very probably occupies the site of the ancient pool of that name noticed in the Scriptures. A few hundred feet above this pool the valley enters the modern city, and I believe cannot be traced any further. There can be no doubt that it is the ancient Tyropœon, and we

* Antiq. lib. xv. cap. xi. § 4.

thus get a portion of the northern boundary of Mount *Zion.**

Mount Zion had on the east the valley of Kedron, and on the south and west the valley of Hinnom,† or Gehenna, and these boundaries are now just as described by Josephus, except that the sides of the valleys towards the city are now rendered sloping by the vast quantities of debris or loose stuff from the ancient city, instead of being perpendicular as they were in ancient times. That of Hinnom, on its southern and western sides, still presents that appearance, a bold perpendicular precipice, which it would be impossible to scale. This valley is described by Strabo (lib. xvi.) as having a depth of 60 feet and a width of 250, which are pretty nearly its present dimensions. The wall of the ancient city was built on the edge of the precipice, and, according to Tacitus, was, in the parts thus guarded by nature, 60 feet in height; on the northern side of Jerusalem, where the ground offered fewer advantages, it had the prodigious elevation of 120 feet.‡ It was built in a crooked or zigzag line, "so that they might flank the besiegers and cast darts on them sideways."§

We have thus far had what sailors call plain sailing, for no one can easily be at a loss as regards the eastern, southern, and a portion of the western boun-

* Jos. de Bel. lib. v. cap. iv. § 1.
† Ibid.
‡ Tacitus Hist. Lib. v. cap. xi.
§ Ib.

daries of the ancient Jerusalem. The northern limits offer a subject of greater difficulty, and it is one also of greater importance, for on this depends the question whether the spot pointed out as Mount Calvary be really the place of the crucifixion or not. The objectors, including almost all Protestant visitors, say it is not and cannot be, since this spot was evidently within the ancient city; and both from the Scriptures, and from the well-known custom of the Jews on such occasions, we know that this event occurred without the walls. This subject we will now examine.

The valley of Cheesemongers, commencing, as we have seen, just south of the temple, took a course to the north-westward, and formed the boundary of Mount Zion on the north, separating this hill from another on the eastward, called Acra,* probably from the Greek word ακρος, *high*. Acra was originally a flat† on the summit, except at one part, where it rose

* Jos. de Bel. lib. v. cap. iv. § 1.

† Josephus informs us, that the Jews under Simon, "all set themselves to work and levelled this mountain; and in that work spent both day and night, without any intermission, which cost them three whole years before it was removed and brought to an entire level with the plain of the rest of the city; after which the temple was the highest of all the buildings. Now the citadel, as well as the mountain on which it stood, was demolished." Antiq. lib. xiii. cap. vi. § 7.

By the words, "to an entire level with the plain of the rest of the city," he cannot mean to a level with the plain of Zion; for in another place (de Bel. lib. v. cap. iv. § 1.) he says that the upper city, or Zion, was much higher than this; we must understand him to say, that the peak was reduced to the general level of the rest of Acra.

to a peak of sufficient height to overlook the temple. On this Antiochus Epiphanes (B. C. 168.) erected a citadel, strengthened with high walls and towers, which proved such a serious annoyance to the citizens, that, under the rule of Simon Maccabeus, (B. C. 143.) not only was the citadel demolished, but, to prevent its being rebuilt, the hill or peak itself was cut down to the level of the adjoining ground. In this way the whole of Acra got to be comparatively low ground,* and, to facilitate intercourse between the Temple and the "Upper City," or Mount Zion, a bridge† was carried from a gate near the S. W. corner of the Temple quite across to the neighborhood of the palace of David.

Of the valley of the Cheesemongers after it enters the modern city, there are at present no traces, it having doubtless been filled up at the time when Jerusalem was levelled with the ground by order of Titus; but as Mount Zion was much higher than Acra, we may expect to find some remains of the steep ascent by which they passed from this valley up to Zion, or, as it was called by them, "The Upper City." And of this there are considerable remains. Mr. Nicholayson's house stands about three hundred feet a little east of south from the Jaffa gate, which is designated on this map by the figure 1, at the place where the roads from Bethlehem and Jaffa meet. Sixty feet eastward from his house is a slope about twenty-

* Jos. de Bel. lib. v. cap. iv. § 1.

† Ibid. lib. vi. cap. vi. § 2, and cap. viii. § 2.

16*

five feet high, and so steep as to make it difficult even for donkeys to ascend. Standing on its edge, we are still able to overlook a large part of the city to the east of it. This slope continues thence to the south-eastward, keeping parallel to some extensive ruins now to be seen there, the remains of a hospital belonging to the time of the Crusades; the slope being separated from them by a narrow bazaar. This slope is undoubtedly the north-eastern edge of Mount Zion, and I have so expressed it in the map which we are endeavoring to form. I have not been able to trace it further than to the end of this bazaar; but as it passes in the direction of Siloam, or the opening of the valley of Cheesemongers, I have marked it in the map as continuing down to that place, as I have no doubt that it does. This gives us the northern boundary of Mount Zion exactly as described by Josephus, who says that "this city laid over against the temple in the manner of a theatre."* At the place where this slope approaches the nearest to the valley of Hinnom, or near Mr. Nicholayson's, I have placed the tower of Hippicus, which stood at the northern angle of the city of Zion.†

The "old wall," as it is called by Josephus, first erected by David and Solomon, and strengthened by succeeding kings, commences at the tower of Hippi-

* "For the city lay over against the Temple in the manner of a theatre, and was encompassed with a deep valley along the entire south quarter." Antiq. lib. xv. cap. xi. § 5.

† Jos. de Bel. lib. v. cap. iv. § 2.

cus, and had its course on the west and south, directly along the edge of the valley of Hinnom. On reaching the valley of Kedron, it bent to the northward, and curving again to the east just below the pool of Siloam, joined the temple wall nearly at its south-eastern angle. On the northern side, starting again at the tower of Hippicus, it kept along the edge of the bank above the valley of Cheesemongers, until curving opposite the Xistus, it here crossed the valley, and passing by the Xistus and the council-house, joined soon after the western wall of the temple, probably at the south-western angle.*

He does not tell us what is meant by "the Xistus," but it is probably from the Greek word χιστος, "a division" or "separation;" and I suppose refers to the branching of the valley of the Cheesemongers, one part keeping along by Mount Zion, and the other just on the west of Mount Moriah; the latter branch, as I have already said, was filled up by the Maccabees. Just south of the temple, on the ground sloping down to the pool of Siloam, was a small section of the city called Ophlas.†

It is probable that a wall separated also Mount Zion from Ophlas; for we find, that when Titus had possession of Acra and the Temple, he had still to bring his engines against the northern wall of Zion;‡

* Jos. de Bel. lib. v. cap. iv. § 2.

† Ibid. Also cap. vi. § 1.

‡ Ibid. lib. vi. cap. viii. § 1.

which would not have been necessary if he could have passed at once through Ophlas into that city.

Mount Zion was called by David "The Citadel;" it afterwards frequently went by the name of "The Upper City," in contradistinction to Acra, the latter being frequently styled "The Lower City."*

Acra, we are informed by Josephus, was "in the shape of a moon when she is horned;"† and though he gives no intimation to that effect, I suppose the horns must have been to the northward, for I do not see how it is possible that they could have been otherwise. On the west they certainly could not have been, nor on the south, nor on the east; and there remains only the position which I have given them. The northern wall of Acra, sometimes called "the second wall," commenced at the gate Gennath, (i. e. "gate of the gardens,") and then making a curve,‡ terminated at the castle of Antonia.§ I have placed the gate Gennath about five hundred feet from the tower Hippicus, and have carried the wall, in the first place at right angles across the valley of the Cheesemongers, and then placing a tower at the angle, have there commenced the course over towards Antonia. My reasons for this arrange-

* Jos. de Bel. lib. v. cap. iv. § 1. et passim. † Ibid.

‡ Κυκλουμενον is the word used by Josephus; Whiston has translated it "encompassed;" L'Estrange, I think, translates it "passes along;" it means simply making a curve, either inward or outward, and so I have used it.

§ Jos. de Bel. lib. v. cap. iv. § 2.

ment are as follows. When Titus had set down with his army before Jerusalem, and came to select a spot for his assaults, he determined to commence at the tomb of John the High Priest, because the outer wall (marked here by the zigzag lines) was weakest at that place; and here, too, he could pass at once to the "old" or "third wall," without the necessity of first taking the second;* which expectation "of an easy passage to the third wall" would not have been reasonable, had the gate Gennath and the branching of the northern wall of Acra been nearer to the tower of Hippicus than I have placed them. And when the Romans had taken this outer wall, and the Jews were driven to their next line of defences, they immediately commenced a line of fortification, which seems to have been from the second wall to the tower of Hippicus; for which reason, as well as because it is a more rational way of carrying a wall across a valley, I have made this angle in the outer wall of Acra.

These walls, namely, those of Mount Zion and Acra, are all that were standing in the time of our Saviour. The outer wall, marked here by the zigzag lines, was erected by Agrippa, not till eight years or more after the crucifixion; a circumstance that seems to have escaped the attention of those who maintain that the spot now marked as Calvary was then within the city. At the time of our Saviour, a

* Jos. de Bel. lib. v. cap. vi. § 2.

very large suburb extended northward from the temple and the tower of Antonia, occupying a hill called Bezetha, but *it was not yet walled in.* Speaking of this outer wall, Josephus says, "It was Agrippa (Agrippa ruled over Judea from A. D. 41 to 43.) who encompassed the parts added to the old city with this wall, which had been all naked before; for as the city grew more populous, it gradually crept beyond its old limits; and those parts of it that stood northward of the temple, and joined that hill to the city, made it considerably larger, and occasioned that hill, which is in number the fourth, and is called Bezetha, to be inhabited. It lies over against the tower Antonia, but is divided from it by a deep valley, which was dug on purpose. * * This new built part of the city was called *Bezetha*, in our language, which, if interpreted in the Grecian language, may be called *The New City.* Since, therefore, its inhabitants stood in need of a covering, the father of the present king, and of the same name with him, Agrippa, began that wall we spoke of; but he left off building it when he had only laid the foundations, out of the fear he was in of Claudius Cæsar, lest he should suspect that so strong a wall was built in order to make some innovation in public affairs; for the city could no way have been taken if that wall had been finished in the manner it had been begun; as its parts were connected together by stones twenty cubits (thirty-six feet) long and ten cubits broad, which could never have been either easily undermined by any iron tools, or shaken by any engines. The wall was, however, ten cubits wide, and it would probably have had a height greater than that, had not his zeal who began it been hindered from exerting itself. After this it was erected with great diligence by the Jews as high as twenty cubits, above which it had battlements of two cubits, and turrets of three cubits altitude; insomuch that the entire altitude extended as far as twenty-five cubits."* De Bel. lib. v. cap. 4. § 2.

The slope which I have noticed as near Mr. Nicholayson's house, and as showing, southward from that, the outline of Mount Zion, does not however terminate at the site of the tower Hippicus. It there bends to the eastward, and again, near the present Latin convent, turns to the northward, but is at that place reduced to an elevation of only five or six feet. For a reason to be seen in Josephus, de Bel. lib. v. c. 7. § 3, as well as on account of the ground, I have made Agrippa's wall, which started from the tower Hip-

* In Antiq. lib. xix. cap. vii. § 2. is a short passage that seems to be opposed to this. It is probable that his predecessors contemplated such a wall, and made a commencement in one or two places; both Pompey (B. C. 63) and Herod (B. C. 37), when they came to attack Jerusalem, found this place quite naked, and made their assaults at once on the temple and the second wall at Acra. Tacitus, Hist. lib. v. cap. xii. has a passage bearing on this subject. "Moreover the covetous temper that prevailed under Claudius gave the Jews an opportunity of purchasing for money, leave to fortify Jerusalem; so they built walls in time of peace as if they were going to war, they being augmented in number by those rude multitudes of people that retired thither on the ruin of the other cities." Claudius reigned from A. D. 41 to 54.

picus,* keep along the upper edge of this slope, and have placed the tomb of John at the angle; the reasons for which may be found also in the above reference. Thence the course of this wall is uncertain; we only know that it proceeded far to the northward, and enclosed the suburb of Bezetha; but, though the course which I have drawn corresponds, as far as I can judge, with the data given us in Josephus, those data are too few to furnish us with any thing positive. I think, however, the outline cannot be far from the truth.

But, as I have just remarked, this wall was not existing at the time of our Saviour's crucifixion. If I am correct in the conclusions which have just been laid before the reader, the castellated walls on the map, together with the temple, were the only portions then enclosed. This would make a small city; but the extensive suburbs around would make up for the deficiency of room. Vienna is an example in our own times, similar to this, where "the city" or fortified portion is of very limited extent compared with the vast stretch of suburb attached to it; these castellated parts of this map have, indeed, just about the extent of the *Burg*, or city proper of Vienna.

The suburb of Bezetha at that time, though stretching a considerable distance to the north, seems not to have extended much to the west of Antonia,

* Jos. de Bel. lib. v. cap. iv. § 2.

for, in addition to the intimation to that effect in Jos. de Bel. lib. v. cap. 4. § 2, we are informed that the wall of Agrippa, when erected afterwards, was left weaker at its south-western extremity than in the other portions, "the builders neglecting to build the wall strong where the new city was not inhabited."* The dense portions of this appendage to Jerusalem were on the higher ground lying directly northward from the temple, the ground over towards the spot which I have marked as Calvary having a few scattered dwellings, and those of the meanest order. The ground west of this suburb was probably taken up with great roads, and such thoroughfares as are usually to be seen in the neighborhood of a populous city.

And now, if we had no tradition whatever as regards the spot of our Saviour's suffering, and were left simply to the guidance of our own judgment, I think I should look for it somewhere in this angle between Hippicus and Bezetha. Public places are usually selected for such occurrences, and in this instance the enemies of the sufferer would be apt to seek for every circumstance that would add to his humiliation. We are told by the Scriptures (John xix. 20.) that the place was *near* the city; and as it is not probable that they would select a spot on the other side of the valley of Hinnom or of Kedron, and the hill Bezetha was covered with houses, we have lef only this angle immediately north of Acra; and in

* Jos. de Bel. lib. v. cap. 6. § 2.

17

Matthew xxvii. 39, we are informed that "they that *passed by* reviled him," which seems to intimate that the cross was adjoining some public roads or thoroughfares.

Our search then is restricted to a narrow compass; and now, if upon this ground we should find a rocky knoll about twenty feet or more in height, it would appear to us that this would be, in all probability, the spot selected for such an occasion. It would elevate the sufferers to a height sufficient to expose them to the eyes of all the multitude, and would in all respects be adapted to a spectacle like this. Just such a rock is existing at this day, and *is the one built into the present church of the Crucifixion.* The place is in Scripture no where called *Mount* Calvary; but simply Calvary, or "Golgotha, that is, a place of a skull," and we have no reason given us there to look for a larger eminence. Indeed this seems just such an one as would be selected for such a purpose, and corresponds, both in elevation and extent, to its ignominious title.

In these remarks it will be observed, I have been guided entirely by the judgment, and have endeavored to see whither it would lead us, without any reference to traditions on this subject. As we have seen, it conducts us exactly to the spot that tradition *has always pointed out as the place of the crucifixion.* This tradition I will now proceed also to notice.

It is not probable that the early Christians would

soon forget a spot of such tender and deep interest to them; for, as I observed at the beginning of this chapter, the subject is also one of some practical character. It was rather to be feared that they would attach to it a reverence that would degenerate into superstition, than that they would entirely forget it. If at our day the idea of the bare possibility of visiting Mount Calvary sends a thrill through the whole system, with what feelings must they have regarded the place when the memory of this event was fresh among the Christians, and when they were able to converse with those who had themselves witnessed the ignominious death of their Lord and Saviour. It does not appear to me at all probable that such a place would be forgotten; and we have a proof of the respect in which it was held, in the fact that Hadrian erected on the sepulchre a statue to Jupiter, and one to Venus on Mount Calvary. This could have been done only to mock their feelings and distress them, by desecrating places held by them in high regard. The fact that he placed these statues on these spots, at all events shows that they were at this time (about one hundred years after the events themselves) considered as the places of the crucifixion and the sepulture of Christ. Helena, the mother of Constantine, two hundred years subsequently to this, erected on the spot a Christian church, which, with some changes not affecting the locality, has continued ever since. There is, therefore, a chain of evidence with regard to these localities of a very satisfactory kind; and as the judgment finds no difficulty in the case, but, independently of tradition, is led to the same conclusion, my own convictions are clearly and decidedly in their favor.

Let us then examine into the circumstances of this affecting event. The place of the crucifixion was about six hundred feet from the city wall, to which the ground from this place had a gentle descent; on the east were the low and straggling outskirts of the large suburb of Bezetha; on the west, the ground, at the distance of a few hundred feet, sloped upward rapidly for a short space, and then stretched off in a long ascending plain; on the northward it also ascends gently for the distance of more than a mile. The rock of Golgotha or Calvary is now about sixteen feet in height, though as the ground around it has been elevated by the ruins of the old city, it was probably at that time a few feet higher. It was of sufficient altitude to bring the sufferer into distinct view before all the crowds that probably at this time covered the walls and houses and the upward slopes of the hills, and to make him visible to those "afar off."* A few gardens were near; but most of the space around this rocky knoll was open, and traversed by the dusty thoroughfares to the populous city.

It was now the Passover, and more than two millions of people had come up to Jerusalem;† the city, the suburbs, were crowded, the country around was

* See Luke xxiii. 49.

† Jos. de Bel. lib. vi. cap. 9. § 3.

covered with the dense multitude; and the ceaseless hum of men, even in their calmer moments, was like the deep hollow roar of the ocean.—And now the multitudes are agitated, and the stormy passions are at work amid the countless throng.—He who had excited the wonder of the Jewish nation, and the rage of the priests and of the stately Pharisees, had been brought forward before the judgment-seat of the high-priest and the governor of Judea, and had been condemned for blasphemy.—He, for blasphemy! The good, the benevolent, the Godlike! who had given sight to the blind, and had caused the lame to walk, and had healed the sick, and had brought the dead to life; who had led their thoughts to heaven, and taught them pure and holy doctrines; and had been among them in his miracles with the power of the Divinity himself. He, for blasphemy? Yes, he had publicly, before their council, declared himself to be the Christ, the Son of God, and that they should see him sitting on the right hand of power, and coming from heaven in majesty; and he had foretold that of their glorious temple, the object almost of their idolatry, not one stone should be left upon another; and had been accused of saying that he himself would destroy it. The passions of the dense multitudes rise; and rumor, with her exaggerations, excites them to phrensy.—And now comes forth the sufferer, bearing his cross; his back lacerated with thongs, his brow dropping blood from the crown placed on it in mockery. Though sinking under fatigue and pain, he meets no commiseration, but is driven on with tauntings and scorn; and they come to the place of public execution, and the victim is nailed to the cross, and between two malefactors is raised up to be a spectacle to man; and wherever he turns his agonized eyes he sees only rage and scorn; and his ears hear only bitter tauntings;—"he saved others; himself he cannot save." "If he be the king of Israel let him come down now from the cross, and we will believe him." "He trusted in God; let him deliver him now if he will have him; for he said, I am the Son of God."

There is a punishment somewhat similar to this of crucifixion, that until lately was practised in Algiers and in various parts of Turkey. The criminal was thrown from the top of a wall and caught by large hooks projecting from its side, and there left to perish. His torments were frightful. A fever seized on the body, and excruciating pains coursed through the whole system; the eyes became bloodshot and glaring, and starting from their sockets; the sufferer was burnt up by a scorching thirst, and begged piteously for drink, and after many hours died in frightful agonies.

Death upon the cross was probably similar to this, for the nails were driven through the hands and feet, where are congregated an unusual number of delicate nerves; and by them the whole weight of the body was suspended. The agonies were probably even greater than those I have been describing.

Such was the price of our redemption. "He hath borne our griefs and carried our sorrows; he was bruised for our iniquities; the chastisement of our peace was upon him; and with his stripes we are healed."

The question with regard to the place of our Saviour's burial is in a measure dependent on that into which we have just been examining, and will therefore not require more than a few minutes' attention. St. John (xix. 41, 42.) tells us that "*in the place* where he was crucified, there was a garden; and in the garden a new sepulchre, wherein never man was yet laid. There laid they Jesus, therefore, because of the Jews' preparation day, for the sepulchre was *nigh at hand*." We are therefore to look for this spot close in the neighborhood of Calvary; and I think that the merriment in which Protestant visitors sometimes have indulged on finding the spot pointed out for the sepulchre, so near that of the crucifixion, to be quite out of place. It certainly is in bad taste; for whatever these places may be, they bear sad and solemn names, and have been regarded by Christians from time immemorial as really the places of our Saviour's bloody death and burial, and glorious resurrection. However, then, we may be disposed to regard their genuineness, we should approach them with solemn feelings; and levity or sarcasm in such a place becomes us very ill.

For myself, I believe that as regards the place of our Saviour's crucifixion, there is no just ground for disbelief, nor can I see much as regards also that pointed out as the place for burial. It is about 110 feet from the rocky knoll, and is not at all too near to have a garden wall intervene, and make this a proper place for Joseph of Arimathea to hew out a sepulchre. *Gennath*, the name of the gate opening from the Upper City to this place, means gardens,* and it is probable that much of this space was originally occupied with gardens. We find also that it was a place of tombs; for the monument of the high-priest John was near this, as were also probably "the monuments of king Alexander."† The circumstances of the case are, therefore, in favor of this spot; the Scriptures in some measure give it their sanction, and tradition from the earliest years has been uniform on the subject. Hadrian over it erected the statue of Jupiter, and here also Helena built a church; and among the rival sects of the Greek and Latin church, which soon after sprung up, and which have been endeavoring to appropriate, each to itself, as much as possible of the holy places, no one has ever attempted to designate another spot.

I confess I take pleasure in believing that the spot pointed out to us as that of our Saviour's sepulture, is the true one; and that, to the scene of his deep humiliation and his agony for us is in close proximity the scene of his triumph over hell and the grave; and though it can be no argument, I confess there

* גנה Esther i. 5, &c. † Jos. de Bel. lib. 5. cap. 7. § 3.

seems to me to be a fitness of things where we are allowed to stand where stood the cross of Christ, and look down on the empty tomb, and say through him, "O death, where is thy sting? O grave, where is thy victory? The sting of death is sin; and the strength of sin is the law; but thanks be to God which giveth us the victory, through our Lord Jesus Christ."

CHAPTER XV.

Commencement of our visits. Hospital of the knights of St. John. Church of the Holy Sepulchre. Reputed tomb of the Saviour. Marble sarcophagus. Effect of this visit on us. Question whether this is the real tomb, or only a representation of it. Removal of the floor two centuries since. Greek chapel "the centre of the world." Origin of the various incredible traditions. Charity to be exercised. Cave where the cross is said to have been discovered. Fissure in the rock. Tradition about the head of Adam. Calvary. Holes for the crosses. Another fissure in the rock. The humiliation in the tomb, and resurrection.

We were glad, on arriving at Mr. Nicholayson's, to find the ladies of the Commodore's family quite recovered from the effects of the preceding day's severe fatigue. Mrs. Nicholayson herself was in a feeble state of health, occasioned by her watchings over Mrs. Thompson's couch, and exposures during the earthquake, and the subsequent fighting in the city; their house, as has already been observed, having been used as an advanced point ot attack on the citadel. The presence of ladies speaking her own language had immediately an astonishing effect on her spirits, and she became rapidly convalescent.

Impatient, and with feelings almost in a nervous state, we soon found ourselves out, and winding along the narrow lane that leads from Mr. Nicholayson's to the slope by which we descend from Mount Zion to the lower city. Standing on the edge of this, we looked down on the ruins of a great edifice erected for the knights of St. John at the time of the Crusades. It is a very large building, I should think near six hundred feet in length by two hundred in width; but the lower story or basement is all that now remains. This forms a suite of vaults, which are now occupied as stores for grain and merchandize; a street of shops forming a kind of bazaar passes along the western side of it, and on the south is the principal bazaar of the city, the exterior range of vaults answering very well for stores. The place where we were then standing was about the spot where I suppose the gate Gennath to have been.

Descending from this eminence, we entered a street which passes along the northern side of this ruin, and is lined with fruit shops and houses, sometimes one, sometimes two stories in height, of stone, the windows small and the exterior very plain. This street is about one thousand feet in length. At its further extremity on our right was an edifice distinguished by its size and massiveness, but presenting on the exterior only a bare wall pierced with a few narrow windows. This was "The Church of the Holy Sepulchre." It forms altogether a block of masonry about one hundred and sixty feet by one hundred in width, in which are included the chapel of the Crucifixion, the church of the Sepulchre, some small chapels, and a monastery, the cloisters of the monks occupying the portions of the building next the street. Just before coming to this building, we entered a low door in a stone wall, and then, having descended along a narrow alley, we turned presently to the left, and had before us the court and grand entrance to the church. On our left was the church tower, but without bells, as, with the single exception of Mount Lebanon, bells are not allowed to Christian churches in Turkey. The height of this tower has also been reduced, from a similar feeling of jealousy on the part of their Turkish masters. Three sides of the court were formed by a mass of buildings of irregular shape, while the fourth, or that looking towards the west, was open; in the central part was an arched portal ornamented with columns of verd-antique, and sculptures of the Norman style of architecture; it was open at the time of our visit, and I believe is so daily for an hour or two in the morning. After this it is closed, the key is returned to the Turkish governor; and admittance during the rest of the day, if desired, must be purchased from him. The monks, therefore, are prisoners in their monastery, except during this short interval, and intercourse with them must be held through a square hole in this door, where also provisions and other necessaries are taken in. We visited the place once in the afternoon, and were allowed to enter after waiting nearly an hour, and at the cost of a dollar or two.

Passing through this door, the visiter finds himself in a hall or vestibule, about forty feet long by twenty in width; and in front of him, on the floor, a slab of reddish marble, with huge candlesticks and candles at either end; they call it the stone of unction, and say that on it our Saviour's body was anointed previous to interment. And here commences a series of legends and fictions, dealt out unsparingly to the visitor, which often produce disgust, and always jar on the feelings of the pilgrim whose mind is not steeped in the grossest credulity. I could fill a book with them, but have no relish for such a task; and during this visit gave but little attention to them, as I wished to keep my feelings free from the effect of such puerilities; and I shall at present trouble the reader with them only so far as to give him an idea of this blot on Christianity at Jerusalem. By doing more, we should only stir up emotions that cannot harmonize with the place, and which will prevent us from feeling the influence of that which is real and true.

Turning now to the left we came, at the distance of about twenty feet, to a large door-way which admitted us into a circular church, quite lofty, and about fifty feet in diameter.*

The lower part of this is lined with a range of pilasters, between which are arched openings into a

* All these dimensions, I wish the reader to understand, are not by actual measurement, but as nearly as I could judge by the eye; I think they are sufficiently accurate to serve as a guide in the present case, but I do not affirm them to be strictly accurate.

dozen chapels, some used by the Copts, Greeks, and Armenians, and some occupied by altars connected with the legends which have just been noticed. Above these runs a corridor, and the whole is surmounted by the large dome which had drawn my attention when on the top of our monastery. In the centre of the area of this church is a structure of masonry, about eight feet wide, eight or nine in height, and about twelve in length; at one end is a marble platform, raised about twelve inches from the floor, with steps quite around, and bordered part of the length with a low marble wall or parapet on either side; the other end of this structure, instead of being square, has three faces, in which are very small chapels for the Copts, Abyssinians, &c. The structure itself is faced with the richest marbles, in compartments, and enriched with mouldings, and has on the summit a little tower like a lantern, used, I believe, as a vent for the smoke from some lamps within the tomb. Yes, this, they tell us, is the tomb of our Saviour, hewn originally in the solid rock; but that the exterior rock has been cut down so as to form a kind of shell, in the shape of a chapel, with its exterior surface enriched in this manner with marble. If this be so, they have sadly disguised the place, for, being lined with marble also in the interior, it has now not the least resemblance to what the Scripture account of it would lead us to expect. The entrance is at the end towards the east. We ascended the marble platform, and entering by a low door found ourselves in a chamber about six feet wide and five in depth, in the centre of which is an upright column irregularly shaped, about two feet in height. They say it is the stone on which the angel sat when he announced the resurrection to Mary Magdalene, and Mary the mother of James, and Salome. At the further end of this room, at the corner on the left, is a low door; and there, stooping down, we entered another chamber about six feet square. One half of this latter apartment was occupied by a marble sarcophagus; and in this, they say, was deposited the body of our crucified Saviour.

For a while we were unwilling, and I believe should have been unable, to enter into the inquiry whether this was really so;—so strong an emotion was created by the annunciation that we were in our Lord's sepulchre, and that before us was the coffin where his body had lain, and from which he rose triumphant, leading captivity captive. We stood for a long time silent, gazing on the marble; and I believe it would have taken little to have caused us to shed tears. The place was lighted only by lamps suspended from the ceiling over the coffin; no sounds were heard, except occasionally of our deep breathing, as our emotions became almost too strong to be restrained. And our feelings, I believe, were of a salutary nature.

There was then in our company, one of whom I am allowed here to speak, but whom the shrinking modesty which she always evinced while living, and which should still be regarded, will allow me barely to notice. She was dear to us all; and although, with such solemn scenes as these around us, it becomes me to speak with humility of worldly accomplishments, I may say she possessed them in an unusual degree, and that she was admired and beloved at home and abroad by every one that knew her. She is now no longer in this world. In the grave, earthly accomplishments, and even earthly love, avail us nothing; but religion does avail; and the religion of the cross of Christ, so full of hope and glory, she was led to adopt by this visit to Calvary and to the sepulchre of Christ. She had been educated by pious friends, and had respected and esteemed the ordinances of the gospel; but this visit, and the scenes here brought before her mind, made her realize as she had not done before, how great was the price paid for her salvation, and how strong are our obligations to give ourselves unhesitatingly to Him who hesitated not to give himself for us. Selecting a proper time, when the act would be free from ostentation, she took out her Bible, which she had brought to the city, and placing it on the coffin, wrote, as was long after discovered, her name and the date of our visit, with the quotation, "Let every thing that hath breath praise the Lord." Not long after her return to the ship she made a meek yet decided avowal of this Saviour as her only hope and trust; and all who knew her witnessed a corresponding exhibition of Christian character. For the change which brought the humble and gentle virtues into striking relief, while hope rose higher and became full of immortality, she always referred to this visit as the immediate cause. She was, at that time, apparently in excellent health; but youth and health are no guarantee for us in this our earthly home. When our ship, eighteen months afterwards, approached our own shore, it bore her a feeble and exhausted invalid; and when land at length rose to our sight, we scarcely heeded it; for she, our companion so long, and so beloved by us, was now a corpse. She had expired suddenly only the evening previous. By her mourning parents in that hour of anguish, I heard this visit spoken of, and they found in its consequences a source of consolation, such as the whole earth could not have afforded them; to her, had she possessed worlds, what would they have been in comparison with her religion?

When we spoke, at length, as we stood by the coffin in this sepulchre, it was involuntarily in low tones, and in brief sentences; and it was a relief to get out where the feelings were less oppressive. I speak of the sensations of others as well as of my own; for I have since frequently heard them speak of this visit and of its effects on their feelings.

Our feelings however, in this case, led captive by the scene around us, by the silent chamber lighted by a few lamps, the marble coffin, and the tradition that this was our Lord's sepulchre, acted without the concurrence of our judgment; or rather, they suspended

18*

for a while the power of judging or the disposition to inquire. Yet, although for reasons already given, I have little doubt that this was the spot of our Saviour's interment, the assertion that this is the sepulchre itself, wants confirmation; and the marble coffin or sarcophagus, I cannot regard as any thing more than a mere *representation* of the grave, or the place where the body was deposited; and for this it is by no means happily chosen. This *may* be the sepulchre, cut on the outside into the form of a little chapel; but as nothing but marble is seen both within and on the outside, the native rock, if it exists, being no where allowed to appear, we have no means of satisfying ourselves that it is so; and the circumstances are altogether suspicious, particularly when taken in connexion with the many other assertions with regard to sacred places in Jerusalem which are manifestly beyond belief. The coffin is of white marble, slightly marked by a few veins of a light blue color; it is rectangular, six feet long within, about three feet broad, and two feet two inches in depth; being in all respects exactly like the ancient sarcophagi found all over Greece and in Asia; the cover remains, and the whole exterior has a slight degree of roughness, as if it might once have been exposed to the weather. This is entirely at variance with the ancient tombs still to be seen in great numbers about Jerusalem, and particularly in the district lying north from the present city. They are composed sometimes of a single chamber, sometimes of a succession of chambers, cut in the solid rock, with a rectangular cavity large enough for a body, in the floor, at the side of the chamber; in the larger chambers, there are more than one cavity, and in a few cases, instead of being cut in the floor, they form a box against the side, but cut also out of the solid rock. In no case that I have heard of, has a marble sarcophagus been found within them, none would be needed; and even in the tombs of the kings of some magnificence, northward from the city, the native rock has been exclusively employed. The evidence is altogether against this marble sarcophagus, and I cannot yield it my belief.

But still, whether it was that I had some lingering doubts on the subject, or whether it was the name it bore, and the silent and lamp-lit chamber in which it is presented, I cannot say; but though I visited this chamber repeatedly, it was always with a feeling of awe mingled with a degree of reverence.

There was in the city, at the time of our visit, an English gentleman, who had become a Roman Catholic, and was now a priest, but was a man of enlightened and liberal views; he had been residing some time at Lisbon, and had now been sent to Jerusalem with the contribution of the Portuguese churches for this year. He visited us frequently at Mr. Nicholayson's; and we were all struck both with his intelligence and very gentlemanly manners. He informed me that a short time previous to this, when occupied one day in examining the library of the principal Latin convent, he lighted on an old musty book, written in Latin by the father guardian of Jerusalem about three centuries since. The author said, that during his residence here it was found necessary to take up the pavement of this church in order to make some repairs; that he watched the process with deep attention, and that his satisfaction can scarcely be imagined, when, on coming to the native rock, he found, immediately under this spot, a chamber cut in the rock, and corresponding exactly to the tombs we find about the city. That on further research among the old records of the convent, he (the father guardian) found it stated, that in ancient times the sepulchre had stood open and exposed; and was beginning to be greatly mutilated by pilgrims, each one being desirous of carrying away some portion of the sacred rock. In order to preserve it, a strong railing was built around; but that now, the visitors being debarred from touching the sepulchre, votive offerings, rags,* &c. were thrown in by them in such quantities that the place soon become offensive; and that finally, to prevent this new evil, the tomb was filled up, and a small chapel was erected over it, with a sarcophagus, as a representative of the real sepulchre beneath.

* Such a custom still prevails in the east. In Turkish burying grounds, we frequently see bits of rags suspended about the tombs of the dead whom they regard with reverence. The monumental enclosures in Pere la Chaise, near Paris, are often rendered offensive by the heaps of decaying garlands within them, the offerings of friends.

The account of the father guardian has the appearance of probability, but the reader is left to take it for what he may consider it worth. I tried to get sight of the book; but as the convent was in quarantine on account of the plague, could not succeed; and I regret to say that I have forgotten its title.

The light which we can gain from the Scriptures on this subject, joined with the uniform tradition, lead me to suppose that this is the spot; whatever may be the fact with regard to the sepulchre itself, whether it be now beneath the structure going by its name, or whether it has been cut away to make room for a heathen temple erected by Hadrian, or for the present church.

The little chapel of the Sepulchre stands in the centre of the great church, facing the east. Directly in front of it is a large opening into a church owned by the Greeks, and no wise remarkable, except for a ball suspended from the ceiling, and a plate beneath it, on which is an inscription, telling that this is the centre of the world.

The authority for this is in Ps. lxxiv. 12. "For God is my King of old, working salvation in the midst of the earth;" and here I must warn the reader that his feelings will sometimes be shocked in the course of these visits, and I must be allowed to warn him also against allowing his disgust to operate so as to make him reject the truth with the error. This is not consistent with the principles of sound judgment, but the contrary. Where truth is, error will generally come; and error, as I have already remarked, is to a certain degree a proof that there is truth somewhere; for man could not hang up such a mass of fictions if there was not something real to hang it upon; and generally, the more important the truth, the more earnest is error to draw advantage therefrom.

I cannot, however, join in the frequent outcry of imposition, craft and falsehood against the sects who hold these places, and recite these traditions to the visitor. That such things as these are to be found in high and sacred seats, is doubtless true, and that they are sometimes practised here is also very probable; but I can find, for a great many of these traditions, an origin of a more charitable nature, and I believe one more consonant with the real state of the case. We live now in an age of light and knowledge, and find it hard even to imagine the darkness that once covered Europe and all these lands. We can form only some idea of it from the books of the middle ages—books full of fable and false philosophy on every subject. These fables on medicine, on alchemy, on astrology, and on a multitude of other topics, grew up, we are willing to believe, from men's ignorance; in some cases there may have been deliberate deception; but in most, their origin was in the gross ignorance of the times; they show the strivings of minds shorn of their strength by diseases hereditary and for ages universal; men saw but dimly, and wandered into the ways of error when really and honestly in search of truth. And if we are willing to extend this charity to the other sciences, why not also to that of religion, where men's feelings are apt to be more warmly affected, and even in a good cause, to warp the judgment, particularly if it be weak, than in any other? In this very city, the Mahomedans have a great variety of traditions with respect to the mosque of Omar, and some other of their sacred places about Jerusalem, quite as wild as any thing among the Christian sects; yet when we listen to them, we do not at once cry out "craft and roguery," and believe the narrator to be wilfully imposing on us. We are willing to suppose him honest. We look at him; his face is grave; he has the appearance of sincerity; and we attribute the error to the deep and dark ignorance in which these people are known to live. Now I wish to claim for the Christian traditions just what we are willing to give to those of the Mahomedans. The principle of charity may, it is true, be carried too far, but I wish to see it carried further than it is. Let us go among these sacred places cautious, as cautious as you choose; but not sneering, or cultivating bitter feelings towards one another; let us pity the ignorance of our brother and commiserate him, but not load him with harsh epithets. Uncharitable insinuations are certainly very much out of place in this region, which should excite only humble and tender feelings; where, amid tauntings and contumely showered upon him, the Saviour prayed, "Father, forgive them, *for they know not what they do.*"

After leaving the Greek chapel, we crossed to the western side of this circular church; and here entering a narrow winding passage, came presently to a floor of naked rock with two graves cut in it, called the Sepulchres of Joseph of Arimathea and of Nicodemus. They are just deep enough to contain a body; that of Nicodemus is only about four and a half feet in length.

From this place we were taken to a chapel on the northern side of the church, where, they say, our Saviour appeared to the Virgin after his resurrection; and next, by a winding passage, to a place in the rear of the Greek church, where are altars marking, it is said, the spots where they cast lots for his garments; where he was confined till they had prepared the cross; where occurred the conversion of Longinus, the officer who pierced his side with a spear, &c. Here also we were conducted, by a descent of forty steps, into a large cave, the place where Helena discovered the cross. They tell us that the Jews, in order to stop the adoration of the cross by the early Christians, cast it here into a hole called the "Valley of Corpses," where it remained three hundred years; that Helena, on digging for it, discovered three crosses, and, unable to distinguish which was the one she was searching for, had them carried to the place where is now the chapel of the

Virgin, and where was then a woman at the point of death; and that the sick person being made to touch them, two produced no effect, but the third or true cross restored her immediately to health.

Ascending from the cave and following another dark passage, we came presently into a chapel about fifteen feet square, one side of which is formed by a bare precipitous rock. This is a portion of the rocky knoll of Golgotha or Calvary; and here they showed us a rent or fissure about sixteen inches in width, telling us that it was formed at the time of the crucifixion, when the veil of the temple was rent in twain, and with the quaking of the earth the rocks were rent. They tell also a story, which I feel loth to repeat, that here, at the time just spoken of, the head of Adam was discovered; and that when the Saviour's side was pierced, the blood and water flowed down upon it; that, as Adam had been the first to sin, he might be the first to experience the benefit of the redemption.

After giving an impatient glance at these various spots, we passed on; and soon after, emerging once more into daylight, found ourselves in the vestibule, and at the foot of the staircase leading to the summit of Calvary.

I have mentioned, that on entering the vestibule from the outer court, we had before us the stone of unction, and on the left the entrance to the circular

Church of the Sepulchre. On the right, at the distance of about thirty-five feet, is a narrow stairway of eighteen steps, cut in the solid rock, and leading to a platform elevated about sixteen feet above the lower church, and nearly square, having about forty feet on each side. This is Mount Calvary. The surface is now level, and paved with red marbles; and, by a kind of partition formed of two arches with square columns between, is divided into two chambers, one being nearly square and the other oblong. They are surmounted by a dome, more peaked than that over the church of the Holy Sepulchre. When we reached the top of the stairway, we found ourselves in the first of these chambers, or the square one; but were first taken across it into the other, where a large star, formed of marble mosaic work in the pavement, was pointed out as indicating the spot where the Saviour was nailed to the cross. That designated as the place where the crosses stood during the crucifixion is in the first chamber, at its northern side.

Returning to this place, we found there a platform against the wall, running the whole way across the church, and sixteen inches in height by about three feet in width. It was also covered with marbles, and half way across had a large embossed silver plate with a hole in the centre; and this is said to be over the very spot where stood our Saviour's cross. On each side are similar plates, said to be over the holes for the other two crosses; but the holes are so near together, that the arms of the three crosses could not have been in a line, unless, as might have been the case, that of the Saviour was higher or lower than the others. I put my hand several times through the hole in the central silver plate, and found beneath it a hollow of rough sides, rather large, and about a foot or fifteen inches in depth. Half way between it and the hole on our right, as we stood facing them, is another plate of silver about thirty inches in length, and with a narrow slit in it, corresponding, they informed us, to a fissure in the rock, the commencement of the crevice which we had seen below. There is something very much like a crack, about two inches wide, the opposite parts of which appear to correspond; but a close examination is prevented by the silver plate above; its direction is across the natural stratification of the rock. The object of these silver plates is probably to guard these places from violence, as pilgrims or other visitors are much given to chipping off fragments from such spots* for friends at home. Whether these are really the holes where the crosses stood, and whether this is a real fracture or "rent" in the rock, it is impossible to say; there can be no doubt, however, that this is really a mass of native rock; and its elevation is just such as

* Many parts of Jerusalem bore testimony to our itchings for such relics; fresh fractures were to be seen in a great many places on the walls and along the streets.

would be desired for the infliction of death by crucifixion. It is now so built around, and so, covered with marbles, that it is not easy to form an exact judgment of its original altitude or extent; but if I may venture a rough estimate of the former, I should say it was about twenty or twenty-five feet. It appears to be nearly precipitous at the northern end.

Our feelings while standing on Mount Calvary were of that high-wrought but solemn kind that we had experienced while at the Sepulchre, but not perhaps so strong in degree; for although this was a place of agony and shame, and yet of the highest moral grandeur, there was connected with the other a depth of humiliation, a completeness of abandonment, that was extremely affecting. The grave had received the body of the sufferer, cold and stiffened in death; the winding sheet was around those mangled limbs, and over the temples where the blood stood on many a wound. Nature that day had sympathized and shuddered,—but this now had passed; the taunters, after praying that his blood might be on them and on their children, had gone their way; the disciples were appalled and had fled; the tomb was sealed up, and the moon threw its mild rays on a scene forsaken apparently of God and of man, except the silent sentry pacing to and fro. The humiliation was now complete; the price of our ransom was paid to the utmost, and then glory from heaven poured down upon the spot. The God-Redeemer rose, and death, who, though conqueror, had set trembling to see the Creator of all things prostrate and beneath his sway, was now himself led captive, and made a ministering servant to bring the redeemed to eternal glory.

CHAPTER XVI.

Dimensions of the Modern City. Ground within the city, and in its environs. Its picturesque appearance. Continuation of our visits. Via Dolorosa. Sentence of the Saviour from Salignatius. House of Veronica and Picture of the Napkin. House of "the Rich Man." Arch of the Ecce Homo. Pilate's House. Mosque of Omar. The Locked-up Stone. Pool of Bethesda. Place of Stephen's Martyrdom. The Golden Gate. The Emperor Heraclius in a dilemma.

THE modern Jerusalem is about three fourths of a mile at its greatest length, and about two thirds of a mile in width.* It contains a population of about 20,000 persons; namely, 10,000 Mahomedans occupying principally the northern and eastern portions;

* I paced the circuit of the city, taking notes and plans of the whole, and marking the towers; but the paper has been unfortunately lost.

The following are the dimensions in detail, as furnished by Messrs. Fisk and King:

	paces.	
From N. W. cor. to the Jaffa gate,	300	768 on the western side,
" thence to the S. W. corner,	468	
" " to Zion gate,	195	1149 on the southern side,
" " to bend in S. W. wall,	295	
" " to S. E. corner,	659	
" " to St. Stephen's gate,	583	943 on the eastern side,
" " to N. E. corner,	360	
" " to Damascus gate,	759	1419 on the northern side,
" " to N. W. corner,	660	

which, at their computation of five paces to a rod, makes the whole circuit two miles and seven tenths, or nearly two thirds of a mile; Sandys made it nearly the same, namely, two miles and a half.

6,000 Jews living on what was formerly the Acra; 3,500 Greeks and Catholics, around the church of Calvary; and about 500 Armenians, in and about their great convent on Mount Zion. Of the last eminence only a small portion is included within the limits of the present city.

Seen from the Mount of Olives, Jerusalem appears to stand on a plain declining gently towards the east; but the ground is far from being an unbroken level. On the contrary, it is quite uneven, though in no part rising into hills, unless the remains of Mount Zion be entitled to this name. The steep descent from Zion on the eastward I have already noticed. Passing from Calvary to the south-east, we begin immediately to descend, and towards the site of the ancient castle of Antonia the slope is very rapid; then succeeds a piece of low ground for the space of 100 feet; and next as we reach the site of the castle is an eminence fifteen or twenty feet in height, with a rapid ascent from the west, but sloping gradually down towards the gate of St. Stephen (marked *c*) in the eastern wall. From Calvary, northward and westward, the ground ascends by a gentle inclination, with the exception of the rapid slope already mentioned, at the line which I have marked for Agrippa's wall. But this slope does not continue far.

Without the city on the south and west, after crossing the valley of Hinnom, we find ourselves on an open and rather barren plain ascending gently as it recedes from the city, and stretching off for a distance of two or three miles; on the northward the ground is rolling for a few miles, when it begins to ascend, and at the distance of about five miles attains considerable elevation; there was probably the *Scopus* of ancient times.

On this, the northern side, Jerusalem as it is approached appears to the best advantage, as the cultivated grounds, the olives scattered thickly around, the verdant slopes of the Mount of Olives, towering upward just on the left, impress the visitor favorably with the environs of the city; while the walls of the city itself, at the northern end battlemented in a fanciful manner, and by numerous angles broken in a picturesque form, produce, with their numerous towers, a very favorable effect. Jerusalem, however, seen from a great many points of view, is a highly picturesque city; and I can say for myself at least, that I found it presenting on the outside a more imposing appearance than I had anticipated. War and the earthquake had left the interior wretched indeed; nor, as far as we could judge, have its narrow streets, and its low rude houses, even in better times, any thing very attractive; but from numerous places without, and particularly as we wound along the valleys below, its battlements, and castles, and towers, rising from the edge of the high steep bank, and brought into strong relief against the sky, sometimes overhanging our path, and sometimes stretching off to a distance, appearing and disappearing along the uneven ground, had a very picturesque effect.

When viewed from the Mount of Olives, the whole city appears like a map at our feet. The houses, which are of stone, are seldom more than two stories in height, and on the exterior are rude and without any pretensions to beauty; but when seen from an elevated spot, the city has a singular appearance, in consequence of the domes, with which every dwelling is covered. Sometimes every chamber in the house has its dome; and as these are whitewashed on the exterior, when we look down upon it from the Mount of Olives, the whole city appears dotted over with these excrescences. A couple of open green spots just within the walls, a few trees rising here and there, the tower of the church of the Holy Sepulchre and its large domes, several minarets, and close to us the extensive open court of the mosque of Omar, with its trees, and in the centre the handsome mosque itself, complete the view as seen from the Mount of Olives.

The walls of Jerusalem are twenty-five or thirty feet in height, and are flanked with numerous towers, both circular and square; and at the Jaffa gate are still further strengthened by a mass of buildings forming a castle. There are four principal gates; and on the north and south two smaller ones or posterns, which, however, I believe are seldom used.

Leaving the church of the Holy Sepulchre, we turned down a street at right angles to the one by which we had come, and leading towards Mount

Moriah. It forms a portion of the "Via Dolorosa," or way by which, they tell us, our Saviour came, bearing his cross, from the judgment hall to the place of his suffering. The street is narrow and badly paved, and at the distance of about 600 feet from the church, is crossed, for a space of twenty feet, by a low heavy arch, which, they say, is a remnant of the ancient gateway. I suppose this arch is near the line of the northern wall of Acra, but, apart from what is said in Josephus, (de Bel. lib. vii. cap. i. § 1.) this arch wants the massive character of that wall; and the account is not at all probable. They call it the *Puerta Judicaria,* and point to a broken column as one on which the Roman authorities were accustomed to stick the sentence of persons condemned to death; and they quote from Salignatius that of our Saviour as posted here. "*Jesus of Nazareth, a subverter of the kingdom, a derider of Cæsar, and a false Messiah, as is proved by the evidence of the chief men of his nation, is to be led to the place of common punishment, and with mock majesty is to be crucified between two thieves; hasten, Lictor, and prepare the crosses.*"

We pass on, and again they try to tax our credulity by pointing to a house on the left, about two hundred feet below this gate, as the veritable house of Veronica, a pious woman living at the time of the crucifixion. They say that as Jesus passed by this dwelling, his face covered with blood streaming from the crown of thorns, Veronica offered a napkin, which, having been pressed against his face, when given again to her was found to present an exact copy of his features. Pictures of the Saviour are to be seen in all Catholic countries, represented as painted on a towel, and said to be copies from this.

Though we cannot believe it, yet there is something pretty in the tradition; and the same may be said of a great many of the traditions which they relate to us, but it would require an excess of credulity to suppose that this is her house, when we know that by the infuriated soldiers of Titus every dwelling was destroyed;* and the appearance of the building itself must satisfy us that it is comparatively a modern dwelling.

Still lower down they put a climax to all this by pointing out the very house in which dwelt "the rich man," and the spot (on the opposite side of the street) where Lazarus used to recline. The house is a large good looking edifice, and I believe is now occupied by Aboo Ghoosh.

Here the Via Dolorosa bends, for a short space, to the left, and then, turning again in the direction of St. Stephen's gate, ascends a low eminence, and terminates at what they call the ruins of Pilate's house. At this place is a lofty arch over the street, with two windows above, in which, they tell us, the Roman

* In addition to the passage of Josephus just referred to, see also de Bel. lib. vi. cap. ix. § 1.

governors were accustomed to address the people; and which they call "Ecce Homo," from a tradition that the Saviour was there brought out before the Jews, when they cried out, demanding his crucifixion. (John xix. 5.) Here, too, they showed us the place from which were taken a suite of marble steps, now shown at Rome, as then belonging to the Judgment Hall, and which I have seen in that city, where no one is allowed to ascend them except on his knees. Indeed, all the region around this spot is fruitful in their traditions; some of which are sufficiently curious, but the reader has probably by this time had enough of them. I will only add, that the windows over the arch had formerly a pillar between them; but that on one occasion a deputy of the Sultan being on a visit to the cities of Syria, on his arrival at Jerusalem the Father Guardian of the Latins neglected to carry him a present, on which the deputy ordered him to carry this pillar on his shoulders to the mosque of Omar. "But for this he was well chastised; for, on departing from Jerusalem, he fell from his horse and broke a leg; so at least it is affirmed by many."*

Pilate's house stands a short distance from the street leading to St. Stephen's gate; and we turned aside to it, not to speculate upon their traditions, but for the advantage offered by the lofty terrace that forms its roof for getting a good view of the mosque

* El Devoto Peregrino.

of Omar. The Turks will allow no Christian to enter even the court of this mosque, and as the edifice from which we had our view forms a part of its boundary, we were able, from our elevated position, to overlook the whole of it.

This court stands at the south-eastern angle of the present city, the walls of which bound it on the east and partly at the south. Its dimensions are 1500 feet by 1000; and it therefore occupies considerably more ground than the ancient Mount Moriah, which was, I suppose, towards its southern extremity. Its clean grounds, and the shade trees which are scattered over them, make a very pretty appearance. The platform in its centre is ornamented along the edge on either side by a species of triumphal arch; and the mosque itself, which stands towards the southern end of this platform, is a very handsome building. It is octagonal, and is built of light colored marble with blackish veins, into which are set pannels of a darker shade. The other portion of the building, and the lofty cupola, are ornamented with various colored tiles disposed in fanciful patterns; and below, at each of the entrances, is an ornamented porch attached. The interior is enriched with twenty-four columns and pilasters, and also with carving and gilding.

The mosque of Omar, called by the Arabs *El Sakhara*, or the "Locked-up," owes its high sanctity to a large stone in the centre, apparently a portion of the native rock of the mountain. It is rough as

20

when hewn from the quarry, is surrounded by a wooden railing about four feet high, and covered by a cloth of green stuff and satin. This is the *Hadjr-el-Sakhara*, or the "Locked-up stone." The Turks relate that it fell from heaven when the gift of prophecy was bestowed on man, and was used as a seat by the ancient men who were thus endowed. But when the prophets were at length compelled to abandon it and fly to other countries, the stone showed also a disposition to take its departure; on which the archangel Gabriel came, and, grasping it with his hand, held it in its place until Mahomet had flown from Mecca, and firmly attached it to the mountain. The Caliph Omar afterwards built around it the present mosque. They show on it the marks of the archangel's fingers, made in the struggle to detain the rock.

Beneath the mosque is a cave about eighteen feet square, with niches, called by the names of Abraham, David, Solomon, Elias, Gabriel, and Mahomet, but containing nothing remarkable.

In the south-eastern angle of the large court is another edifice of an oblong shape, 162 feet in length and 32 in width, called by the Turks *El Aksa*, and used by them as a mosque. It is enriched by a great number of columns within, but has a plain exterior; the Latins say it was the church used in the Presentation, but it probably belongs to the times of the crusades.

Immediately without the court of the mosque of

Omar, on the north, is a rectangular pit, about 150 feet long and 40 wide, and 12 or 15 in depth, walled around with hewn stones, evidently placed there in very ancient times. It is called the Pool of of Bethesda; but though I should like to consider it so, I know not of any sufficient evidence. The sides are perpendicular, and the plan is altogether different from that which the Scriptures would lead us to expect. See John v. 2.

A little beyond the Pool of Bethesda we come to the eastern gate of the modern city, called after St. Stephen, from a belief that this proto-martyr met his death on the slope, by which, just without this, we descend to the brook of Kedron. A rock about half way down the declivity, projects a little; and some stains, produced by an oxide of iron in the rock, are pointed out to the pilgrims as caused by his blood.

This gate is at present the only outlet on this side of the city; but there was formerly another gate opening from the court of the mosque, about 230 yards further south. It was called from its splendor "the Golden Gate;" but it is now walled up, in consequence of a tradition current among the Turks, that the city will one day be taken by the Christians, and that they will make their entrance through this gate.

Connected with it is also a Christian legend, somewhat fanciful, and of no bad moral, but destined to little credit in these severe and searching times.

In the year 608 Coroes, king of Persia, conquered

Jerusalem; and after plundering the city and desecrating the holy places, returned to his kingdom, carrying back with him the true and venerated cross. The emperor Heraclius, fourteen years after this, was fortunate enough not only to regain possession of the city, but following up his conquests, recovered also the sacred relic. Returning to Jerusalem, his intention was to enter the place by "the Golden Gate;" and after having proceeded in grand cavalcade to the churches, and having purified them, to restore the cross to its original site. Attired in robes all glittering with royal gems, and followed by a long train of courtiers and nobles, he advanced with gladness, and was about to enter through this splendid gate, when an invisible but steady hand pushed him back. Twice again he essayed to enter, but as often was brought suddenly to a stand; nor could any force succeed against this unseen and mysterious power. At this moment Zacharias, the patriarch of Jerusalem, came up; and seeing at once how matters stood, exclaimed, "Say, O emperor, art thou adorned with these splendid robes, and in this triumphant procession,—art thou imitating *Him* who, in humlity and sorrow, bore on his shoulders this sacred wood? Doff thy jewelled garments, put on a coarse and humble dress, and quickly shalt thou find an entrance, and be able to effect thy pious desires." The emperor hastened to comply, and the invisible hand ceased to obstruct his way.*

* El Devoto Peregrino.

CHAPTER XVII.

Valley of Hinnom. Potter's field. Singular properties attributed to its earth. Will not act on the citizens of Rome. Gloomy character of the valley. Job's well. Pool of Siloam. Fountain of Siloam. Periodical in its flow. Stones and columns belonging probably to the court of the ancient temple. Monuments of Zachariah and Absalom. Tomb of Jehoshaphat. Burial-place of the Jews. Valley of Jehoshaphat. View from the Mount of Olives. Plain of Jordan, and the Dead Sea. Garden of Gethsemane. Tomb of the Virgin. Tradition about her death and ascension.

ANOTHER interesting excursion was along the valley of Hinnom or Gehenna, thence up the valley of Kedron, or, as I shall hereafter call it, of Jehoshaphat, (its present name,) to the summit of the Mount of Olives, and to the reputed Garden of Gethsemane.

We left the city by the Jaffa gate, and began immediately to descend into the first of these valleys, which here widens considerably and then terminates. At the distance of about 500 feet from the extremity we came to a causeway, stretching quite across, and supposed to be an ancient embankment for confining waters that were discharged from an aqueduct still to be seen in the rocks above. This aqueduct may be traced for some distance on the western side of the valley where the rocks have in some places been cut with great labor to make way for it; it passes on towards Bethlehem, and I was informed, has its commencement at the Reservoirs of Solomon, about two miles beyond that city. This causeway and aqueduct probably belong to the very few remnants of the ancient Jerusalem now to be seen.

Our road laid near the bottom of the valley, upon the debris of the ancient Jerusalem, consisting of loose earth mingled with pottery; immediately over us, on the left, rose the frowning battlement of the city; on the right at the distance of about 200 feet were the perpendicular cliffs which on that side bounded the valley; they are composed of parallel strata of limestone, and are pierced with numerous sepulchral caves belonging to the times of the Jewish ascendancy. Near the bend of the valley, in a recess among the cliffs, was pointed out the spot supposed to be the Aceldama or field of blood. It belongs now to the Armenians, and if we are to believe numerous strong affirmations, the soil has the property, miraculously bestowed, of destroying the flesh of any body deposited in it in the short space of twenty-four hours. Earth from this place has been transported both to the famous Campo Santo at Pisa in Italy, and to Rome; and in both is said to retain its miraculous properties, with the single exception, that in the latter city, though it acts on the corpses of strangers, instead of eating, it indignantly thrusts out from it the bodies of the citizens themselves. For this distinction the Romans have to thank themselves. The earth was sent to them in 270 ships by Helena (or St. Helena according to the Roman calendar), who expected that it would be joyfully received. On its arrival, the strangers then in the city joyfully proffered their services in assisting to unload it, but the citizens took the liberty of declining, saying that they had already sacred earth enough, since the whole of their soil had been consecrated by the blood of the numerous martyrs who had suffered there. "For which act of contempt it is permitted of heaven, that if the body of any Roman is interred in the Campo Santo of Rome, the earth thrusts it out, fœted and deformed, but operates on that of a stranger as has just been related. There are many books which treat on this subject; and when I was myself in Rome, I inquired with great diligence into it, so as to inform myself about the matter; and all affirmed it to be the fact."*

This valley, which had presented a somewhat cheerful aspect at its upper extremity, became more sombre as we advanced; and our path, winding at last among large fragments of stones, was tiresome enough. We had lost sight of the city walls; the hill on our left was solitary and deserted, and around us were the ruins of habitations that had once covered it; the vegetation that had carpeted the bottom of the valley higher up had now ceased, and on our right were the rude large cliffs of the opposite

* El Devoto Peregrino, p. 68.

precipice. The scene was adapted to recall to our minds the ancient times when parents here caused their children to pass through the fire to Molech; it was a place well suited to such abominations. The valley is about a mile and a quarter in length; and, wearied with its rudeness and dreary solitude, we were glad when we emerged at last into the more open valley of Jehoshaphat, and found ourselves in a wide space, and by a well of cool delicious water. It is called Job's well, from a tradition that Job, when recovering from his diseases, came and facilitated his cure by washing here.

The valleys both of Hinnom and Jehoshaphat were quite dry at the time of our visit, but the numerous rounded pebbles in the bottom, particularly of the latter, gave evidence of rapid torrents in the rainy season.

Following up the latter valley on the western side, we came, at the distance of about 1200 feet from Job's well, to the outlet of the valley of Siloam, and our road was here crossed by the first stream of water that we had seen any where in or about Jerusalem; it is a mere streamlet however, a few drops oozing among the clods, and these soon lost in the thirsty soil. They come from the *Pool of Siloam*, which was a hundred yards on our left, and presents a chamber once apparently arched, and walled on either side, but open at the lower end, while from the upper part of the other extremity, a small stream drops in a light cascade, and forms a pool below, still much resorted to for water and for washing. Whether it presents the same appearance as in ancient times it is impossible to say; but there can be no doubt that the site is exactly that* of the pool to which the man blind from his birth was sent to wash, and whence he returned with his sight restored. There is great satisfaction in being able to identify a spot so highly interesting, and connected with such tender associations as this.

About 150 yards further on, as we were passing along the steep descent to the valley of Jehoshaphat, an opening in the rock suddenly presented itself on our left, and we found here the *Fountain* of Siloam—the spot from which the *Pool* is said to draw, by a subterranean channel, its supply of water. It is called the Virgin's Fountain, from a tradition that she used to resort to it frequently, and its waters are still used for diseases of the eye. It may, perhaps, have some medicinal qualities; for it is brackish, and not very pleasant to the taste. The fountain is subterranean, and is reached by a descent of thirty steps cut in the solid rock. At my first visit the water was gushing out at the bottom of this in a full stream as clear as crystal, and in this land of drought was really an attractive object. At my second visit, I could scarcely recognize it to be the same. The flow had ceased, and it was a stagnant pool; which a lad, filling some jars on a donkey alone, had defiled with

* See Josephus de Bel. lib. v. cap. 4. § 1. lib. vi. cap. 9. § 5.

sediment so as to give it a yellow muddy color. Its flow is periodical, and my visits must have been at times when the phenomenon is most striking in its operation. The waters of the Pool of Siloam have always been represented as sweet and pleasant, and those of this fountain are brackish. Can the former be supplied from this? It appeared to me also that the latter is lower than the *Pool* of Siloam; but my time did not allow me to settle the question. The water is conducted off from it by a subterranean channel deeply sunk in the hill.

Not far from this fountain is the south-eastern angle of the present city; and the wall here, projecting a little into the valley, is on this account about twice the usual height. Even at a distance our attention is attracted by some remarkable stones at this corner; and an examination satisfied me that they belonged to the ancient Jerusalem. I have frequently been asked, since my return, whether I could see any remains whatever of the ancient temple. These stones probably did not belong to the temple itself, but there is little doubt in my mind that they were a part either of its cloisters, or of the huge wall that supported its courts. They are just at the foot of Mount Moriah, and are in all respects quite different from the stones that form the remainder of the present city wall. The latter are of irregular shape and of no great dimensions, such as are to be seen in any common wall. These are all rectangular, with a remarkably fine joint, and are sometimes of very great size; I noticed some, the length of which would measure twenty-one feet; and they were all of considerable dimensions. Though the stones are of the common compact limestone found northward of the city, the joints are so closely fitted as to be perceptible only on a close inspection. On the outer surface of each stone, is a pannel, raised one fourth of an inch, and approaching to within two inches of the joint; there is an edifice at Baalbec, supposed to belong to the time of Solomon, the stones of which are all ornamented with a panelling similar to this; the castle or citadel of Damascus is also in the same peculiar style of architecture. Josephus, when speaking of the wall that supported the court of the temple, seems to refer to something like this when he tells us that, although the stones were neatly fitted together, yet "the vastness of the stones in the front was plainly visible on the outside."*

Built into the wall, at different elevations, from this angle on to the Golden gate, are also a great many columns, that appear to have belonged in ancient times to some splendid edifice. They are in a horizontal position; their extremities, which alone are visible, projecting two or three inches beyond the face of the wall. Some of them are of verd-antique of remarkable beauty, some are of a common kind of cipoline, and others are of a very hand-

* Antiq. lib. xv. cap. 11 § 3.

some rose-colored marble. Their position, directly under the site of the ancient temple, and their beauty, lead me to think that they belonged once to the courts of that splendid edifice.

In front of us, on the opposite side of the valley of Jehoshaphat, were now two remarkable objects, and descending, we crossed a bridge which here spanned the dry channel of Kedron, in order to examine them. They are two square monuments, lying about thirty feet above the bottom of the valley, and seem to be partly imbedded in the side of the Mount of Olives. In fact they are cut out of that mountain, being composed each of the solid undetached rock, but isolated from the hill by a channel ten or twelve feet wide, cut at the back and sides. They are called the monuments of Zachariah and Absalom.

The first of these is ornamented on each face with four semi-columns of the Ionic order, and a pilaster at each angle, crowned by an entablature, making, with the columns, an elevation of about twenty feet; all of this is one solid piece of rock. The whole is surmounted by a flat pyramid of masonry, the sides of which are smooth, and come down to the edges of the cubical mass. We can discover no opening of any kind in this monument, though there is doubtless a cavity beneath the pyramid.

The monument of Absalom stands about one hundred feet north of this, and is nearly of the same dimensions; the columns in this, however, are of the Doric order, and with an entablature to correspond. These are also cut in the same mass of rock, but are surmounted by a square block of masonry edged with mouldings; this again by a circular mass similarly enriched, and this by a sharp pointed dome, which, finally, is crowned by a stone ornament resembling a flame of fire. In the hinder side of this monument is an opening about ten feet from the ground, giving access to a chamber in it, which is now nearly filled up with pebbles. Both Mahomedans and Christians, as they pass along, throw a pebble at the monument, to show their detestation of the unfilial conduct of him whose name it bears. The authority for calling it after Absalom is in 2 Samuel xviii. 18. "Now Absalom in his lifetime had taken and reared up for himself a pillar, which is in the king's-dale, 'for,' he said, 'I have no son to keep my name in remembrance;' and he called the pillar after his own name; and it is called unto this day Absalom's Place."

It has been conjectured that the columns and other exterior ornaments are of more recent date than the rest of the work; but the parts all correspond so well, and harmonize also so well with the shape and proportions of the main body of the rock, that I can see no room for such an opinion.

Between the two monuments is a cave, called the Tomb of Jehoshaphat, on what authority it would be difficult to say; it consists of three chambers, one of which borders on the front of the precipitous rock in which they are situated, and is there adorned with two Doric columns, placed so as to support the roof. Back of the tomb of Absalom the face of the rock is also ornamented with scrolls and other sculptures, in bas-relief, covering, apparently, the entrance to a tomb cut in the mountain.

Turning here into a footpath that by zigzag lines begins to ascend the Mount of Olives, we found ourselves soon in a scene of pathetic interest. Yearning ever after the holy land of his forefathers, the Jew, as life begins to wear out, often collects together his earnings, and rouses up his sinking strength to carry him hither, that he may die in Jerusalem, and have his bones laid beneath the mountain of the ancient temple. They are not permitted to set foot within the enclosure of Mount Moriah, but in pleasant weather they may be seen just without the outer wall, seated on the ground, and reading in their devotional books; and even for this privilege they have to pay the Turkish governor. Sad and humbled people! They come hither from the ends of the earth, and, excluded from the Holy Mountain, sit down in the dust without its walls to mourn over their desolations, and cry, "Lord, how long, how long?" And the mark that is set upon them follows them, even in death. The Moslems occupy the slope down into the valley of Jehoshaphat for their own burying-place; and the Jews, desirous of having the shadows of Moriah fall upon their graves, have to take the opposite side of the valley along the slopes of the Mount of Olives. The ground there is whitened with the humble slabs that cover their graves.

"And the Lord shall scatter thee among all people, from one end of the earth even unto the other; and among these nations shalt thou find no ease, neither shall the sole of the foot have rest." The sleep of death! The graves of such a people here by the relics of the ancient city, are a touching spectacle!

The valley of Jehoshaphat, which takes its name from the monument we have just been noticing, is about two miles in length. It is the belief, both of Mahomedans and of the eastern Christians, that the Last Judgment will be held in this place. The authority given by the latter is in Joel iii. 2 and 12. "I will gather all nations, and will bring them down into the valley of Jehoshaphat," &c.—"Let the heathen be wakened, and come up to the valley of Jehoshaphat; for there will I sit to judge all the heathen round about."

I have already, I believe, mentioned that the Mount of Olives is about a mile in length, and about seven hundred feet in height. To a spectator on the west, it has a gently waving outline, and appears to have three summits of nearly equal height. On the top of the centre one is a Christian church, erected over the spot where, they inform us, our Saviour ascended into heaven; and, in confirmation of the fact, point to a stone with the impression of the left foot, made, as they say, as he was about leaving the earth; that of the right foot has been carried away by the Turks. On Ascension day they come up in great crowds, and have service here. The chapel had been shaken down by the recent earthquake, and the floor was covered by rubbish, so that we did not see the stone, nor did we care about it. In Luke xxiv. 50,* it is very clearly stated that the ascension occurred near Bethany, which is on the eastern side of the mountain, more than a mile from this. The Turks have a similar tradition with regard to Mahomet in connexion with this spot, and close to the Christian chapel have a mosque, also nearly laid in ruins by the earthquake.

From this central height a ridge stretches off towards the east for a distance of three fourths of a mile, when it terminates by a bold descent. We were conducted to the end of it in order to enjoy the view eastward, which is very extensive. The plain of Jordan, the mountain beyond, the Dead Sea, and the dark and singular chain of mountains on the east of it, were in full view, as well as all the country intermediate between them and us. Some of us thought that they could see the waters of the Jordan; but although this was uncertain, we could easily trace the course of the river through the plain

* Compare this passage with Acts i. 12, where the ascension is also spoken of. There are two roads to Bethany; one around the southern end of the Mount of Olives, and one across its summit; the latter being considerably shorter but more difficult. It was probably on this latter road, in the descent to Bethany, that the Saviour was taken up from the Apostles.

by the verdure; and where this failed, by the broken nature of the ground. Beyond it towered the lofty mountains of Moab, rising peak above peak in great majesty, including among them Mount Nebo; and as I stood gazing upon them, I took pleasure in repeating the hymn which I had often sung among friends in my own father-land,

"There is a land of pure delight."

It had a been part of our design to visit the Jordan and the Dead Sea; but the country was then filled with bands of people driven from their homes by the incursion of Ibrahim Pasha, and in a high state of excitement, as well from disaffection to the government as from their sufferings in consequence of the war; and when we proposed this journey, the men who owned our horses refused absolutely to let them go. The Governor of Jerusalem said that a guard of 300 men would be necessary, and offered to furnish us with such an escort, if the Commodore desired it; but this polite offer was of course declined. So we made the most of our mountain view, which was a very extensive one. The atmosphere in these lands of scanty exhalations is so clear that the Dead Sea and the Jordan appeared to be close to us, and we wondered that the journey to them should be esteemed so toilsome. But glancing at the country between us and them, we saw hill succeeding hill, till the detail swelled out into a distance of at least thirty miles. The country below us was a scene of complete and utter desolation; the hills were bare and red, and cut into deep ravines, and in the whole stretch between us and the Dead Sea, scarcely a spot of verdure could be seen. The mountains east of that lake of death have a very unique aspect, rising to a great height, and presenting an outline as smooth and even as if they were an artificial wall.

It was a relief to turn from this dreary prospect to the fertile and verdant mountain on which we were then standing. And as we returned, and, gaining the summit towards Jerusalem, looked down over its graceful slopes, and at the city, all displayed before us, no one could wonder that the Saviour often sought the Mount of Olives for meditation; and that the view around, then so varied, so rich, so beautiful, and soon to be changed by a fearful war into utter desolation, should incite to prayer.

The sun was now beginning to approach the western horizon. We descended by a steep zigzag path leading directly down towards the gate of St. Stephen; and near the foot of the mountain, now immersed in the broad shades of the city, came to a spot, that, as soon as it was named, excited a universal and powerful interest. It was the Garden of Gethsemane. It lies near the foot of the mountain, at an angle formed by the branching of the lower road to Bethany and that to Jericho, by which we had just been descending; and is marked by eight olive trees, that look as if they may have stood almost as many centuries. The Latins, to whom they belong, say, indeed, that they were here in the time of our Saviour, and would punish with excommunication any person of their order who should venture to break a limb or otherwise injure them. They allow pilgrims to peel off any loose pieces of bark that they may find on the huge trunks; which accordingly are kept white and raw looking by the frequency of such visits. They are very large; and as the olive tree is of very slow growth, there may be some truth in the declaration, that the Turks, on regaining the city from the Crusaders, having imposed a yearly tax of ten cents on every olive tree then standing, and half as much on any that should be planted, the records of the monastery show that the former sum was then paid for these trees; but as to the statement that would carry their age to the early times of Christianity, we cannot believe it; for if the olive tree itself were ascertained to last so long, we know that Titus had all the trees within several leagues cut down* for the construction of banks and instruments of assault.

As to the query whether this is the Garden of Gethsemane, I do not see that we have any reason for deciding in one way or the other, the notice of its location in the Scriptures (and I believe we have no others) being so very slight. The ground here slopes off more gently than in most other places, and is favorable for a garden; but it is quite near the foot of the mountain, and I think the expression

* Jos. de Bel. lib. vi. cap. 1. § 1.

(Luke xiv. 26.) "they went out *into* the Mount of Olives," would have led me to look for it higher up; and it seems probable, also, that a spot more retired than one so immediately adjoining the thronged city would have been selected on such an occasion. But these objections are not entitled to much weight, and I feel loth to disturb the belief in a spot of such tender interest. I broke off a few of the branches, and gathered up some of the earth, which I have brought home with me.

Although few of these places can be identified, and all have changed, it was still a high gratification to know that we were among scenes often blessed by the presence of our Saviour and Lord; that here, in this region, he had healed the sick, making joy spring up in bosoms where it had been long a stranger; here had given sight to the blind, and hearing to the deaf, and had taught his pure and benevolent doctrines; and that from the scenery around us, and now in our sight, had drawn elucidations and found the subjects for his parables.

About twenty paces northward from this, is a cave twenty-five or thirty feet in diameter, to which we descend by eleven steps; and here they say our Lord retired for prayer on this occasion; and they show also the spot where the three disciples reclined and slept.

Proceeding again to the northward, we come, at the distance of thirty yards, to a large subterranean chamber called the Tomb of the Virgin. It was lighted up for us; and having descended by a noble flight of steps, fifty in number, and twenty feet wide, cut in the solid rock, we found ourselves in a lofty apartment, branching off into small chambers on the right and left. The latter chamber is used as a chapel by the Copts, while in the other is the reputed Tomb of the Virgin, together with an altar. On either side of the flight of steps, about half way down, is also a recess, containing the reputed tombs of her parents, Joachim and Anna, and of Joseph the husband of Mary. This region is fruitful in traditions connected with the virgin and the apostles; but I pass them by, with the exception of one that is so full of poetry that I trust I shall be pardoned for noticing it.

The Virgin being sick, and now at the point of death, prayed her Son that the apostles might all be permitted to be present at her departure; and they were accordingly transported in a moment from all parts of the world, whither they had travelled preaching the gospel; and found themselves together by her bedside at Jerusalem; all except Thomas, who by a particular judgment was left behind.

She died, and was buried by the apostles in this spacious tomb, which they left not for three days and nights; during all which time sweet music from unseen angelic harps was floating amid the vaults and through the air above. At the end of this time, Thomas was placed among them, and was disconsolate when he found he had been denied the privilege of witnessing her death. He begged, however, that as he had not been allowed to see her while yet alive, he might be permitted to look at the corpse; they complied, and the tomb was opened for him; but the body was gone, nothing remaining but the grave clothes and winding sheet. At the same time the music of the angels ceased, by which they knew that the body was ascending to heaven. Thomas, with tears, gazed upward, and caught a glimpse of the ascending form; and to comfort him she dropped for him a girdle of marvellous beauty, which fell upon a rock adjoining the tomb; "which rock," says the book, "is held in the greatest veneration by all persons, and has granted for it indulgences, like those of the other sacred places of Jerusalem."*

Maundrell says of this stone, that there is "a winding channel upon it, which they will have to be the impression of the girdle when it fell, and to be left for the conviction of all such as shall suspect the truth of their story."

* El Devoto Peregrino, p. 105.

CHAPTER XVIII.

Visit to the Mount of Olives to procure olive root. Cabinet work from it. Attempt, by a Fancy spell, to raise up again the ancient city of Jerusalem. Its appearance. Fortifications. Towers. Royal palace. Stupendous wall supporting the Courts of the Temple. Outer Cloister. Solomon's Porch. Court of the Gentiles. Inner Cloister. Gate called "Beautiful." Court of the Jews. Court of the Priests. Altar. The TEMPLE. Its dazzling façade. Noble entrance. Skill of the Architect. Vestibule. Grape-vine of Gold. The Sanctuary. Its furniture. Holy of Holies. Effect of this place on Pompey. Walls of the edifice. Stones of amazing size. Frame work of the city. Villages and gardens around. Effect of the contrast between the Temple and Mount of Olives. The millions coming up to the Passover. Their Hymns. The Roman army. Titus takes a view of the city. Events foretelling its doom. The horror-stricken prophet.

THE olive root makes beautiful cabinet work; and, desirous of procuring some from the Mount of Olives to be worked up for my friends, I took one day an intrepreter and a couple of natives, and ascended the mountain to see if I could purchase some. Southward of Absalom's monument is the village of Siloa, standing in what appears to have been a quarry; and consisting partly of houses erected on the rocky platforms, and in part of caves cut in the side of the declivity. This was quite deserted; but near the summit of the mountain I was fortunate enough to find a house with occupants, from whom I purchased the privilege of cutting some roots.* It may afford an idea of the state of the arts at Jerusalem, when I mention that the best axe which we could find in the city was a species of blunt grubbing-hoe; and that we actually grubbed through the thick roots ; and this, they informed me, is the usual way of cutting wood in that country. Mr. Nicholayson had owned an English axe, but his Arab guards had carried it off at the conclusion of the siege.

Soon after commencing operations on the trees, we found ourselves surrounded by a dozen wild looking men, who seemed to have started up from beneath the ground, where probably they had been concealed in the caves and artificial pits with which the country abounds. They were induced, by the offer of a trifling compensation, to assist us; and while they were tugging away at the wood, I sat down a few yards off to make some plans and sketches of the city. In half an hour the interpreter came to say that they had all fled ; and on returning I found that not an individual of them was to be seen.

* I trust that I shall be pardoned if I add that the Commodore and myself had some of it worked at Mahon into tables representing, in Mosaic work, the hills and valleys of Jerusalem, a plan of the city, and a view of the Mount of Olives, its buildings and roads. The workmanship was well executed, and they make handsome pictures. The ingenious workman, Juan Rivdavetz y Prieto, just before we left that city, contrived a method of staining on plain apple wood, pictures of fruit, &c., with a very rich back-ground, forming beautiful cabinet work. The Commodore offered him a passage in the Delaware to America; but the love of his native island prevailed, and he remained.

The soldiers at the city gate below had spied them out with their glasses, and a detachment had been sent up to seize them; but they were too cunning, and escaped; and as we stood by the tree, we heard them, in their flight, calling to the soldiers, and using epithets that were any thing but complimentary. I have introduced this simple circumstance, however, not so much for its own sake, as to give me an opportunity of carrying the reader once more to the top of the Mount of Olives. And here I wish him to sit down at the spot which I have just been occupying on the central eminence, and gaze down on this place of wonderful history, and of tender and thrilling association. But my object is not to speak of the present city of Jerusalem; I wish to blot out all that picture, defaced in so many places by wretchedness and unsightly ruins, and to place before his imagination the ancient city of Jerusalem, when she sat upon these hills in her jewelled ornaments,—when "glorious things were spoken of thee, O city of God."

Often as that city is upon our lips, I believe there are few persons who have an idea of its extraordinary splendor in the olden times; for it was a place not only unique, and of strange religious interest, but also of wonderful magnificence. The period of Solomon's reign might perhaps be selected as that when its effect was most imposing; but I prefer for our picture the time of the Agrippas, because, while the splendor of Jerusalem was scarcely less than in

22

the reign of Solomon, we have, by the aid of Josephus, more ample materials for forming a judgment of its appearance; and this, too, with a slight exception, was the city whose streets our Saviour trod, and over which, while observing it from a spot just below us here on the Mount of Olives, he wept in the sad anticipation of its downfall.

And now look northward, and westward, and southward, and notice how, from these distant heights, the land slopes gently downward; bending hitherward as if in reverence, and to add dignity to the consecrated spot. Now look downward. Behold now I spread over the place the spell of a sober and chastened Fancy. I call up again the buried objects of other days. City of the olden time—arise!

See, this is the ancient Jerusalem!

Truly it is a magnificent place; a picture of rare and exquisite beauty set in a frame of brilliants. Recovered from our surprise, and the eye having grown more familiar with the unique spectacle, we turn now to examine it in detail. And, first, observe the walls by which it is begirt; what a proud and formidable array of strength is here. The massive battlements seem to set all earthly power at defiance, while the stones of immense size excite our wonder, not only by their prodigious size, but by their peculiar and careful finish. That wall on the north is eighteen feet in thickness, and with its battlements and turrets is forty-five feet in height; it runs zigzag, so that each part may be raked from the towers, of which there are ninety in this wall. The towers, thirty-six feet square, are of solid masonry, and are crowned each with two stories or suites of rooms, in which architectural beauty is consulted as well as strength, and which are of great magnificence. The angles in the wall are acute, receding considerably from the towers; and the whole structure, as it sweeps around the city, looks like a mountain of solid and immoveable rock. At its north-western angle, high above all the rest, rises the tower of Psephinus, massive below, but in its upper part marked by graceful, though still heavy architecture; it is octangular, and attains an elevation of one hundred and twenty-seven feet.

Within this, separating Acra from Bezetha, is another wall, a solid mountain of masonry, presenting high angular walls, battlements, and towers of exceeding strength; and here, south of Acra, on the edge of Zion, is a third line of similar defences, making, with the steepness of the ascent, a bulwark by no means less formidable than the rest; and on the southern and western sides of this mountain, grow up from the edge of the high rocky precipice, by which it is there begirt, lines of broad and high stone-work, presenting an utterly hopeless barrier to an assailant. "Walk about Zion, and go round about her; tell the towers thereof; mark ye well her bulwarks; beautiful for situation, the joy of the whole earth is Mount Zion. The kings were assembled, they passed by together;

they saw it, and so they marvelled; they were troubled, and hasted away."

The chief glory of these defences of Zion, however, is a nest of towers there at the north-west angle, "which, for largeness, beauty, and strength, are beyond all that are in the habitable earth." They were built by Herod, and called after his friend, his brother, and his wife. They stand at a point where the elevation of Mount Zion, contracting into narrow limits, becomes more remarkable, and thus presents their altitude and elaborate architectural beauties in a more striking point of view. One of them is placed in the sharp angle, and is called the tower of Hippicus. It is 46 feet square; and to an elevation of 55 feet is composed of firm and solid masonry, the stones with which it is built being 36 feet in length, by eighteen in width, and nine in height; above this enduring mass is a reservoir 36 feet in elevation; next above this is a double range of magnificent chambers of ornamental yet massive architecture, making an additional height of 46 feet; and above these rise battlements and turrets, the whole height of the tower being 146 feet.

A short distance from it we behold the tower Phasaelus, 72 feet square and 164 in height. Seventy-two feet of this elevation consists of stones like those in the tower just described; and the rest is composed of heavy stone work faced with colonnades; of richly ornamented chambers, and of battlements and turrets.

The third tower of Mariamne, named by Herod after his wife, is smaller than these, but of exquisite beauty, and richly adorned with ornaments; it attains an elevation of 91 feet.

All these look immediately down upon the royal palace, also on Mount Zion; and here the eye is wearied with tracing the labyrinth of courts, the succession of porticos adorned with rich and curious pillars, the ranges of lofty windows, giving light to halls where statuary and carved work have added their embellishments, and where the vessels are of silver and gold. And in the courts below and in the gardens are rare trees, and fountains, and brazen statues, and winding streams. No cost or skill has been spared in this palace by a prince whose resources were of the most ample kind. These palaces and courts and towers are the *Kremlin* of Jerusalem.

Observe now that long bridge, with its lofty arches, a striking feature in this scene, and adding greatly to its picturesque effect. It rises high above the dwellings of Acra, and, stretching quite across that portion of the city, connects the precincts of this palace with the Temple. But let us hasten to turn our attention to the Temple. The city has yet many striking objects that solicit our attention; the lofty and frowning castle of Antonia, palaces in great numbers, private edifices of remarkable architecture, brought out into strong relief by the uneven nature of the ground, invite our notice; but the wonderful Temple, grand, mysterious, awful, is here before us,

22*

and the eye glances impatiently at other objects. Let us turn then, and suffer our eyes to dwell and feast on this.

And it is indeed a glorious sight. It stands here all before us, the walls that support its courts rising from the very depths of the valley of Jehoshaphat, and towering aloft to an astonishing, a giddy height. It was a bold and daring conception—that of carrying up this mountain of stone-work to such a stupendous elevation. This wall here fronting us is 729 feet in height !* On the northern and western

* Jos. Ant. lib. viii. cap. 3. § 9. Ib. lib. xv. cap. 11. § 15. Ib. de Bel. lib. v. cap. 5. § 1. The height of these walls must strike the reader as almost beyond belief; and I confess that I hesitated about repeating them from the Jewish historian, till I came to reflect on the size of similar structures in other eastern cities. The walls of Nineveh are reported on good authority to have been 100 feet in height, and to have been strengthened by 1500 towers 200 feet in elevation. The height of the temple of Belus, at Babylon, formed altogether of bricks, is computed by Major Rennel at 500 feet, and by Prideaux at 600; its ruins still form a mound 200 feet in height. The royal palace in the same city was nearly as large as the temple; and the ruins of a castle are still seen 140 feet in height, and half a mile in circuit. The walls of this city were 34 miles in circuit—according to some writers 60; and were broad enough for six chariots to drive abreast upon them; and appear to have been originally 300, or 350 feet in height; having been reduced from this to 75 feet by Darius Hystaspes in order to check the rebellious spirit of the inhabitants.

The Egyptian pyramids still afford us a proof of the colossal nature of such undertakings in ancient times. The largest two of these, as has been already stated in this work, being 470 and 456 feet high, by 704 and 654 on each side.

When we reflect on the sacred character of Jerusalem in the eyes of all the Jews; how deeply the temple worship was wrought into all their systems, both civil and religious; how earnest their zeal, how entire their devotedness as regards this structure—we are prepared for something extraordinary.

sides, owing to the inequality of the ground, the elevation is somewhat less.

You perceive that in order to obtain greater strength, the walls are not perpendicular, but somewhat slanting, so that with the ascending nature of the ground in the courts above, the whole structure has somewhat of a pyramidal form. The stones of which it is composed are of prodigious size, yet are fitted together with the greatest care, and in addition to the security afforded by their magnitude, are strengthened internally by means of iron clamps. This wall is above 730 feet in length on each side; it forms an exact square, and the whole interior space being filled up, we have thus a vast mountain raised by human labor, a stupendous structure that must excite the astonishment of all succeeding ages. But this is only the ground work, the substructure for the great Temple and its sacred courts. Look up-

Josephus computes the number of "pure" persons who came up yearly to the feast of the Passover at about 3,000,000. (De Bel. lib. 11. cap. 14. § 3. lib. vi. cap. 9. § 3.) The vanity of the historian may have led him to some exaggeration, but still the number was prodigiously great. Many of these brought rich presents to the temple, and all were ready to contribute their labor as well as means whenever called upon. Agrippa, at one time, had 18,000 men employed in repairing the Temple. (Jos. Antiq. lib. xx. cap. ix. § 7.) Solomon employed 80,000 men to cut stone; 70,000 to transport the materials, and 10,000 men constantly on Mount Lebanon to cut wood for the Temple, and was seven years in completing it.

The space comprehended by these lofty walls was not entirely filled with earth, a large portion being occupied with vaults and subterranean passages. Their extent and the subsequent violence will acount for the complete abrasion of this mountain. See Jos. de Bel. lib. v. cap. iii. § 1. Antiq. lib. xv. cap. ii. § 7.

ward now; you see along the edge of this wall, far up at its giddy elevation, where the brain reels as it attempts to measure the depths below, you see a cloister or ornamented colonnade, on the outside ornamented with architectural embellishment, and yet more remarkable still for massiveness and strength, as if to guard from the assaults even of the wildest fancy the sacred precincts of the Temple. This cloister is 55 feet wide, and consists on the outside of a range of chambers, and within or towards the Temple, of a double row of marble columns 46 feet in height, each column consisting of a single block of white marble; the entablature gives to the whole cloister or colonnade an elevation of more than 60 feet. At the southern end, instead of two, are four rows of columns, each column six feet in diameter and 27 in height; the heaviness of the shaft being relieved by fanciful flutings at the base, and by rich leaf-shaped capitals, like those which we consider as belonging to the Corinthian order. This end is called Solomon's Porch;* it consists of a nave, if I may use the term, 45 feet wide, and in height 100 feet, with side aisles, each 30 feet wide, and 50 in height. It is an enchanting spot, and fanned at that high elevation with a perpetual breeze, and is a favorite resort; but, indeed, where, in this whole colonnade, forming a complete circuit of 2900 feet, is a spot that is not marked by exceeding beauty and magnifi-

* Thrice referred to in the New Testament, John x. 23. Acts iii. 11. and v. 12.

cence? At each angle you perceive towers of elaborate architecture, crowned with turrets or pinnacles, where, gazing downward, the senses recoil with horror from the frightful depth.

But this is only the commencement of the grandeur of this wonderful Temple. Within this cloister is an open court, running also quite around; it is paved with marble, and its level is broken by a few steps of ascent, also passing along the whole circuit of the court. This is the court of the Gentiles; and inscriptions on columns are seen at intervals, forbidding this class of people to advance nearer to the Temple. Along the inner edge of this court runs another cloister, consisting also of a row of chambers, with a single colonnade in the interior, or looking toward the Temple. In the space allotted here to the chambers, the ground has taken an ascent of seventeen feet from the court of the Gentiles, but the colonnade itself is on level ground, the pillars being, as in the outer colonnade, forty-six feet in height, and making, with the entablature, likewise a full elevation of more than sixty feet; but from the rise of the ground this colonnade is twenty feet higher than the other.

In this cloister, fronting us on the east, is the "Beautiful Gate;"* and truly, no one need be directed to mark its surpassing magnificence. It is ninety-one feet in height by seventy-three in width; the doors are of massive Corinthian brass, covered on both sides,

* Acts iii. 2.

as are also the jambs and lintels, with plates of gold and silver, sometimes plain, sometimes in fretted work, or raised into figures in low or in high relief. On either side of the doorway is a tower, seventy-three feet high, adorned with columns twenty-one feet in circumference. On the northern and southern sides of this cloister are eight other gates, of less magnitude, but covered in a similar manner, as are also their jambs and lintels, with plates of gold and silver; and strengthened also like the former, with towers and massive columns.

Passing through this, we are once more in an open court, paved with marble, and rising by steps towards the central point. The eastern side of this court is allotted to the worship of the Jewish women, while that on the north and south is divided off for the men. At the inner edge of this court is again another wall; it is of marble, only a few feet in height, and is richly ornamented with sculpture; it separates the court of the Jewish worshippers from the inmost court of all, the court of the Priests.

And there, at the eastern side of this inmost court, in the open air, at the apex of this stupendous Pyramidal structure, canopied only by the heavens, stands the Altar of Burnt Sacrifice. It is a colossal structure, being twenty-seven feet in height and ninety-one feet on each of its sides. The ascent is by an inclined plane on the south.

And just beyond it, is the TEMPLE. This looks also to the eastward, and as we attempt to gaze upon it in this bright morning sun, now darting its rays across the Mount of Olives, our dazzled eyes turn away, pained by the glorious sight. It presents a front one hundred and eighty-two feet long and of an equal height, *all of which is covered with thick plates of gold.* What a magnificent spectacle! What a grand termination to this stupendous structure, towering upwards from the deep valley towards the clouds. Cast your eye downwards, and let it range over the immense masses of chiselled rocks, wrought into regular shape, enriched with architectural device, and piled on each other till the senses are pained in endeavoring to take in the colossal fabric of more than seven hundred feet in height; glance at the huge mouldings into which the wall swells at its termination; mark the high colonnades of pure showy marble, that are ranged along the edge of this mighty structure; see within this the marble tesselated pavement, ascending by flights of steps, and encircling the mountain; and then again another range of light marble porticos sweeping quite around; mark the pavement, again ascending by unbroken flights of marble steps; and here, at length, crowning the whole magnificent work, is the gorgeous Temple, its front one hundred and eighty-two feet high, decked with elaborate architectural embellishments, and covered with massive gold.

And "the Lord is in his Holy Temple, let all the earth keep silence before Him."

Yes, in this gorgeous edifice, raised to such a

stupendous height, wrapped in a splendor that the eye can scarcely look upon; deep within the edifice in a spot of mysterious darkness and solitude, is shadowed forth the presence of Jehovah; and this Temple belongs not to Jerusalem, but to the whole world. And He, the Deity, whose very name is awful, and should be used with reverence, hath blessed this spot with his peculiar presence; and it is meet that man should look upon it with deep and solemn feeling. "How amiable," said the Psalmist, when far distant, "how amiable are thy tabernacles, O Lord of Hosts. My soul longeth, yea, even fainteth, for the courts of the Lord; my heart and my flesh crieth out for the living God. For a day in thy courts is better than a thousand. I had rather be a door-keeper in the house of my God, than to dwell in the tents of wickedness."

In this eastern front of the Temple is an open and ornamented door-way, 46 feet wide and 128 feet in height. The architect of this edifice was a man of skill. He knew well the powerful effect produced by the prevalence of high ascending lines in a building, and in the Temple he has taken advantage of this effect, and with the best results. How fine is the appearance of this grand and lofty door-way, open also so as to give a view of the rich vestibule just within! Our thoughts and our feelings, whatever they may be, are not checked at the very threshhold, but are allowed to penetrate to a short distance; they are not excluded from the edifice; they enter sufficiently to make us a part of it; and yet it is not made common by being all exposed; sufficient of it remains shut up to excite our wonder, to cherish feelings of respect, to inspire that awe which arises from mystery.

He who may enter this lofty door-way, will find himself in a vestibule at right angles with his path; it is 36 feet wide, 92 in length, and 164 feet in height. The wall in front of him is all covered with plates of gold, which, like that on the exterior front, is in various forms, smooth and highly burnished, or in patterns of embossed work, or in figures of various kinds. From the lofty ceiling, which the eye is pained in attempting to reach, hangs down a golden vine, with leaves and fruit of the same metal, and so colossal are its dimensions, that the clusters of grapes are six feet in length.* Our foot may not be placed within this vestibule; but through the large open door-way we can discover much of the splendor by

* I have been unwilling to break the thread of description by references; but my authorities are in Josephus, Antiq. lib. xv. cap. 11. lib. viii. cap. 3. de Bel. lib. v. cap. 5.

If the reader should think this account of the richness of the Temple incredible, he is requested to consult ancient authors about similar structures in other countries. The Parthenon at Athens cost sixty millions of dollars; the Propylaea, or entrance to the Acropolis, on which it stands, cost half as much; the statue of Minerva in the former was of ivory and gold; the gold alone cost more than half a million of dollars. The statue, decorations, and utensils in the Temple of Belus, according to Diodorus Siculus, were equal in value to more than 200 millions of our dollars. When Titus had taken Jerusalem, gold was so abundant among his soldiers, that in Syria a pound of it sold for half its former value. See Jos. de Bel. lib. vi. cap. 6. § 1.

23

which it is distinguished. In the golden wall that bounds our vision at its further side, is a door-way twenty-nine feet wide by 100 in height, covered by a Babylonian curtain, of blue and scarlet and purple, richly embroidered, and of wonderful workmanship. Its ample folds conceal a door, which, like the wall, is covered with plates of gold, plain or in various patterns, and of exceeding richness.

He who enters this door will find himself in *The Sanctuary*. This is a chamber thirty-six feet wide and seventy-two in length, and 109 in height; its height, however, cannot be reached by the eye; for this chamber is in darkness, except the obscure light shed upon it by several lamps. Daylight cannot penetrate it, unless occasionally a feeble glimmering through the door-way; a mysterious obscurity is left to pervade it, and the vision, turning upward, combats for a while the deepening shadows, and is then repelled by utter darkness. The furniture of this room is simple, for it contains only the Table of Shew-bread, and the Golden Candlestick, and the Altar of Incense. While the incense ascends silently, and keeps the chamber filled with perpetual odours, the softened light of the Seven Golden Lamps of the Candlestick falls upon a table with twelve loaves of bread, one for each tribe; as if, by this simple emblem, the staff of his life kept here in memorial, man would gratefully acknowledge by whom his existence is prolonged, and whence are derived its blessings. There is something in this quiet and simple scene, a subdued and humble, yet grateful character in its speech, that is very impressive.

At the further end of this chamber is again a doorway covered by a thick veil of many folds. It opens into a square chamber thirty-six feet on each side, and 109 in height. In this chamber there is nothing at all. *It is quite dark;* and its deep obscurity and its vacancy are fit emblems of HIM who is invisible to mortal eye, and whom mortal thought can never reach. This is the Holy of Holies. It is entered only by the High Priest, and by him but once a year. Unadorned, and deeply shut up within the Temple, it is left to darkness, and silence, and impressive solitude.

When Pompey, after a toilsome siege, at length took this mountain by assault, he hastened to the Temple, incited both by curiosity, and by a desire to feed his eye on the wealth that had at length become his own; but when, having examined the Sanctuary in its dim mysterious light, and then, raising this veil, he stood in the Holy of Holies, and found no object, nought but an obscurity that his eye, as he gazed upward, sought in vain to pierce, a feeling of awe and dread seems to have come upon him; he left the Temple, having touched neither its furniture nor its treasure, and, calling off his troops, he gave orders to repair the injuries that had been occasioned by his assault.

The walls of this building are fourteen and a half feet in thickness, and are composed of stones forty-six feet long by twenty-one in width, and fourteen in thickness, interspersed with some that have the astonishing length of eighty-two feet.* The main body of the edifice, containing the Sanctuary and the Holy of Holies, is so narrow in proportion to its elevation, that it would be in danger from earthquakes if that were not guarded against by an outer wall nine feet from this, with which it is connected so as to form between them three tiers of cells, thirty in each tier; the upper part of the building is used as store-rooms for the furniture and utensils of the Temple. The vestibule, being at right angles with the body of the edifice, projects thirty-six feet on either side. The stone employed here appears to be a pure white marble, for those portions of the building which are not covered with plates of gold are of dazzling whiteness, so as to appear at a distance like a mountain covered with snow.

The whole mass, the foundation walls, the porticoes, the Temple, are indeed a wonderful structure; and with the sacred and solemn associations connected with them, form an object of surpassing interest and grandeur.

And now look down again upon the city and upon the fair region stretching all around. The ground on which Jerusalem is built, assists greatly, as you perceive, in giving it architectural effect. Babylon, Nineveh, Thebes, Memphis, those cities of ancient

* Stones are still to be seen at the Great Temple of Baalbec sixty-four feet in length.

renown, were built on level plains, and with all their riches and greatness were in most parts tame and monotonous; but here the picturesque is added to greatness and splendor; the walls and towers overhang deep precipices; the lofty palaces are brought into stronger relief by their situations; each portion of the city, by harmony or by contrast, adds a charm to every other; and the Temple, like another sun chained to the dizzy heights of Moriah, sheds an effulgence over all.

Gaze now around. What a frame-work is there for the city of Jerusalem! See the villages, embosomed in gardens of deep verdure, sprinkled thickly over all the plains, which, ascending as they retire from the city, expose every object to our view. Here the houses stand in thick clusters, there they straggle along amid the overhanging trees; and the whole immense extent of country seems only a continuation of the city in a more cheerful form. And this Mount of Olives, what a beautiful object it must be when viewed from the city. Its graceful slopes, its gardens, its deep shade, its white cottages, its villas, where the wealthy love to retire, half exposed, half concealed, by the dense verdure; its groves and public walks; what an admirable picture they form; and alongside of the stupendous and glittering pyramid of Mount Moriah, each by contrast gives new beauties and new charms to the other. Where in all the world shall we find a scene equal to this?

And now glance your eye along these roads that

come winding over the hills by which Jerusalem is encircled. See! The whole country seems awakened into an intensity of life and animation. *It is the Passover.* Far off as the eye can reach, the great highways and the narrow paths are covered with masses of living beings, thousands upon thousands pouring onwards, and still succeeded by other thousands, till it seems as if the whole habitable globe was sending its inhabitants and its tribute to this sacred city. And it does. Here are "Parthians and Medes, and Elamites, and the dwellers in Mesopotamia, and in Judea, and Cappadocia, in Pontus and Asia, Phrygia and Pamphylia, in Egypt and in the parts of Lybia about Greece, and strangers of Rome, and Cretes, and Arabians," in their various costumes, and speaking their various tongues. The number that assembles here on this occasion is about three millions. They come, some purely from religious feeling, some also for commerce; for the occasion is seized by dwellers in far distant countries for the interchange of commodities. As they approach the city, however, a common feeling takes possession of all of them, delight, reverence, awe, wonder, admiration. As they gain the summits of the distant hills, and catch a view of the Temple, they burst into shouts of joy, they prostrate themselves upon the ground, they break out into hymns of praise. The air seems burdened by the noises that unceasingly ascend; one while they are like the roar of the ocean; at another, they rise, and sink, and swell upward again into lofty strains of wonder and thanksgiving; the earth trembles under the moving to and fro of these countless multitudes. See--still they come, thousands and yet still countless thousands pressing onward towards the city. The eye is wearied with beholding them; the senses are pained and overwhelmed.

And now the sounds abate and sink into a deep but continuous murmur. They are preparing for the Paschal sacrifice. The multitudes are divided into companies of from ten to twenty, and each company, by a deputy appointed for that purpose, is to offer in the courts of the temple a lamb without blemish or spot; the blood is to be sprinkled at the foot of the great altar, and the fat is to be cast upon it for a burnt offering. There will be 250,000 of these sacrifices.

See! the courts of the Temple, the flat roofs of the colonnades, are covered by the dense throngs; the walls and towers of the city, the terraces of the lofty dwellings of Jerusalem, are crowded by the multitudes; and the ascending plains around, and the slopes of the Mount of Olives, are all animated; it is an ocean of living beings.

And now they are silent all. Soon you will perceive a great cloud of smoke roll up from the altar and envelope the Temple, and then you will hear their hymns. There it is! and astounding! the millions of voices that ascend seem to burst the very heavens; the mountain shakes under the strange concussion. —Their Hymn.—

Hallelujah! Hallelujah!
O praise God in his holiness,
Praise him in the firmament of his power.
Praise him for his mighty acts,
Praise him for his excellent greatness.

Instrumental music accompanying.

Praise him in the sound of the trumpet,
Praise him upon the lute and harp.
Let every thing that hath breath praise the Lord.

Children of the Levites, from the Temple.

Thine ordinances, O God, how glorious they are.
But tell us, fathers of Israel, what mean ye by this service?

Solemn recitative, from the Elders.

It is the sacrifice of the Lord's Passover, who passed over the houses of the children of Israel, in Egypt, when he smote the Egyptians, and delivered our houses.

Hymn from Mount Moriah.

Sing unto the Lord, for he hath triumphed gloriously.
He has brought us in and planted us in the mountain of his inheritance;
In the place, O Lord, which thou hast made for thee to dwell in,
In the Sanctuary, O Lord, which thine own hands have established.

Full chorus of all the multitudes.

The Lord is our strength, and he is become our salvation.
He is our God, and we will honor his habitation.
Our father's God, and we will exalt him.
Hallelujah. The Lord shall reign for ever and ever. Hallelujah.

Full company of instrumental music, on Mount Moriah.

Now listen, this is the hymn of solemn invocation.

From the Priests in the inner Court.

The Lord hear thee in the day of trouble.
The name of the God of Jacob defend thee,
Send thee help out of the Sanctuary, and strengthen thee out of Zion.

Remember all thy offerings, and accept thy burnt sacrifices.

Grant thee according to thy heart's desire, and fulfil all thy mind.

Be merciful unto us, O God, be merciful unto us; for our soul trusteth in thee.

Response from the deputies in the surrounding courts.

Hear our cry, O God; give ear unto our supplications.

From the ends of the earth will we call upon thee when our heart is in heaviness.

Our souls wait only upon God; for our expectation is from him.

He is our salvation and our glory; he is the rock of our strength and our refuge.

Response from the full multitude.

Also unto thee, O Lord, belongeth mercy; our souls wait only upon thee.

Thou art our salvation and our glory; thou art the rock of our strength and our refuge.

HYMN THIRD.

Voices of the full multitude.

O sing unto the Lord a new song; for he hath done marvellous things.

With his own right hand, and with his holy arm, hath he gotten himself the victory.

The Lord hath declared his salvation; his righteousness hath he openly showed in the sight of the heathen.

He hath remembered his mercy and truth towards the house of Israel;

And all the ends of the world have seen the salvation of our God.

Show yourselves joyful before the Lord, all ye lands; sing, rejoice, and give thanks.

Praise the Lord upon the harp; sing to the harp with a psalm of thanksgiving.

With trumpets also, and shawms, O show yourselves joyful before the Lord, the king.

Full outburst of instrumental music on Mount Moriah.

HYMN FOURTH.

Voices of the strangers.

How amiable are thy Tabernacles, O Lord of Hosts.

I was glad when they said unto me, let us go into the house of the Lord.

Our feet stand joyfully within thy gates, O Jerusalem.

Voices of the citizens.

Pray for the peace of Jerusalem, for the peace of Jerusalem; they shall prosper that love thee.

Full chorus of all, both strangers and citizens.

Peace be within thy walls, and prosperity within thy palaces.

For my brethren and companions' sakes, I will wish thee prosperity.

Because of the house of the Lord our God, I will seek thy good.

Hallelujah! The Lord shall reign for ever and ever! Hallelujah!

* * * * * *

City of Jerusalem! art thou then to be a heap of ruins? Land of glory! art thou then to be a desolation? Temple of the living God, to which exceeding beauty and wonderful associations draw our hearts, art thou then to be laid in the dust, till not one stone shall be left upon another? It is even so.

The voices of the worshippers are suddenly hushed, for upon yon distant hills, to the northward, is the glitter of armor; and see, the heights are now all covered with a dense array of the legions of Rome. Their leader comes here to reconnoitre, and from this mountain looks down upon the glorious city.

"It must be—
And yet it moves me, Romans! it confounds
The counsels of my firm philosophy,

That Ruin's merciless ploughshare must pass o'er,
And barren salt be sown on yon proud city.
As on our olive-crowned hill we stand,
Where Kedron at our feet its scanty waters
Distils from stone to stone with gentle motion,
As through a valley sacred to sweet Peace.
How boldly doth it front us! how majestically!
Like a luxurious vineyard, the hill-side
Is hung with marble fabrics, line on line,
Terrace o'er terrace, nearer still, and nearer
To the blue heavens. Here bright and sumptuous palaces,
With cool and verdant gardens interspersed;
Here towers of war, that frown in massy strength,
While over all hangs the rich purple eve.
And as our clouds of battle, dust, and smoke,
Are melted into air, behold the Temple,
In undisturbed and lone serenity,
Finding itself a solemn sanctuary
In the profound of heaven! It stands before us
A mount of snow, fretted with golden pinnacles!
The very sun, as though he worshipped there,
Lingers upon the gilded cedar roofs!
And down the long and branching porticoes,
On every flowery sculptured capital
Glitters the homage of his parting beams.
By Hercules! the sight might almost win
The offended majesty of Rome to mercy."

MILMAN.

It is a wonderful city, wonderful in its origin, in its history, in its present character; strange events, too, have been foretelling its doom, and terrible is to be its downfall.

A flaming sword was seen night after night, for the space of a year, suspended over the city; the inhabitants crowded to the Temple, they offered sacrifices, but still that bloody sword was over them; the timid buried themselves in their chambers and wept; the gay tried to forget it in debauch, but still it hung above the city, and the hearts of the stoutest at length quailed before it. It has lately disappeared, but they do not know whether to consider this as an omen for good or for evil.

Also the Beautiful Gate of the Temple, which requires twenty men to move it, one night, though secured by heavy bolts, opened of its own accord, as if to show that the spirits which had been keeping guard in the Temple were leaving it.

Also one night at Pentecost, as the priests were going to their duties in the inner court of the Temple, they felt a quaking of the earth, and then, as they stood to recover from their dread, they heard a whispering noise as of a multitude of people, saying, "*Let us go hence.*"

Even now, as we have been sitting here, a lonely and mournful, but loud voice, has been repeating in the lanes and in the high streets of the city, "Wo, wo to Jerusalem!" And for four years, by day and in the deep stillness of night, that melancholy cry has been unceasingly heard denouncing wo to the affrighted and cowering inhabitants. A plain countryman came up to the Feast of Tabernacles four years ago while the country was prosperous and at peace; and while engaged in the duties of this occasion became suddenly a changed man, and before the multitudes cried aloud, "A voice from the east, a voice from the west, a voice from the four winds, a voice against Jerusalem and the Holy House, a voice against the bridegrooms and the brides, and a voice against this whole people!" A dead weight of fear has ever since lain upon the spirits of the inhabitants, crushing the timid, and oppressing even the boldest. They have tried by every means to stop his mournful cry; they have beaten him till his bones were laid bare, but he made no supplication and shed no tears; they have carried him before the rulers, but he has not been awed to silence, nor to their queries and threats has he made any reply; he has associated with no one, but in the crowded city has made himself a solitary and a lonely man; he has not complained when ill treated and abused from day to day; he has not thanked those who gave him food; to each he has replied only by his usual exclamation of, wo to the city; the channels of all feeling, except a deep and dreadful horror, seem to have been frozen up. He rests but little; something within him hath murdered sleep. At midnight, when all nature is hushed in death-like repose, from amid the deep darkness his mournful voice is heard; and the mother starts and draws her infant to her breast, and the sentry on his post trembles at the prolonged and melancholy cry, "Wo, wo, wo to Jerusalem!"

* * * * * *

The wo hath been poured out upon the unhappy city.

* * * * * *

Eleven hundred thousand persons perished dur-

24

ing the siege, by famine, pestilence, or by human violence. Ninety-seven thousand at its close were carried as captives into distant lands.*

* See Jos. de Bel. lib. vi. cap. v. § 3. Ibid. cap. ix. § 3; and for the prodigies, see also Tacitus, Hist. lib. v. cap. xiii.

CHAPTER XIX.

Visit to Bethlehem. Well of the Star. Monastery of Elijah. Rachael's Tomb. Plain of the Shepherds. Town of Bethlehem. Character of its inhabitants. Church and Cave of the Nativity. Traditions. The Turpentine Tree, &c. Manufactures of the Bethlehemites. Tattooing. Country northward from Jerusalem. Cave of Jeremiah. Hill of Bezetha. Tombs of the Kings. Dr. Clarke's subterranean Chapels. Ancient quarries. Tombs of the Judges. Thorn from which the Saviour's crown is supposed to have been made. Difficulty at the Gates. Yaoub and the Soldiers.

On the morning of the 18th we started for Bethlehem, which lies at the distance of about five miles from Jerusalem on the south. Leaving by the Jaffa gate, and crossing by difficult paths the valley of Hinnom, we had then before us an elevated plain bordered eastwardly by the valley of Jehoshaphat, about two miles wide, and extending three miles toward the south, in which direction it has a slight ascent. As we passed on, a troop of cavalry, which had been out at their morning drill, came sweeping along on our left; but when they had passed us, we were left alone in the open country, where scarcely a sign of cultivation appeared. A blight has for a great many years been upon this doomed and unhappy land. At the distance of about two miles from the city, we came to a well, called "the well of the kings," or, "the well of the star," from a tradition that when the wise men had left Jerusalem for Bethlehem, and had reached this place, the star (Matthew ii. 9.) appeared again, and led them on to the couch of the infant Messiah. At the extremity of this plain, and on a height commanding a view both of Jerusalem and Bethlehem, is the Greek monastery of Elijah, where is one of the sacred places of the country. "Here," says el Devoto Peregrino, "is a rock impressed by the body of the holy prophet, as natural as if it had been stamped there; for we see the head, the shoulders, the ribs and body, extended horizontally. This is the place to which the holy prophet retired to contemplate the future Messiah; and where, looking towards Bethlehem, he saw him enveloped in coarse swaddling clothes, but surrounded by angels, singing glory to God in the highest; and, looking towards Jerusalem, saw him nailed to the cross and crowned with thorns, while the multitude around were blaspheming and insulting him."

Sandys, in his quaint style, remarks of it: "Hard by is a flat rock, whereon they told us that the prophet was accustomed to sleepe, and that it beares as yet the impression of his body. Indeed, there are certaine hollowes in the same, but not by mine eyes apprehended to retaine any manly proportions."

I speak of the place from the authority of others, for I felt no disposition at the time to trouble myself with matters of this nature. Indeed, it requires a constant effort in travellers among these places to keep the mind free from disgust, and from the baneful effects of the errors, that, like leeches, have fastened themselves to the truth, covering and deforming it, and exhausting its power, while they themselves live on its fading strength.

The monastery is surrounded by a strong wall, and looks as if it might be a place adapted as much for defence as for devotion.

Bethlehem here came into full view, though more than two miles distant; the country between it and us, although broken, being rather low, and the town itself being situated on an eminence of steep ascent. On the way, we left, at a short distance on our right hand, a small square edifice surmounted by a dome, evidently a modern structure, but called the tomb of Rachael, and regarded by Moslems as well as by the Christian sects here with high respect. Further on to our left, and below the town of Bethlehem, was a small valley, covered even at this hot season with a refreshing verdure; and here they inform us the shepherds were watching their flocks by night, when the angel appeared to announce glad tidings of great joy, the birth of "a Saviour, which is Christ the Lord." Near this is also a well, said to be the one from which David's three "mighty men" procured him water at the risk of their lives. Passing these spots, we soon after arrived at the outskirts of Bethlehem; and as our large cavalcade wound up the steep ascent, the whole population of the place came crowding along the way, hanging over the rude

24*

walls, and filling every door and window. They are all Christians in name, though they bear an indifferent character; and, what in these countries strikes one with surprise, the women appeared with their faces exposed, and frequently very good-looking faces they were. Our arrival seemed to excite a very unusual sensation, which I was able to account for by and by, when one of the men, taking me aside in the convent, asked seriously whether the report was true, "that we had come to take the place from the Egyptian Pasha." They bear no good feeling towards the Moslem power, and have always been refractory and troublesome subjects to the Porte; their insulated situation, and the facilities for retiring to mountain fastnesses in the wild country around, encouraging in them bold and independent habits. We were informed that when the general order from Mohammed Ali for disarming the populace of Syria was carried to them, they sent in about a dozen muskets, saying, that these were all they had; nor could any threats wrest more from them, though the place has three or four hundred fighting men well equipped. The town is situated on a piece of isolated table land, of sudden elevation on every side. On the east this runs out into a narrow tongue, and at the extremity of this projection, 200 yards distant from the village, are the monastery and church of the Franciscans, covering the spot where the Messiah was born.

The recent earthquake had rent the massive walls of these edifices, but not so as to endanger them, and we met with a ready and hospitable reception beneath the roof. The door of entrance is low and strong, and every where in this country is the traveller reminded of the insecurity of life and property; and, unless people would live there with a martyr's spirit, of the necessity of being constantly prepared for defence.

Having entered the building, we were carried along some winding passages, and found ourselves presently in a church that had once been splendid, but which is now in a dilapidated state, owing partly to the effects of time, and partly to the spoliations of the Turks. It has four rows of columns, ten in each row, and still imposing objects, the effect of which is heightened by gilding and paintings on the wall; but the colors are dim, and the pavement is torn up, and the place has a melancholy grandeur that chills and oppresses the feelings.

They took us from this, after a short period for resting, into some side passages, and we soon found ourselves descending into the Cave of the Nativity. It is reached at one end by a tortuous underground passage, but on the other by a flight of steps that brings us at once to the spot. We were introduced by the former of these, and after winding along for a distance of about fifty feet, we turned short to the left, and a flood of light bursting suddenly upon us, we knew that we were in the Chapel or Cave of the Nativity. The main body of this subterranean apartment is about thirty-five feet long by twelve in width, with a height of ten or twelve feet, but it is irregular in shape. On either side, as we advanced, were benches or seats for those who may choose to come here for meditation. Having proceeded about twenty feet, we came to a small apartment on our right, about ten feet square, the floor of which is lower by eighteen inches than the remainder of the cave; it is open in front, where are two pillars to support the roof. On the three remaining sides are shallow recesses; one of which, they inform us, is the manger in which the infant Messiah was laid; in the recess opposite the Magi sat, and in the third they deposited the gifts of "gold, frankincense, and myrrh." The rock over this apartment is bare, and visitors are allowed to break off small fragments; the other portions of the cave are all lined with precious marbles.

Just beyond this spot the cave branches to the right and left, a broad flight of steps, on either hand, leading, at the distance of about twenty feet, to the surface of the ground; at the angle formed by this branching is another recess, about three feet deep and six in length. It is occupied by an altar, over which is a handsome painting of the Adoration; the altar is in form of a table, and beneath it, at the centre of a star formed of marble mosaic work, is a silver plate inscribed,

HIC DE VIRGINE MARIA JESUS CHRISTUS NATUS EST.

Here Jesus Christ was born of the Virgin Mary.

I suppose there can be no reasonable doubt that

this is actually the cave of the Nativity. Hadrian, in derision of the Christians, placed here a statue of Adonis, and Helena, not long after, erected the church, the remains of which we have just been examining. Jerome speaks of the place as undisputed in his day; and as he resided here a while, we must suppose him well acquainted with the subject. A subterranean chamber, on the right of the winding passage by which we had reached this cave, is still pointed out as his study; they show, adjoining to it, also, the place where the bodies of the Innocents were cast, the sepulchre of St. Jerome, that of Eusebius, and that also of St. Paula and her daughter Eustoquio, persons distinguished in the Romish calendar. Over the small chamber in which the manger is situated, they show also what they call a picture of St. Jerome, stained miraculously in the natural rock.

It is sad, when we enter a place of such powerful interest, to be met at the very threshold with things that we cannot believe; and instead of being left to indulge in salutary reflections, to be compelled to commence separating truth from error, and fixing their boundaries, or else to feel the repulsive and chilling effect of scepticism settling upon the whole. The great error of the Romish and Greek churches here has been in endeavoring to fix upon a locality for every event noticed in Scripture; and even the parables of our Saviour have not been suffered to escape from this spirit of blind and injudicious zeal.

They point out upon the Mount of Olives spots as those where the Saviour taught the Lord's Prayer, where the Apostles composed the creed, where Christ wept over Jerusalem, where he preached the Judgment, &c.; and on Mount Zion, where the last supper was held, where Peter retired to weep, where Isaiah was sawn in two, and a great variety of other places with which it is not necessary to fatigue the reader.

And as if this were not enough, they have got up traditions of the wildest and most startling nature, and the whole country is full of the localities with which these are connected. On the way out to Bethlehem are two which I have not yet noticed, and at which I will now barely glance. One is a place where formerly stood a turpentine tree. As the Virgin was going to Jerusalem with the infant for the Presentation in the Temple, this tree bowed and did reverence as they passed; and to make its show of respect more lasting, did not return to its former position, but remained thus inclined. It was worthy of observation, too, that ever after, though the air might be sultry and stifling in all the region about it, yet under this tree was always a refreshing breeze. Indulgences were granted to those who recited prayers beneath it; wood was cut from it by night (through fear of the Turks), and carried, in the form of crosses, all over Europe. The Arabs, at length, in a fit of ill humor, cut it down.

As we descend the hill toward Bethlehem is another spot made sacred by their traditions. The Virgin passing by this place, saw a man sowing or planting beans, and asking him what he was employed at, received for answer, that he was sowing pebbles; on which, the beans in his basket turned to pebbles, nor has any care since that availed to make the field produce any thing else than stones.

These are only specimens of the superstitious legends with which the whole region is filled.

On our return to the convent, we found an excellent dinner in a state of preparation by the monks, who indeed, during the whole of our visit, treated us with great hospitality and attention; on leaving it, we, in return, made them a present of some gold coin, which, as was perfectly proper, they accepted. During the recent troubles in the country, the strong walls of their monastery had afforded protection to the persons and property of many of the inhabitants of Bethlehem; and we found several of the chambers and passages still filled with furniture and bags of grain. While dinner was in preparation, the natives of the town crowded in with a great variety of articles which they are in the habit of making for pilgrims; crosses, inkstands, boxes of mother of pearl, huge clasps for girdles made of a complete shell with figures cut in relief, and beads of the same material, and of a substance called Mecca-stone, which is sometimes colored red or black. Most of these objects were rude enough, but some of the figures in relief were conceived and executed in a manner that would not have disgraced an Italian artist. The pilgrims place these things first in the Cave of the Nativity, and then carry them to the Holy Sepulchre, where, being deposited on the tomb, prayers are said over them, which are supposed to give them a supernatural power over evil spirits, so far as to protect the persons and property of the possessors.

While most of us were laying in large stores of their bead and pearl manufactures, some of our younger companions were submitting to the painful process of having figures, from Scriptural subjects, pricked and stained in the arm with blue or black pigment, a species of tattooing, at which, it seems, the Bethlehemites are expert, and to which pilgrims very often submit. It is not often that they have such a market for their commodities, and I believe our visit to Bethlehem will long be remembered; to us it was certainly a very interesting epoch.

Taking our usual interpreter, an intelligent young Armenian, for a guide, and accompanied, whether we would or no, by a half crazy and yet very shrewd fellow, called Yaoub, a party of us made an excursion one day to "the Tombs of the Kings." They lie about three quarters of a mile north of the city, amid olive groves and fields; and we found the walk there pleasanter than we anticipated.

We passed out by the Damascus gate, so called from the circumstance that the great road from Damascus enters the city here; and soon after leaving it, turned to our right to examine a huge cavern that stood yawning upon us. It is called the Cave of Jeremiah, from a tradition that he made it his residence; it is above 100 feet deep, by seventy in width and thirty in height, and is a gloomy, desolate place, such as we may suppose would have been chosen by the author of the Lamentations; but I presume there is no other authority for its name.

We were now on the hill Bezetha, where stood the Neopolis, or New City, inclosed by Agrippa's wall. The hill is still marked with tolerable distinctness, though it is in no place very high. It is ridge shaped, declining gently towards the east and west, and ascending gradually towards the north. Passing on, we reached, in a short time, a square pit with smooth perpendicular sides, about 100 feet on each side and fifteen in depth, cut in the solid rock, and resembling a quarry, which it may have originally been. An inclined plane at the north-eastern angle leads to the bottom; and having descended by this, we had opposite to us, on the south, a portico about twenty-five feet long by ten in depth, cut out of the solid rock; this is surmounted by an entablature, enriched with flowing sculpture of plants and fruits, in bold relief, and of very superior execution. At the eastern end of this portico was a hole, formerly a door-way of easy passage, but now so filled up that we could enter only by prostrating ourselves flat on the ground, and pushing ourselves forward by the feet. Having entered in this manner, we found that we were in a room about twenty feet square, cut entirely out of the solid rock. It appears to have served as a vestibule to other chambers, of which there are six in number, each with one or more receptacles for the dead. These consist of troughs cut out of the native rock, not sunk in the floor as is generally the case in the ancient sepulchres about this city, but on its level; fragments of the covers of one or two were scattered about the rooms; these were enriched with flowing sculpture, very well executed in strong relief; the coffins or sarcophagi were in other respects entirely plain.

The doors by which these chambers were closed are very remarkable objects. They are of stone, and are in dimensions about forty by thirty inches, and are six inches in thickness. Above and below are projecting knobs, forming a portion of the same stone, four inches in length; these were inserted into corresponding sockets, and formed the pivots on which the door revolved; but the question, how they were inserted into the grooves, is one that it would be difficult to solve. It is said that the ancients had a mode of fastening these doors so that no one who had not the secret could open them without breaking the stone. I have seen similar grooves in the gateway of the citadel of Mycenæ in Greece; and the sculpture belonging to these tombs, so strongly resembling the Grecian, appears to indicate for them an origin in the latter days of the ancient city. They are probably what by Josephus are called Herod's Monument, and in another place, "the sepulchral caverns of the Kings;"* and I think we may reasonably suppose them to have been formed by Herod. If this surmise with regard to their name is correct, they receive an additional interest, as showing us the northern boundary of the "new city" of Bezetha.

From this we proceeded to visit "the Tombs of the Judges," which lie nearly a mile further, in a course somewhat west of north. The ground was still cultivated in patches, and was covered with olive trees; the surface undulating. We passed, on the way, several subterranean apartments like that which Dr. Clarke discovered on the Mount of Olives, and which he supposed to have been a chapel for the secret and forbidden worship of the false gods. They are in shape like a bee-hive, are plaistered, and are entered by a small hole at the apex, which is the only opening. To our judgment they seemed designed to be reservoirs for water, or for granaries, but were most probably the former. Several years since I discovered one exactly similar to these, on some heights overlooking the site of the ancient Abydos at the Dardanelles.

We were now getting into an interesting region, evidently that from which were procured the huge blocks that formed the walls of the ancient city. The rock here is compact and solid, and of a fine texture; and for a great distance, and in every direction, exhibited the appearance that rocks would do

* Jos. de Bel. lib. v. cap. xiii. § 2. and Ib. cap. iv. 2.

from which large rectangular blocks with smooth surfaces had been cut. The vertical sections were regular and smooth, and sometimes fifteen or twenty feet in height. In the face of them were a great number of tombs, such as I have already described; sometimes consisting of a single chamber, sometimes of a succession of chambers, and with from two to four burial-places each, generally without ornament, and, as far as we observed, without inscriptions.

The largest of these chambers are called the Tombs of the Judges; but as the name is probably fanciful, we gave it little attention. Nor are the tombs themselves, except in size, more interesting than the others. These tombs are scattered over a surface of about a square mile, and are numerous.

In the interval between this and the city grows abundantly a thorn, which is considered to be the species from which the Saviour's crown of thorns was made. It is called the *Rhamnus Paliurus*, and consists of a bush with long slender twigs, on which are, alternately, a long and a short thorn, slightly curved and very sharp. It is found all over Syria, and also in Asia Minor.

We set out from this on our return; but the sun had set, and when we reached the city gates we found them closed; nor, in the strict vigilance which the recent dangers had taught them, was it at that time easy to get them opened again. Our crazy friend, Yaoub, who had been acting the merry-andrew along the road, now, however, interfered, and was more serviceable than a more sensible person would have been. He hailed a soldier, whom, in his walks about, he spied reconnoitring us through a loop-hole, and the man of gunpowder and bullets, perhaps thinking him sufficiently crazy to be a Turkish Santon or Saint, was at length brought to a parley. A messenger was despatched forthwith to the Governor; and Yaoub, now once more quite at ease, called to the soldiers to pass him a pipe beneath the gate, which having been done, he sat down to enjoy its fumes and his own importance. The messenger at length returned, and the guard having been mustered, and the gates having been thrown wide open, we were about to advance, when we were met by a couple of dozen fixed bayonets directly at our breast. We were brought to a stand till a more careful scrutiny of our faces had satisfied the officers that we were not wild Arabs in disguise; when the ranks opened, and we were allowed to enter. And we found that the prospect of spending the night in the open fields, that for a while was staring upon us, was sufficient to give a charm even to our hard and uneasy quarters in the convent.

25*

CHAPTER XX.

Departure of the first party. Mohammed Ali's firman, and alarm of the Governor. Sickness of Mr. M. and Mr. Nicholayson. Trials of Missionaries. Their general character and qualifications. Moonlight view of Jerusalem, and reflections. Arrival of the second party. Interview with the Governor. Visit to Bethany. Departure from Jerusalem.

Our party, with a good store of relics, olive canes from the Mount of Olives, and other memorials of their visit, left Jerusalem on the morning of the 20th; their early departure being occasioned by a desire to give the officers, who had remained in charge of the ships, also an opportunity of visiting the city.

While we were preparing to sail from Alexandria, the Egyptian monarch had ordered to be prepared for Commodore Patterson a letter of introduction to Ibrahim Pasha, and a firman for all Syria, worded in strong terms of kindness, commanding all persons, whether in authority or otherwise, to treat him, and those with him, with the same respect and attention that they would show personally to Mohammed Ali himself. The Commodore, during his stay in Jerusalem, had made an official call on the Governor, but not finding him at home, had made no use of the firman. Just, however, as the party were preparing to leave the city, the Governor heard of it, probably through the Pasha of Jaffa, where it had been used, and in great alarm sent immediately to apologize for not having shown the party greater attentions. When they reached the gate this morning, they found on the outside a double file of soldiers, who presented arms, and the Governor himself here joined the Commodore, and accompanied him some distance from the city. He regretted that he had not had official notice of our coming, so that he might have prepared accommodations for the party; and said that when the second company should arrive, they would find a commodious house ready for them. We certainly, however, had no cause of complaint; for we had every where been treated with respect and kindness; and the Governor's offer of a large escort to the plain of Jordan I have already noticed. The anecdote will show the dread in which the Egyptian Pasha is held through all his dominions.

I did not accompany the party back, having received permission to remain till the second company should conclude their visit. Mr. M., our sailing-master, who was ill of a fever, and unable to ride, was also left behind; and as the fever began to increase rapidly upon him, we accepted Mr. Nicholayson's invitation, and had him placed in more comfortable quarters at the Missionary house. But Mr. Nicholayson was now himself becoming seriously ill. His health had been for some time feeble; and recent exposure to the sun, and fatigue, had brought on sickness. It was now evident that a violent fever was burning in his veins. There was no nurse in the house, and I removed also from the convent to this hospital, for such Mr. N.'s dwelling had now literally become.

I shall not soon forget the night that followed these changes, a night of the deepest anxiety and distress. In the lower part of the house was a little girl, daughter of the Armenian patriarch of Beirout, put here to board, sick with the ophthalmia; two servants were also ill of fevers, and unable to help themselves; Mrs. N. was just recovering from a long sickness, and durst not expose herself to fatigue. In one corner of the room with me was Mr. M., restless, and in a burning heat, and on an adjoining bed was stretched Mr. N., now in a high fever, and quite delirious. For the others we could find some medicines tolerably appropriate, but the case of the last gentleman baffled our judgment, and there was not a physician to be had in the place. It was sad to be compelled to sit and listen to his ravings, and to see the disease hourly taking stronger hold upon him, and know not what to do. The ruling passion of his life was still prevailing, even in his wildest fancies; and his language was about the mission and its friends, or else he was disputing with the Jewish Rabbis, and quoting Hebrew from their voluminous authors. Thus wore the night away, a long and distressing night; and the day brought no relief, for we had the grief to see our friend sinking fast under his fiery disease. The fever left him towards evening, but as weak as an infant, and now particularly needing assistance which we knew not how to give; for the disease appeared to be of a complicated nature, and the little medicine which we ventured to administer, had done harm rather than good. If I could picture that missionary family as I saw it there, the scene would, I think, be a refutation of the charges of those who seem to think that missionaries go abroad for selfish and unworthy purposes. They had just passed through times of alarm and distress, such as persons seldom, and in our homes are never, called to witness; a city for days rocked and shattered by earthquakes, till the affrighted inhabitants knew not where to fly, and then plundered by fierce and lawless men. Their house had been pierced with cannon balls, and they were compelled to fly from one place to another for shelter; one of their company, whose health had been too feeble for these rude shocks, they had carried to the tomb, and had buried her beside another martyr in the same cause of missions.* In the house were now six invalids, some very ill, and one, the head of the family, apparently at the point of death; nor was there a physician to be any where found.—And the grave which we expected to dig for him was soon after this, dug for

* Dr. Dalton, from England.

another of the mission family, Dr. Dodge, whom we met on the way as we were returning to Jaffa. Yet they keep their ground, undismayed by dangers and death; suffering discomforts with cheerfulness; patient amid rebuffs, and with a zeal that tries, even in subjects of disappointment, to find new sources of hope, and that "fainteth not, neither is weary." Nine months after this, as our ship was lying in Gibraltar bay, I heard that Mrs. Nicholayson was on board an English brig that, after suffering severely in a storm, had just come in and anchored; and procuring a boat, I went within speaking distance, for the brig was in quarantine, and we were not permitted to go on board. She was then taking her little children to England for the purpose of putting them to school, and among society less hurtful to youthful minds than that of the east; and after thus leaving them, was to return to her far distant and now childless home. If in all this is not a picture of self-denial, and patient endurance, and Christian boldness, and painful sacrifice, I do not know what is; and yet it is only a plain statement of facts. In our ships we are apt to complain of discomforts; and yet we have plenty of medicines, and good surgical attendance, food such as we are accustomed to at home, and society and abundance of comforts of every kind; and yet it seems a hard case to be three years from home; and I now speak of ships in particular, because their inmates know what it is to be a long time from one's native land. But suppose it were for life; and a life separated from the comforts to which we have been accustomed, shut out in a great measure from intelligent society; a life of drudgery too, offering knowledge to those who care not for it; simplifying its nature, and bringing it to the capacities of all, and yet exciting little interest, and perhaps a sneer? Is this a life to be sought for, for the sake of worldly considerations? I think not. There is only one way in which we can reconcile it even with common sense; and that is, by supposing that missionaries are sincere; that they love their work; that the promises of the gospel, and the cheering influences of heavenly grace, support them; and that they look to eternity for their exceeding great reward. And when we look at them in this point of view, how engaging is their work, and how Godlike the errand on which they are gone? And it was a truly noble act in that church which I now love doubly to call my own—the Episcopal church,—when, at the last General Convention, its clerical and lay deputies from all parts of the country unanimously resolved that the whole Episcopal church be hereafter a Missionary Society; and declared that the cause of missions is the cause of religion, and a love for missions an essential part of the Christian character.

As regards the missionaries themselves, I do not know any class of men that presents, as a body, a more respectable array of talent or intelligence than this; and if any one should be disposed to doubt the fact, the proof is very easily to be found. He has only to take their reports to their several societies, their letters and published addresses to the public, and when he has read them, I will challenge him to produce from any other class of men, productions so uniformly correct in style, so free from puerilities, and so abundant in useful facts and valuable sentiments. In geography and statistics, in mineralogy, in geology, and in various other matters of science, they have furnished us with a mass of most valuable information from all parts of the world; their observations are minute, and generally very correct; and if the world were to receive no other benefit than the knowledge which their papers have scattered among our community, it would be recompensed for the money bestowed upon them. I do not wish to write their panegyric, but to defend them from charges which I have often heard brought against them; and the defence is a simple statement of facts which are before the public, and to which any man who chooses may have access. As to the charge that the pictures they give of their successes are over-wrought, I believe it often to be just; and it is not strange that men who have given their lives to one great subject, and are filled with zeal and are in earnest about it, should sometimes over-rate their influence, or, in the excitement of supposed or real success, should draw a picture more highly colored than a cooler observation of facts would warrant. But this, I believe, is the extent of their offending; they themselves appear to have been taught by experience greater distrust and caution in these matters ; and their recent accounts will be found to be more stamped with prudence, and more the result of cool and calm observation, than they formerly were ; while they show no diminution of interest in their great work. I cannot help again earnestly recommending their letters and reports home, and repeating that these reports, coming from so large a number of men, and so variously situated, are remarkable for perspicuity of style, and for simplicity and yet force of expression.

The night of the 21st passed away like the preceding one, a long night, and one of great anxiety ; life seemed to be hanging by so brittle a thread, that the least shock appeared capable of breaking it. I stole now and then from the sick man's couch, and looked out upon the city, bathed in moonlight, and hushed in the deepest repose. How quiet! how tranquil! Could this be the Jerusalem where, in a short time, 1,100,000 had perished amid the horrors of war?

The view from my window took in the Mount of Olives, the dark wall-like range beyond overhanging the Dead Sea, the mosque of Omar, the church of Mount Calvary, and a large portion of the city; and offered subjects for solemn and useful contemplation.

Could we have the history of all nations written by men to whom God had condescended to unfold the reasons for his acts, would it—would it not—appear like those of the Jews? Should we not find what

26

we call man's doings very often the doings of God; and man only the agent, a free agent, and yet, by the mysterious combination of His Omnipotence with our freedom, man only an agent in working great events; and those events acts of reward or of retribution from Heaven on kingdoms for their observance or neglect of His commandments?

Over yon mountain David passed, dethroned, expelled, a fugitive from his own son; attended only by a small train of attached but desponding friends. If we knew not the cause of this, it might have been passed as thousands of such acts pass in history, leading us to as little useful reflection; but we are informed why it was; and these thousand other acts in history, are they not retributive too? And will not the same apply to nations? And, could we see into Heaven's councils, should we not find what appears to be the entangled web of national events all plain and simple—a few simple and general rules, as in the works of nature, pervading and governing the whole? And would not the first of these be that the fear of God and respect for his commandments are the only source of national happiness and national stability?

On that mountain Titus also stood, and formed plans for the destruction of the ancient city. To himself and to his Roman army the son of Vespasian was there for his own purposes; but be this as it may, *we* know that there were also other purposes to be effected. In the 28th chapter of Deuteronomy, though the application is complicated, yet a simple principle stands at the head of it all; "If thou shalt hearken diligently unto the voice of the Lord thy God, *to observe* and *to do* all his commandments, blessed shalt thou be;" "if thou wilt not hearken diligently to observe and to do, cursed shalt thou be; and the Lord shall bring a nation against thee from afar," &c. The passage is too long for quotation, but I beg the reader to turn to it and read from the 49th to the 58th verses inclusive, and compare them with Josephus' account of the siege of Jerusalem; and ask himself if the same rule does not probably apply to us, and if we have not reason to "fear this glorious and fearful name—THE LORD THY GOD."

About five o'clock on the following afternoon a second party from our ship, consisting of about fifty persons, arrived; and were met at the gate by an officer from the Governor, who came to say that a house had been provided, and was ready to receive them. This was indeed doing things on a handsome scale; and the party gladly accepting his hospitality, were shown to a large edifice not far from the entrance of the city, which, after sundry ablutions, proved to be a very comfortable and convenient lodging place. In the party was Doctor B., who immediately came over to see Mr. Nicholayson, and on examining, spoke very doubtfully of his case. Tired, however as he was, he immediately offered his services for the night; and he afterwards persevered in a course of most assiduous attentions, which, doubtless, were the means of saving a valuable life. When we left the city on the 25th, Mr. N. was yet very weak, but convalescent; and, we were happy to hear, afterwards entirely recovered. We were glad, also, to be able to send the mission family, from the ship, some wine and other comforts, which their circumstances urgently required.

Captain Nicolson, who came with the second party, took an early opportunity of calling, with most of his officers, to pay his respects to the Governor of Jerusalem. He resides in a large, but by no means splendid house, near the centre of the city; and on our arrival we were detained a short time till the servants could get his women out of the way. We found him a tall and fine-looking man, with marks of old age creeping upon him; which, however, did not seem to affect his gallantry towards the ladies, as he told us that he had lately added another wife to his household. The usual compliment of pipes, sherbet, &c., was paid; and while the odoriferous fumes were ascending in graceful curves, a rambling conversation was carried on, sometimes about this country, and sometimes about our own. The frank address of Captain N. soon thawed the old gentleman's gravity, and the interview was more lively and full of humor than is usual in a Turkish divan. The officers all took part in the conversation, each with proper respect; and the Governor seemed to be quite surprised at the accounts we gave him of the extent and resources of our country, the length of our rivers, and our rapid growth as a nation. If we did not convince him that America is the greatest country in the world, I think we must at least have satisfied him that we have a very high opinion of it ourselves. He seemed to be amused and gratified, and we parted right good friends.

During the stay of this party, I took Yaoub as guide one day, and went out to make a visit to Bethany. It lies on a pretty steep declivity on the eastern side of the Mount of Olives, and I believe I have already stated that there are two roads to it, one directly across the mountain, and another, much less difficult, winding around the southern extremity. By the latter it is about three miles distant. There are now only a few miserable houses remaining, together with the ruins of a large and massive building, which, they tell us, was the house of Lazarus. They take the visitor also to a cave, in which, they say, he was buried; but in all these assertions I have little confidence.

The 25th was fixed upon for our departure, and at two o'clock in the morning our cavalcade was formed without the gates, and we began to move forward towards the ship. As we passed on, I turned often to take another look at the city, whose white domes and minarets were still visible above the serrated walls, and were now shining with silvery lustre in the quiet moonlight.

26*

Farewell then, Jerusalem, city of marvels; wonderful, awful, enthroned in the hearts of men, making a part of the very soul and life-blood of thy people. City of God! when shalt thou revive again? Terrible has been thy fall; wo upon wo was poured out upon thee; thou art stricken to the dust; and yet in thy humiliation, in the very depths of abasement, thou still art great! Thou drawest to thee pilgrims of three religions, whose empires stretch east and west till they meet again in the opposite confines of our globe; they come to thee to worship, they come to thee to die! In lands far distant and of recent birth, we are taught to lisp thy name in our childhood; thy scenes and thy history mingle in our earliest dreams; and in the moments when we most need comfort, our thoughts turn towards thee!

Mount Calvary! the atmosphere does not more closely invest our globe, and enter into and support our systems, than does the comfort that flows from thy bloody cross encircle, and penetrate, and support our souls. Without it we gasp and perish. Mysterious! that to such a bloody scene we should have to resort for consolation. Wonderful religion, that teaches us that by the deep and awful humiliation of God we are elevated to glory; and, after leading us amid creation, and showing us that He is wise and powerful, takes us here and at the foot of the cross shows that He is also of boundless goodness.

Saviour, who hast ransomed us, be thou enthroned

in our hearts! We descend the winding pathway, and the city of our redemption is shut from our sight: help us to enter the New Jerusalem, and to come to that Zion where is everlasting gladness, and from which sorrow and sighing for ever flee away!

CHAPTER XXI.

Accident on our return. Visit to St. Jean D'Acre. Also to Tyre. Prophecies respecting Tyre fulfilled. Visit to Sidon. Lady Hester Stanhope. Her letter of invitation to us. Visit to her residence at D'joun Beirout. Missionary families at Beirout. Striking feature in the Protestant Missionary operations. Their schools and printing presses.

An accident, by which one of our party was seriously hurt, on our way back, damped the gratification of our visit and retarded our progress; but having left the invalid officer and Dr. B. at Ramla, we were able to reach the ship in good season the same evening. Some seamen were despatched during the night with a litter; and having thus got our companions on board, we weighed anchor on the afternoon of the 26th, and with a light breeze stood northwardly along the coast.

As we passed Cæsarea, about thirty-five miles distant from Jaffa, our glasses enabled us to distinguish a few masses of masonry, which is all that remains of that once large and magnificent city. A few hours after this we came opposite to the northern termination of Mount Carmel, on the summit of which the monastery of Elijah* was a very conspicuous object.

* 1 Kings, chap. xviii.

The French ensign was flying on the top of it, probably in answer to our colors. The mountain was green, and had an agreeable appearance; it thrusts itself some distance into the sea, and forms the southern extremity of a large bay, at the northern end of which is St. Jean D'Acre, the ancient Ptolemais.

We dropped our anchor a few miles from this latter city on the evening of the 27th, and some boats, with parties, were despatched to the shore. I have seen no place exhibit so strikingly the ruthless and destructive character of war as did this city at the time of our visit. It was at this place that Mohammed Ali first began to put in execution his ambitious designs upon Syria. Under pretence of assisting the Sultan in putting down a refractory Pasha, he brought his army and navy against the place; but met what Bonaparte had here met before him, a fierce and determined resistance. It was subjected to a long bombardment, and at length, on the last of May, 1832, was taken by assault, when his soldiers are said to have been guilty of the greatest excesses.

The city is built upon a point of land running into the sea, and is surrounded by strong walls; those on the land side being assisted by ditches and by other lines of defence.

Scarcely a house was any where to be seen that had not suffered from the shot. We were particularly struck with a very high wall, the remains of some important edifice, that was completely riddled, and now stood between us and the setting sun, which was pouring a stream of light through every crevice, and making the ruin look still more desolate. We made the circuit of the walls, and walked through the city, but did not see more than thirty inhabitants in the whole place.

Leaving our anchorage early the next morning, we glided up towards Tyre, which lies about thirty miles distant from St. Jean D'Acre, being separated from it by a strip of low but sufficienly fertile land, beyond which the mountains of Samaria commence. Our visit to this country had put our Bibles in more than usual requisition; and I had been pointing out to some friends the prophecies concerning Tyre, and comparing these with the accounts given by travellers of the utter desolation of the place, had endeavored to strengthen the argument for the Scriptures. The spot is spoken of by Shaw as utterly abandoned, except "by a few poor wretches, harboring themselves in the vaults, and subsisting chiefly upon fishing, who seem to be preserved in this place by Divine Providence, as a visible argument how God hath fulfilled his word concerning Tyre." Volney speaks of it as reduced to a miserable village, consisting of "fifty or sixty wretched huts, ready to crumble into ruins;" and Joliffe, a more recent traveller, says, that "some miserable cabins, ranged in irregular lines, dignified with the name of streets, and a few buildings of a rather better description, occupied by the officers of government, compose nearly the whole of the town."

Approaching it with these impressions, I was surprised to see a walled town of tolerable dimensions, and with houses no worse looking than is ordinary in these countries, above which, in answer to our ensign, were waving the flags of most of the European nations, together with our own star-spangled banner. The ship was hove to, and we were thus enabled to make a hasty visit to the place. Our boats passed some ruins, probably remains of the times of the Crusaders, which help to guard the harbor from the wind and the sands. This looks as if it had once been spacious, but it was now so choked up with ruins of various kinds and with sand, as scarcely to admit even our boats.

Our consul, accompanied by some of the representatives of other nations, met us at the landing, and conducted us to his house, where we were welcomed with the usual forms of eastern hospitality. The present population of Tyre, or *Tsour* as it is called by the natives, I should judge to be about 3,000 persons; it occupies about half of the ancient island, which since the time of Alexander has been a peninsula. It is surrounded by a wall of no great strength, nor at present of any great utility, as the sands on the eastern side, after covering over the isthmus to a considerable depth, have reached the city and have been filled up nearly to the height of its battlements. The sand is the only enemy, therefore, from which the fortifications are protecting them, for any other would only have to walk up this inclined plane and let themselves down into the city.

In a corner of the wall, about the centre of the island, they showed us a large ruin, probably of a church belonging to the times of the Crusaders, who had possession of the place from the year 1124 to 1289. Near these ruins were some very large columns of Egyptian granite, which looked as if they might have been taken from some of the ancient temples.

I passed out of the gate, and made the circuit of the peninsula. The shore on the southern side is formed of masses of bare rock, much eaten by the waves, and in some places undermined. The foundations of buildings are to be traced all over the ground, and also extending out some distance into the sea. The isthmus has become very wide, and now presents nothing but hills of loose sand, driven about by every wind, and destined perhaps to cover the entire peninsula. The shore opposite, for an extent of miles, is now also nothing but a bed of sand, amid which, any traces of the ancient city that may have been left by Alexander, have entirely disappeared. It was of this old city, of sixteen miles in circumference, and whose walls were 120 feet in height, that the prophecy was uttered: "I will make thee a terror and thou shalt be no more; though thou be sought for, yet shalt thou never be found again, saith the Lord God. All they that feared thee among the people shall be astonished at thee; thou shalt be a terror, and never shalt thou be any more;" and in vain amid that plain of yellow drifting sand should we seek for any memorial of it, or expect to see it rise again. Of this great mistress of the sea, the mother of many colonies, some, as for instance Carthage, of prodigious wealth; of the city that distributed crowns, "whose merchants were princes, and whose traffickers were the honorable of the earth," nought now remains, and its site would probably be unknown but for this island and the village that stands here, as if in mockery of the greatness of ancient Tyre. "Is this your joyous city, whose antiquity is of ancient days?"

After walking about a short time among the dull streets, we were glad to escape and get back to the ship. The commerce of Tyre now consists of tobacco, charcoal, and fagots;—what a contrast to former times!

A gentle breeze wafted us on towards Sidon, which being only fifteen miles distant, was soon distinctly in view; the bold and towering chain of Mount Lebanon forming a striking background to the picture. This mountain commences just above Tyre, and the greatness of that city in ancient times, was probably owing, in some measure, to the outlet afforded between the southern end of Lebanon and the mountains of Samaria, to the trade from the great plain of Damascus and the cities east of it. Sidon, called by the natives *Seyd*, is also a walled town,

27

and is larger than Tyre, containing a population of about 8,000 persons; but its harbor is most wretched, and our boats were near being swamped in endeavoring to get in. A boat from the shore hastened out to assist us, as soon as they found we desired to land; and placing itself before the Commodore's barge, guided us along the shallow and tortuous channel, alongside of which a heavy surf was rolling and breaking, and covering the water with foam.

After all we were poorly rewarded for our pains, unless it may be something to say that we have been at Sidon; for it is a poor miserable place. We desired, on entering the city, to be taken to whatever objects there might be of interest; and they immediately started off with us for "the gardens;" the concourse gathering fresh numbers as we advanced. So we proceeded out of the town, and up a hill, and then down; and there were the gardens, naked earth planted with mulberry trees and vegetables; a spot that would have delighted B——, our steward, had he been with us, but was not exactly to our present taste. I ought to do the place justice, however; for it appeared to be extremely fertile, and as far as our eye could reach down the side of the eminence, there was the deepest verdure, and a refreshing luxuriance of foliage. We returned to the town as soon as possible, as the sun was getting low, and walked around and through it, but without finding a single object worthy of note. The houses are generally low and mean looking, and it appears to be a place of few manufactures, and of little trade. Its rich and beautiful back country, however, gives it a decided preference over Tsour; and its population, I thought, looked as if they might be more comfortable. We have a consular agent here, also, whose kind offers of hospitality the shortness of our time compelled us to decline. On returning to the ship we filled away and stood for the city of Beirout, which lies about twenty miles to the northward of Sidon.

It had been our intention to call upon the celebrated Lady Hester Stanhope, who we were informed was living at Manlius, about four miles back of Sidon; but learning that she had changed her residence to D'joun, three miles further in the interior, we were forced by the lateness of the hour to relinquish our purpose. We met, however, at the consul's, a person who had been connected with her household, and the Commodore requested him to inform her ladyship that we had landed with the wish to pay our respects to her, but had been prevented by the distance and want of time. Soon after our arrival at Beirout we received a very handsome and polite invitation to make her a visit; and as I find that she has excited considerable interest in our country, I will give the letter as the best mode of presenting her to the reader.

To the American Admiral, Officers, and Ladies, who did me the honor to inquire after me.

D'JOUN, 31st Aug., 1834.

You all ought to know how much I love and respect the American nation. If the individuals did not command by their merit these sentiments, I must naturally inherit them from my grandfather.[*] I should be too happy to invite to D'joun the whole of the party; but my premises will not admit of their being comfortable. My house is in a dilapidated state. My thoughts, as well as my finances, for these last three years, have been wholly dedicated to one object—that of the relief of the unhappy persons, which the situation of the country increases every day. The body of the house at this moment can only contain me, very ill lodged; and all I have at my disposal is two pretty good rooms in a court, or rather a small garden, dedicated to strangers alone, that might lodge pretty comfortably, the Admiral and three other gentlemen. I could not well propose it to ladies, being a place which, from its public situation, I never frequent. But should the Admiral's lady and her daughters wish to see something of the surrounding country, I offer them Manlius, where, however, there is only one room furnished. The house is only inhabited by an old woman and a servant; but by bringing their travelling beds and their cook, they might be more comfortable than in any other house in the neighborhood. I can also furnish them with a very civil old man, known to Mr. Guys, called Lewis Marson, who can talk French, and who is very capable of attending to all their little wants.

I send Mr. Bertrand with this letter, that he may further explain about the houses, or answer any other questions relative to them, and to bring me your decision upon the subject.

I very cordially salute you all.

Hester Lucy Stanhope

Accordingly, after our return from Damascus, a party was formed and spent four or five hours with her at her residence at D'joun. The house is tolerably capacious, and is situated in a large garden, laid out after the English style, but the premises are somewhat out of repair. I fear she finds ungrateful subjects among the

[* The Earl of Chatham.—AUTHOR.]

natives whom she has patronized, and among whom she has spent a large part of her fortune. A few years since she sent for our excellent consul at Beirout, Mr. Chassaud, a gentleman of great integrity of character and of business tact, and entreated him to save her from the rapacity of the people around her, who, by exorbitant demands, and by various kinds of roguery, were rapidly reducing her finances. He went and saved her fortune from a complete wreck, and I believe, has now a high place in her confidence.

She is a very extraordinary woman. Her person is tall and commanding, and is shown by her costume, the Turkish trowsers and vest and turban, to the best advantage; she is still handsome, and appears to take pleasure in showing her arm, which is remarkably well turned and beautiful. Coffee, pipes, &c. were brought in, and while she encircled herself with the aromatic fumes, she conversed on various topics—politics, literature, manners, and religion. She appeared to have a good knowledge of our country, and the intelligence she displayed about the politics of Europe was extraordinary for a person shut out as she is from society, and seldom getting even a newspaper. On most subjects she showed excellent sense, and a strength of judgment seldom witnessed in either of the sexes; but when religion was broached she became instantly changed, and was as wild as a maniac, both in language and to some degree also in manner. She believes in magic and astrology, and also that the Messiah will shortly appear, and has in her stables a horse, with a natural sinking or indentation in the back like a saddle, on which she says he is to ascend up into heaven. She formerly allowed visitors to see this animal, but has for some years kept it more secluded; and though the party on this occasion threw out hints as far as politeness would allow them, they were not successful.

She was, it is said, a great favorite with her uncle William Pitt, for whose society the acute and masculine character of her mind well qualified her. Soon after his death she suddenly resolved upon withdrawing to this country, and sailed in a short time, taking a large part of her fortune with her in the vessel. She was wrecked near the island of Rhodes, and her treasures were lost; but she was not to be driven from her purpose; she returned immediately to England, gathered together some more funds, and again set sail for the east, where she has ever since resided. At first she led a somewhat wandering life; and at one time had unbounded influence over the Arabs of the desert; but for some years she has been residing at Manlius and D'joun; and with the diminution of her funds has been also a decrease of her power. I understand that lately, even her life has sometimes been in danger.

It is probable that her mind, originally strong though given to eccentric flights, in these wild retreats where she has been shut out from intelligent society, has turned and preyed upon itself, and that a species of derangement has been the consequence. With her commanding form, her intelligent and somewhat masculine face, her fanciful costume, and the bright unearthly sparkling of her eye, she would make a fine subject for a picture of an ancient Sibyl.

On the 29th we dropped our anchor at Beirout, not opposite to the city, but in a large bay some miles to the northward, where were afforded conveniences for procuring water, of which our ship was in need. Opposite to our anchorage are some rocks at the foot of Lebanon, with a bold perpendicular front, on which are cut some inscriptions in ancient characters, probably Phœnician; and near this is a cave, said to be the one where St. George of merry England met and killed the dragon. The fancy of the reader is fired at the mention of this; and he is now most truly in the region of poetry; for more poetical objects than this mountain of Lebanon, with its wild glens, its rich valleys, its precipices, and even its inhabitants also, are very seldom to be seen.

Beirout is situated on the outer edge of a strip of comparatively flat land about four miles across, which commences at this place, and goes tapering off to the southward, until it terminates somewhere not far from Sidon. A large part of this plain, and every accessible spot on the mountain, is under cultivation; and as Beirout is also at present the seaport of Damascus, it is a city of some consequence, and, for this country, of considerable trade. It contains about eight thousand inhabitants, and on the land side is walled; the harbor will admit only small vessels, but a seventy-four may find safe anchorage in the roadstead, as near almost to the shore as it may choose to come. The country produces great quantities of silk which is worked up in the city; and here, particularly, are manufactured the fanciful variegated scarfs used all over this region for sashes, and sometimes for turbans.

In addition to the pleasures we received in the family of our excellent consul, Mr. Chassaud, another gratification awaited us here, in the society of three of our countrymen, and their ladies, the Rev. Messrs. Bird, Smith, and Whiting, missionaries, who have been several years in the east, and during the last five or six at Beirout. They speak the languages of the natives with great fluency; and are men of intelligence and talents sufficient to give them a high standing in any society, no matter where. They came on board immediately to welcome us, and readily proffered such hospitality as their circumstances would allow; their residence at that time being on the mountain, for the sake of the superior salubrity of its atmosphere in summer. Strangers residing below in the hot season are subject to fevers, and in the summer following that of our visit, they had to lament the death of Dr. Dodge, a physician connected with this mission and that at Jerusalem. They have schools in the villages of the mountains, and in Beirout; and at the time of our visit, were making arrangements for a printing press which has since arrived, and with which they are commencing operations.

It must strike every one, even those opposed to missions, as a pleasing circumstance, that in all such establishments belonging to our country, the communication of knowledge, not only in religious matters, but on all topics, is one of the earliest and is ever a constant object. Religion that comes thus associated cannot wish to hood-wink or lead the people blindfolded. It enlarges the mind, it teaches the people to think, and gives them useful objects of history and science to think about; it strengthens the judgment; and to this judgment, thus strengthened and thus rendered acute, it now appeals and asks for admission to the heart. No man need be afraid of a religion that comes in such companionship. It gives us the very best proof possible that it considers itself based on reason, and that it will bear the test of scrutiny from enlightened and intelligent minds—which scrutiny it ever invites. There is no jargon of the schools here, no throwing of dust into men's eyes, no trying to blunt the intellect that nonsense may be forced upon it. The missionaries come with geographies, and arithmetics, and apparatus for easy and simple lectures, and compendious histories; or where such books are not to be had in the language, they go to work immediately and translate them; and they circulate them; and they gather the children from the streets, and seek for the adults, and they teach them *knowledge*, not religious knowledge only but knowledge of all kinds. Their object, it is granted, is to introduce religion into the heart, *their* religion, if the reader may choose to like the phrase; but then it comes preceded by and associated with *knowledge; it loves the light;* light is created, diffused, and in this light it comes, and in it addresses and appeals to us; and let him who opposes these efforts, look and see if he does not oppose them because he himself loves darkness rather than light, and that because his own deeds are evil.

I visited a missionary house at Malta, belonging to the English [Church?] Missionary Society, but under the care of some gentlemen from Switzerland. I found them striking off maps for an atlas in modern Greek, and making Arabic globes to be sent to Egypt, where, if I mistake not, it will astonish the natives when they are told that the world is round, and that they have been such prodigious travellers on its surface, when they were thinking themselves all the while sitting still. The shelves of this house were also filled with a great variety of books, translations of the most approved modern works for schools; and these they were scattering around the Mediterranean as fast as they were able. And when I went to the dwelling house of one of them, (the only one married,) I found his lady in a school with a room full of children, many of whom had been common beggars in the streets, and had been taken in here and clothed; she was teaching them to read and sew, and had a small cabinet filled with their work, each article with the maker's name—the money for which, when sold, was to be delivered to the child itself. Though their garments were often "of many colors," owing to the strange mixture of patches, yet there was not one ragged child, and all were clean, and they looked cheerful and happy.

And all this is only an example of the Protestant missionary operations at Syra, and Athens, and Constantinople, and Smyrna, and since they have got the press, at Beirout, and in the islands of the Pacific, and in India, and every where, wherever our missionaries are to be found.

CHAPTER XXII.

Party to Damascus. Ascent of Mount Lebanon. The roads. English carriage. Scenery of the mountain. Its inhabitants. Maronites. The Druses. Aaleih. Horns worn by the women. Princesses of the mountain. Beautiful night scene. Bhamdoon. Plain of Coelo-Syria. Anti-Lebanon. Characteristic of Americans. A dilemma. First view of Damascus. The great plain. Gardens. The city. "Street that is called Straight." St. Paul.

About noon on the first of September, a party of us might have been seen winding along the streets of Beirout, and then starting off in high spirits for Damascus. That city is the present capital, and residence of the Governor of Syria, and the Commodore had determined, while the ship was taking in water, to make it a visit.

Our company consisted of Commodore Patterson and two daughters, nine officers, and about twelve attendants and muleteers, and was headed by an Armenian gentleman, Mr. Farrah, whom Mr. Chassaud had just appointed American agent for Damascus. Mr. Farrah was accompanied also by a relative of his, so that we numbered altogether twenty-six persons; a large cavalcade for visiting a city where, only a year previously, it was extremely hazardous for any one to be seen in the Frank dress, so savage and bitter was the hatred of the inhabitants towards all the Gaiours, or Christians. Mr. Smith and his lady were also with us, intending to accompany us as far as his house on the mountain, where we were to stop for the night.

Our road, on leaving the city, laid across a small plot of open ground bordered with trees, and immediately after this entered a region of gardens and vineyards, which appeared to be very productive. Among them, on the right, is a substantial stone house, recently erected by the missionaries for their press and books. It had, in some respects, an American look, and was an unexpected and welcome sight. We kept ascending gently for about two miles, when we came, at the summit of the eminence, to a fine grove of large venerable looking pines. The Pasha of Egypt is disposed to cultivate this tree for the use of his navy, and not far off has planted a little forest, which seems to be in a thriving condition.

This spot commands a fine view of the mountain, and plain, and sea, and is the one to which De La Martine has given a pathetic interest. About three miles beyond it we commenced the ascent of Mount Lebanon, at first by a gently inclined plane, which, however, did not continue long; soon we came to steeper ascents, and then to yet steeper; and then commenced a series of experiments in vaulting, flying, and tumbling, which lasted quite across the mountain, and were sometimes near costing us life

28

or limb. I believe there was but one person in the party who had not at least one fall, many of us could count three or four; and one of the ladies was saved from sliding down a precipice only by our springing to her help, and holding rider and donkey against the side of the bank till they had recovered foot-hold. I had thought that in Indiana, a few years previously, I had seen the very worst roads in the world; but they are equalled by those over Mount Lebanon, that is, if the reader can be made to understand clearly a comparison between mud-holes and rocks, which I confess I cannot exactly do myself. There is no mistake, however, about this road, which is certainly the most toilsome and dangerous one that I have ever met with. And yet it is the great thoroughfare between Damascus and its seaport, Beirout, and is every day traversed by camels with heavy loads of merchandise. The British Consul General for Syria, residing at Damascus, a few years ago had a carriage transported across this mountain from Beirout. He first had it taken to pieces, and then had the body slung between two camels; but the swinging motion, in consequence of the roughness of the roads, soon put the poor animals on beam ends; and they said, as plainly as camels could say, that they had no inclination for such work. He then put the vehicle together again, and employed sixty men to pull it up and lower it down the precipices, and at last got it safe home at Damascus, where now he may go an airing over a plain 500 miles in length. He offered the ladies of our party to carry them in it to Palmyra. A ride in an English coach to Palmyra! it would have been something new under the sun, and we should all have made that interesting journey, if our time would have permitted. But back again —we have not arrived at Damascus yet, nor even at the summit of Lebanon, and many a weary mile is before us. Up, up we went, sometimes almost perpendicularly, wondering, when we could catch a breathing spell, at the power and wonderful surefootedness of our animals. After a while the scenery around us became truly grand. It is a mountain with more poetry than any other that I have ever seen. Grander I have met with, and richer, and more beautiful; but I have seen none that contains so much of all of these combined. The reader is perhaps aware that it is inhabited by a race of people that from time immemorial have kept themselves free and unsubdued; they form an enigma and a wonder in this land of sloth and imbecility. Hardy, industrious, and healthful, they have spread over the mountain till it is teeming with inhabitants, and have been compelled, wherever, by terrace or otherwise, it can be cultivated, to erect their dwellings, and break up or make a soil. They retain also their peculiar institutions; and this is the only place in all Turkey where Christians are allowed for their churches the use of bells.

The inhabitants of Mount Lebanon branch off

into three religions : Mahomedans, Druses, and Maronite Christians. The last of these had their origin in the seventh century, and take their name from Maro, their first bishop, who, at this time, came from the banks of the Orontes and taught here the heretical doctrines of the Monothelites, which he had adopted. In the year 1182 they gave up these doctrines, and were united to the Romish church ; at least they have ever since acknowledged the supremacy of the Pope, but as they never allow him to interfere with their doctrines or forms of worship, and have their own distinct class of ecclesiastical rulers, their subjection to the Roman Catholic jurisdiction is little better than nominal. They have a patriarch whom they elect themselves, and who takes uniformly the name of Peter ; but his appointment, to be valid, must be confirmed by the Pope. Their number at present is about 120,000.

The Druses, who amount to about 70,000, are a strange and mysterious people. Their religion seems to be a compound of Paganism, Mahomedanism, and Christianity; but it is kept a profound secret, and we have few means of forming a judgment respecting it. They are divided into two classes, the *Djakils*, or *ignorant*, about 60,000 in number, and the *Aakils*, or *intelligent*, who amount to about 10,000; the latter alone are acquainted with the mysteries of their religion ; but from the vague answers that are given to all queries by strangers respecting it, I am inclined to think that it is itself vague and undefined, and that except a few leading principles, they themselves scarcely know what they believe.

The Mahomedan population, in some parts of Lebanon, is very numerous.

On our right, as we ascended the mountain, was a large valley, commencing in the elevated parts of the range, and spreading, as it descended, till it formed a theatre among the hills of gigantic proportions. From the highest part to the lowest, it was all under cultivation, and dotted with cottages; while in various parts cascades were seen streaming from the rocks, and contrasting finely with the rich verdure with which the whole seemed to be carpeted, and over which the declining sun was now pouring a flood of mellowed light.

We turned, by and by, around the head of this valley, and delighted with the views, but exhausted by the constant muscular effort to keep in our saddles, we were glad to find ourselves at the door of Mr. Bird's house in the village of Aaleih. In approaching the village, the young beaux of our party had straightened themselves in their saddles, and made their donkeys hold up the head and look smart, in hopes perhaps of making a conquest among the princesses of the mountain, some of whom were residing in Aaleih; but as we passed the houses, nothing but old looking heads, and these with great horns stuck on them, were thrust out towards us, presenting some of the least attractive,

28*

and most singular specimens of woman-kind that we had met with. This is no joke of mine; for it is actually the fashion in this region for the ladies to stick to their heads a horn very much in size and shape like a speaking-trumpet, if deprived of its mouth-piece. They are generally of embossed silver, and are handed down from mother to child through many generations; some are of paste-board covered with gold or silver paper, and some of the more costly ones which we saw, in addition to being of pure silver, were set with precious stones. They are worn generally on the top of the head, projecting a little in front; but are sometimes attached to the side directly over the temple, according as the fancy may take the belle or her ladyship; they are worn not only by day, but also during the night. A white muslin shawl is usually cast over the horn, and tied with a string at its lower part, and is thus made to shade the face; their dress in other respects has nothing peculiar. We priced some of these singular ornaments, and found them valued at about fifteen dollars.

The Druse men have squat figures and countenances, though not very intelligent, yet of rather pleasing expression. They wear a dress considerably like that of the Turks, and in addition, a loose coat, marked with broad white and black stripes running vertically; this coat, I believe, is universal among them, and is one of the characteristics of a Druse. We met them in great numbers along the road, and took pleasure in marking their habits, so different from the lazy, sluggish movements of the Turks.

Mrs. Bird had been good enough to prepare an excellent meal for us, to which we sat down with keen appetites; after which some of us went, in company with Mrs. B. and Mrs. Whiting, to call upon the princesses, the daughters of the late Emir of this district, over which, since his decease, one of them had been exercising the authority of chief.

There was a house full of females and children, and we could not help admiring the sprightly, intelligent faces, and the graceful carriage of all, both old and young. Their costume was also very becoming. One of the lads, about eleven years of age, with a keen resolute eye, wore a handjar* of beautiful workmanship in his belt, and had the bearing of a little king. The young folks came afterwards to visit the ship, with a letter from Mr. Bird; but unfortunately did not reach her till she was under way, and they could not be admitted on board.

Again came our ponies, (alias donkeys, at least most of them,) and again came the tug of this mountain travelling, which soon was rendered doubly unpleasant by a moonless night. We could see nothing of the way, and had no resource except quietly to follow Mr. Smith, our guide, and resign ourselves to the sure-footed habits of our animals.

* A Turkish weapon, like a broad dagger, but usually about a foot in length.

We travelled on in this way for about an hour after dark, when suddenly, and as if by a kind of magic, a scene opened upon us that produced a general exclamation of delight. Mr. Smith had selected a safe spot for the exhibition, and without giving us warning, had led us to the edge of an immense valley, which spread around in the form of a great amphitheatre, and was covered with villages and farmhouses from top to bottom. The houses had lights in them, and all at once, from utter darkness, the whole region, a space of some miles in diameter, appeared as if sprinkled over with stars; it seemed as if we had been suddenly carried upward, and had been placed in mid-heaven, amid the constellations and the bright effulgence of the Milky Way.

But we were yet upon our earth, and in a very rough portion of it; and as we went on, climbing up and slipping down, we began to long for our own beacon light. It appeared at length on the opposite side of a deep valley, around which we had to wind; but at length, about ten o'clock, we were safely deposited in Mr. Smith's hospitable dwelling at Bhamdoon. His house accommodated the Commodore and family, while the rest of us were distributed among his neighbors, where we found pretty comfortable beds.

The rising sun, next morning, found us on our way, and in addition to our baggage mules, another in our company, with a couple of tents provided by Mr. Smith, an accommodation which we found of the most essential service during the journey. Mount Lebanon, at the highest peak, which was not far north of our road, attains an elevation of 10,000 feet; but at our place of crossing was not quite so high. Opposite to Balbec its summit retains the snow, even in exposed situations, all the year.

We reached the highest point of our road at a place about five miles east of Bhamdoon; and after descending into some deep glens, and encountering again a frightful rocky ascent, we stopped for breakfast at 10 o'clock, on the eastern slope of the range. The plain of Coelo-Syria, apparently about eight miles across, but in reality of nearly twice that width, was spread out below us; and on the opposite side of it ascended the more gentle and less formidable looking mountain of Anti-Lebanon. At a peak to the southward of us this latter range was, however, also covered with snow. Numerous streams dash down the sides of both mountains, clothing them with perpetual green, and then discharge their waters into the river Litane, the ancient Leontes, which, after winding through the whole length of this plain, is finally lost in the sea not far from Sidon.

The plain of Coelo-Syria is generally of the breadth that I have mentioned, and is about 100 miles in length, being bounded in the whole extent by the parallel ranges of Lebanon and Anti-Lebanon. It has a rich soil, and might be made extremely productive; but only a small portion of it is at present under cultivation. Our meal was eaten by the side of a brook, beneath some fig trees; and when it had been succeeded by a short season of repose, we finished our descent, and entered on the monotonous and fiery plain. All day we dragged ourselves across, scorched by a fierce sun, and parched with thirst, and finding little relief in the sight of the snowy peaks on either side. We came about two o'clock to a khan, and soon after to the river, which we crossed on a bridge, though at this season it can be forded. Here we met a long string of camels from Damascus, and soon after we witnessed a natural phenomenon, of which we afterwards saw several instances on the great Assyrian plain,—columns of sand raised high in the air, and passing along the ground, in their shape bearing a great resemblance to that of a water-spout, and doubtless produced by a similar cause.

Our course was not straight across the plain, but inclining to the southward. About five o'clock we reached a village near the foot of Anti-Lebanon, and while we stopped for water, our muleteers began very deliberately to unload the animals, concluding to stop there for the night. They were astonished when told that the day's journey was not yet finished, and then remonstrated, and then got angry, but to no purpose; and I believe they thought us a very singular and uncivilized set of beings. I do not know that any traveller has ever yet spoken of the difference between foreign countries and our own with respect to energy and rapidity of movement. With us, "time" literally "is money;" and as we have abundant opportunities of making the most of it, we get a sharpness of look, and a quickness of motion, which is seen no where else, and has at length become a characteristic of the nation.

The contrast is striking every where, but most of all along the Mediterranean. A Spanish lad for whom I lately got an excellent situation with a mechanic in one of our cities, was near losing it because "he did not move fast;" although in his own country he would have been considered smart enough. I pointed out to him the difference, and mentioned the objection, and he immediately improved. There is, in most of these countries, a heaviness of look, and slowness of motion, in strong contrast with the bustling, driving character of people in our cities; but which is easily accounted for by the fact, that there are fewer stimulants to enterprise and activity. The journey from Beirout to Damascus, I believe, usually occupies between three and four days; although there were ladies in our company, we made it in two; and let me here also remark, *en passant*, that as far as endurance of hardships and of fatigue is concerned, I believe ladies are quite as good travellers as men; and as far as my own observation has gone, they are better.

Our determination this evening to proceed, however, soon brought us into an embarrassment. We entered the defiles of Anti-Lebanon, and in the course of a few hours found ourselves shut up in them, and night settling around us, without knowing where to stop; and our Armenian friend, driven beyond his usual land-marks, could now give us no assistance. Tents we had, thanks to the kindness of Mr. Smith, and also provisions; but we had to find a stopping-place where our beasts could get water; and we passed on, mile after mile, without any indications of stream or fountain. This mountain is very different from Lebanon. Though in some places very high, it is generally much lower, and consists of rounded eminences, with here and there deep ravines or glens between. It is also in most places quite deserted. Along this route we passed but one village in the whole way across the mountain, and this was a miserable looking one; nor was there a single house in the whole intermediate country.

We reached a spot at length where the defile was succeeded by a narrow plain, and our company, scattering themselves over the ground in search of water, a glad shout, at length, from some of the party, informed us that they had found a spring. The water came gushing out from the foot of a bluff of rocks, and beneath them we pitched our tents and lighted our fires. Some of us then went to filling the pots for cooking, and some were sent to grope in the dark after dry thistles for fuel; while others seated themselves on the rocks and looked up at the stars, and talked sentiment.

It was a raw cold night; and we were off long before day, traversing a region as dreary and desolate as can be imagined. About ten o'clock we came to the village just noticed; and then again pursued our course over hill and along dale, with not even a butterfly or grasshopper to cheer our course. A large fountain by and by, and a little herbage near it, offered some variety; and not long after this we caught sight of an oasis some miles on our left--a little valley of the most intense green, with trees of majestic form, mingled with the tapering poplar and cypress, all imbedded among hills of a red and yellow color, and of unbroken sterility.

The ground before us now began to ascend, stretching off into elevated plains; and as we advanced, a traveller was now and then met, or seen at a distance crossing the country. These signs multiplying, it was evident that we were approaching Damascus. We gained, at length, the summit of a long sloping plain terminated by a bluff;—and there—there was the city.

And it was a scene strikingly oriental and truly magnificent. We had hit upon the very best way by which Damascus can be approached, for its gardens, though far down, were right under our feet. A sea of intense verdure breaking all at once upon the arid desert; a great city bursting suddenly from amid the completest solitude; and beyond it a plain stretching off—far off—till the eye could follow it no longer;—this was what we saw as we stood upon those heights. I believe the plain of Damascus reaches to the Euphrates, and proceeds on with that river;

and if so, it must be 500 miles or more in length, and as far as we could see, it is a smooth level, without hillock or break of any kind. On the eastward, at a great distance, and forming a dim speck on the horizon, were some inequalities like mountains; but to the southward the plain was as smooth as the ocean in a calm, and apparently as boundless.

The peculiar excellence of the spot where Damascus is situated is owing to the Barraday, a rapid stream, which here breaks out from the mountain ravines; and by numerous artificial as well as natural channels, is made to spread over the plain; it waters the whole extent of the gardens, and when this is done, the little of it that is left proceeds on southwardly through the plain, but amid the arid sands it soon dwindles away and disappears. The stretch of gardens is about nine miles in diameter, and, except the space occupied by the city, is one unbroken extent of the deepest verdure. It is planted with all kinds of trees; mostly, however, such as produce fruit, among which the apricot still holds the ascendency; pomegranate, orange, lemon, and fig trees also abound, and rising over these are other trees of huge proportions, intermingled with the poplar and sometimes the willow. Water is carried into every garden; and as we rode on towards the city, it was our almost constant companion, dashing along by our side or through arched ways under the road, and sending off branches in every direction. It is here quite a rapid stream. The gardens are enclosed by brick or earthen walls; and beside the fruit trees are planted thickly with vegetables and with flowering shrubs. In the centre of this wide stretch of verdure, which, as we gazed upon it from the hills, seemed like an earthly paradise, is the city itself. Its population is estimated at 100,000; but I should judge it to be greater than this.

It presents a great mass of houses, but being situated on the level plain, and having no points of elevation and but few prominent edifices, it would not strike us greatly, if it were not mixed up with so much natural beauty. The great mosque, formerly the church of St. John, towers considerably above the rest of the edifices; and so does the dark massive castle, or citadel, and so also do a few domes and several minarets; but they are not sufficient to give it character. But with the scenery around, the gardens, the adjoining range of Anti-Lebanon, rising in many a peak and presenting bold precipices, and with the great plain, so vast that the imagination is lost in attempting to follow it, *El Sham*, as by this time we had learned from the Arabs to call Damascus, is a place of exquisite beauty. One part of it, which struck us as we viewed it from our elevated position, will interest the Christian. It is a narrow prolongation of the city at the southern end, about three quarters of a mile in length. Commencing in the body of the city and extending along through the whole length of this portion, is "the street which is called Straight," still remarkable for its length and direct course, and still, I was informed, going by its ancient name. It added greatly to the interest with which we contemplated these remarkable and beautiful scenes, to think that here Paul first looked on nature with the eyes of a Christian, and amid this scenery found subjects to animate him in his new and joyful aspirations, and to strengthen him in his high resolves. Here, in Damascus, "he first preached Christ, that he is the Son of God."

CHAPTER XXIII.

Late fanaticism of the people of Damascus. Change. Mr. Farrah's house. Agreeable disappointment. Costume of the natives. The Cobcob. Mr. Farran, the English Consul General. Visit to the palaces. Palaces of Abdallah Bey, &c. Official visit to the Governor, Sheriff Pasha. Handsome reception. Promises of the Pasha with respect to Americans in Syria. Mr. Farran's beautiful country residence. Bazaars. Damascus blades—not to be had. Departure from the city. Night at Mr. Farran's.

Having rested by a stream at the edge of the gardens till our straggling party had all come up, we passed on, and entering one of the city gates, were soon in a labyrinth of bazaars and narrow streets. Our large cavalcade attracted considerable attention as we rode unceremoniously along, our baggage mules frequently brushing the natives and forcing for themselves a wide passage amid the crowds. Many looks of dark and angry import were turned upon us, but no one offered any molestation; and with the exception of their scowling looks, they were sufficiently respectful. It was only about a year before this that De La Martine, on approaching the city, found it advisable to stop at one of the neighboring villages, and change his European for the Turkish dress. The iron hand of the Egyptian

29*

Pasha, wherever it lights, makes itself felt. It is now as safe to travel in Egypt as in our own country; and will soon be so in Palestine, and also about Damascus, which, until quite lately, was, and indeed probably still is, one of the most fanatical cities in the world. In this city there has already been a surprising change. During our visit we went freely among the bazaars, sometimes all in company, and sometimes in small parties or singly; and though attracting such crowds that the streets were often actually blocked up, and it was difficult for the citizens to get along, all were respectful; nor, as far as we know, was even an opprobrious epithet ever used.

The Armenian gentleman who had been our companion in the journey, had offered the hospitality of his house, and now led us on through the city for nearly a mile, when at length we came to a stand. We were in a street, narrow like all the rest, (the bazaars excepted,) and alongside of a house that seemed to give promise of nothing but poverty. Its exterior was rough and coarse; and the walls bulging out here and there, looked as if waiting to tumble on our heads and crush us, rather than to give us shelter. We entered by a low narrow door into a passage, also narrow and dark; and great indeed was our surprise at the scene which broke upon us when we reached its further end. We afterwards visited all the celebrated palaces of the city, and found the exterior of all of them of a character similar to this. On the outside they are coarse and wretched looking buildings, seemingly ready to crumble and fall to pieces; and the appearance of poverty is probably intentional, in order to save the inmates from the exactions of an arbitrary and oppressive government. But for this, ample amends are made in the interior.

The edifice into which we were now introduced formed a hollow square; the open space within being occupied by a court, about fifty feet by forty, all paved with variegated marbles. In the centre of this was a square fountain, fourteen or fifteen feet on each side, and rising about two feet above the pavement. It was filled with gold and silver fishes, and was lined all around with vases or pots with flowers. At the further end of the court; the pavement rose, and here was a recess occupying nearly the whole width of the court, and about ten feet in depth. It was fronted by a lofty pointed arch, richly ornamented with arabesques cut in stone, or painted in a great variety of gay colors. The back and sides of the recess were enriched in a similar manner, every part of them being covered either with arabesques or with parallel stripes of gay colors, either in horizontal, or in zigzag or waving lines. I must except one or two compartments or raised pannels on each side, with rich borders to them; the pannels were occupied by stanzas of Arabic poetry in large letters, either cut into relief, or done with paint. At the back of the recess was a broad luxurious ottoman.

This lofty and magnificent recess, whose effect, apparently unstudied, is yet very striking, meets us at once on emerging from the dark passage, and gives us our first impression of the building; but as we advance towards it a new candidate for our admiration is presented on our left. Just before reaching the angle of the court which adjoins the recess, we come to a door-way, which is ornamented, but has no very remarkable pretensions; but as we approach, the fall of water arrests our attention and invites us to enter; and on doing so our eagerness to take possession of the lofty cool recess is suddenly checked. This room is not very large, its dimensions being altogether about fifteen feet by twenty-five; and the light is permitted to enter only in sufficient quantity to make objects distinct. A short distance within the door is a circular marble fountain, from the centre of which a few streaks of water ascend up into the air, and breaking at the top, fall in a constant shower of gems, creating a delightful coolness, and a noise just sufficient to lull one to repose. The floor here is of tesselated marbles; on each side are marble slabs attached to the wall, supporting China vases and other *bijouderie* of a similar substance. In the window is a salver containing sherbet and confectionary, where any person may help himself whenever his inclinations prompt, the supply being constant but without parade. About ten feet from the door the floor suddenly ascends about eighteen inches, and now it is covered with the brilliant and soft carpet of Turkey or Persia; while quite around the recess thus formed runs a broad ottoman, yet softer and more luxurious than that of the open court. The walls of this chamber are quite covered with arabesques, in stucco, or painted in various colors, among which is also interspersed Arabic poetry. The ceiling is lofty, and is of wood formed into small compartments, usually arabesque patterns, the bottom of the pannels being often composed of mirrors. The wood itself is colored so as to resemble japanned work of brilliant colors.

This description will give the reader a general idea of these two apartments. I am afraid to venture on a more minute description of them, as his mind would only be burdened if I should attempt to give in detail all the ornaments, the projecting cornice in the Saracenic architecture, and the great variety of patterns and colors that decked the sides and ceiling both of the small retired chamber or of the large recess.

The stone walls of the open court were ornamented all around with patterns, sometimes cut in the stone, but usually in paint of brilliant colors,—red, blue, white, and yellow, being those chiefly employed. Sometimes these were put on in horizontal stripes three or four inches wide; sometimes in waving or zigzag lines, and sometimes in interlacing circles; here and there a pannel of fanciful arabesque is introduced. A person is very much struck with the exuberance of the eastern fancy in these patterns, scarcely any two of them being alike; they are generally in excellent taste.

The reader will think me describing the palace of a prince; but it was the residence of a private gentleman—a merchant, I believe; and I have been so minute, because it is not a palace, but one of the edifices common among that class of persons. We saw more of them; they are all wretched looking on the outside, but magnificent and luxurious within.

These two chambers form the "parlors" of the dwelling. At an angle corresponding to that of the small chamber was a room of a plainer character, used during our residence in the house as a dining-room. The remainder of the two sides of the court was occupied by the sitting room of the females of the family, and by entrances to the kitchen and to the offices. Against the end of the court which faced the large recess, two flights of broad steps ascended to the right and left, one to the gentlemen's, and the other to the ladies' private apartments. They were protected from the weather by a broad ornamented projection of the roof. On entering our own sleeping apartment, we had before us a passage about six feet wide, on the left of which was a platform of small elevation divided by a projecting partition into two recesses; while on the right was a similar recess, each of them being about twenty feet square; along the sides were ottomans raised about six inches from the floor, and these being at night provided with covering, formed our beds. The sides of this room were also ornamented with arabesques, and with a great variety of Arabic poetry.

Damascus is by far the most oriental city that I have seen, and this may serve as a specimen of the dwellings of the wealthier class.

The ladies of Mr. Farrah's family came forward to welcome those of our party; we were led to our various rooms and told that they were ours; and then the family retired; nor through the whole of our stay, though their hospitality was unremitting, was there any parade or ostentation of service. Our wants were all supplied, and where this was possible, anticipated; abundant tables were spread, some gentlemen of the family generally taking their seats at them, but seldom eating, giving quiet attention to our wants, and as quiet orders to the servants; but no one pressed us to eat or to drink, or spoke of the dishes, or obtruded any thing on our notice; nor did they come themselves except when we expressed a wish for their society. The business of the family seemed to go on in the usual course, and the only evidence we had that our presence was felt, was in the unostentatious supply of our necessities. This was true hospitality; we received the most essential services, but without their even seeming to imagine that they were conferring an obligation, or making us feel uneasy by allowing us to see that we were disturbing them.

The Moslem inhabitants of Damascus are like

those of Turkey further north both in their dress and habits, except that the turban is better adjusted, and has a smarter and more dandyish look. So at least we thought; but perhaps we should not have noticed this, if we had not been led to expect it from a passage in some book, I believe Hope's Anastasius. And the ladies of the city, I suppose, would scarcely pardon a traveller who should neglect to notice the cobcob, any more than an American belle would excuse an eastern traveller who, in speaking of her costume, would forget to describe the elegant bishops' sleeves by which she adds to her arms those beautiful proportions which stupid nature has forgotten to give her. The cobcob is a kind of—what shall I call it?—stilt? no; this will not describe it—nor will shoe, nor yet patten. It is a combination of the excellences of the stilt and patten. The manufacturer takes a slip of board, which he cuts to the shape of the foot; and across this nails an embroidered strap, through which the foot is to be slipped, and by which it adheres; next he fits to this board near the ends, two upright pieces about nine inches in height, narrowed above to the width of the delicate foot, but spread out to a breadth of eight inches at the lower extremity. The whole is now ornamented with mother-of-pearl in fanciful patterns, and the *cobcob* is finished and ready for use. The height that I have given for them is that of a pair designed for a person of the wealthier classes; the height, however, is in proportion to the rank of the wearer; and if the lady be of superior grade in society, she disdains to walk with a cobcob of less than twelve inches in height; while the vulgar have to be contented with a smaller elevation, say of five or six inches. Slipping her feet under the strap, the Damascus belle now rises into the proper dignity of her station, and is ready to receive her visitors. Would it not be well for our ladies to adopt the cobcobs as an excellent accompaniment to the bishops' sleeves? In some of our towns they would be of real service, as they would settle questions of rank and precedency, by showing us at once in which class of society the lady considers herself to rank; whether among the first, second, or third, or only the ninth or tenth. For an *American exclusive*, we would allow a suitable cobcob of three feet in height.

Joking aside, it was really odd enough to see the ladies of Damascus going about their houses with this singular kind of slipper. I have described exactly the dimensions of a pair which I purchased in a street almost entirely devoted to the sale of them, and abounding in them of all sizes, from the proportions here given, down to those for a child, where the altitude is not more than a few inches. I saw none worn in the streets: they use them in the marble courts of their houses, in the kitchen and nursery, and in the common household occupations.

The morning after our arrival, Mrs. Farran, the lady of the English consul-general for Syria, did us the honor to call, and was good enough to offer to accompany us in our visits through the city. Mr. Farran sent a very kind message, but was unable to come himself; they were residing at a country-seat at the foot of the mountains, and Mr. F. having the day previous to this come to the city on business, was attacked with a fever. Damascus, in summer, is a very unhealthy place, and is dangerous to European constitutions. For the polite attentions of Mr. and Mrs. F., which were unceasing during our stay, any thing that I could say would be but a feeble acknowledgment. We had no claims on them, not even a letter of introduction; but their politeness was unremitting, and certainly contributed greatly to the pleasures of our visit. Mr. Farran, I believe, was appointed to this station by his government in consequence of its wish to open a steamboat communication down the Euphrates with India, and by his intelligence and tact, and the high esteem in which he is held by the Pasha of Egypt, has very materially contributed to the success of that enterprise. Mrs. Farran was the first lady that had ever ventured to appear here in the European costume, and the ladies of our party were the next; lady Franklin, who had visited the place, having, during her visit, adopted the national dress.

Having mounted our ponies, we started, under the guidance of our polite friend, to visit the curiosities of Damascus; and first proceeded to the palace of Abdallah Bey, one of the wealthiest persons of the city. His family is considered the most ancient and most noble in Syria, and, we were informed, had the Pashalik of Damascus for 300 years. Abdallah has declined office under the Egyptian Pasha,* and is now a private citizen. His palace, with the courts and gardens, occupies a large extent of ground; but I will not fatigue the reader with details. There are three or four distinct courts, like that of our own residence already described, but of course much larger, and in a style of far greater magnificence. In this palace we counted eight fountains, several of them with jets. The Bey received us with great politeness, and showed us through the buildings himself, after which we were entertained with coffee, and pipes and sherbet. A hint being here given by Mrs. F. that the strangers would be pleased if they could see the ladies' apartments, the old gentleman gave orders immediately to have them cleared of his women-folks; and when this had been done, led us through the whole establishment. As we proceeded, a rustling and occasionally a titter behind the partitions or screens, seemed to indicate that the females were not far off, and were amusing themselves with watching us while they themselves were unseen. This part of the palace is separated from the rest by a high wall, and consists of a court, with two large fountains surrounded by orange and lemon trees and rose bushes, a garden ornamented also with two fountains and trees, and a range of apart-

* Mohammed Ali got possession of Damascus without resistance, in June, 1832.

ments surrounding the court. These apartments were more splendid than any others in the palace, the architectural finishing of the chambers being of the most delicate kind and in exquisite taste. One room, as we entered, presented a marble fountain in the centre, in which were seven jets; and looking through the shower of diamonds that broke from them, and fell with an unceasing murmur into the reservoir, we saw, at the further end of the chamber, a cascade of six or seven feet in height, the water of which was broken up, and fell amid sculptured marble cut into a variety of fanciful forms.

In the gentleman's receiving rooms of the Damascus palaces is a curious ornament. A few feet below the ceiling is a broad cornice, supported by Saracenic sculptures running quite around the room; and ranged on this is an unbroken line of China bowls of the largest dimensions that it is possible to procure. The wealth of the individual is supposed to be indicated by the number and the size of these bowls. In one palace I counted near two hundred in a single room; they are of the finest China, and are colored; and in rooms where, as in these countries, the only furniture consists of carpets and ottomans, may assist in preventing the apartment from looking too naked; but I did not much admire the taste. Almost every family has some of these bowls; there were several in our sleeping room at Mr. Farrah's, which we put to the desecrating use of wash-bowls.

From this we proceeded to the palaces of Ali Aga

and Abdi El Belzah Aga, which were also splendid, though smaller than that of Abdallah Bey. In one of them was a chamber not more than fourteen feet square, the finishing of the walls and ceiling of which had cost 7000 dollars. They were composed of mirrors in small compartments, and were further highly enriched with mother of pearl, gilding, and with arabesques and Saracenic mouldings in a great variety of forms.

We finished with Mr. Farran's town-house or palace, for such it truly is; and where, to oriental splendor we found united English elegance and comfort. The furniture from his own country was made to harmonize very well with the eastern architectural taste.

The Commodore in the morning had sent his travelling firman to the palace of Sheriff Pasha, the Governor of Syria; and now, while the ladies proceeded with Mrs. Farran to her country residence, he went with the officers to make an official visit to that dignitary. The cavalcade, consisting of the Dragoman of the English embassy, Cavasses, Mr. Farrah, and the American officers, had to traverse the whole length of the city, as the Governor's palace is on the south-western end. Sheriff Pasha had been represented to us as a thorough Turk in his feelings and manners towards Christians; but owing, probably, to the firman, he met the party in the court of his palace, surrounded by his officers, and with a guard of honor. On being conducted to the audi-

30*

ence hall, the party found that *chairs* had been provided for their accommodation, and he even occupied a chair himself. The usual compliment of pipes, &c. was paid; and while smoking, he proceeded to inquire about our country, showing, as indeed did most of the Egyptian officers wherever we visited, a knowledge of our institutions and resources that we had not expected to find. He spoke of our late war and our successes on the ocean; and expressed a strong desire to see the Delaware, of which he said he had that morning received an account by letter. His curiosity, he said, would have carried him over to Beirout to visit the ship, if he had not been in daily expectation of the arrival of Ibrahim Pasha. After presenting Mr. Farrah to him as the agent of our government, and receiving assurances that on this recommendation he should be received without the usual formalities of writing to Alexandria, the Commodore expressed the satisfaction he felt in the protection and countenance that had been afforded by Mohammed Ali and the Governor to the American citizens resident in Syria. The Pasha replied, "That the citizens of all powers residing in the kingdom were entitled to protection—such were his orders, which it afforded him pleasure to fulfil, particularly towards the Americans, who had by their correct conduct and their efforts to do good, merited protection and favor; and that so long as he continued in office they should be his peculiar care, and that he himself would be their *consul*;"

he requested, "if we should hear of an American having suffered injustice or injury, or not having obtained justice for any injury or insult, that the Commodore would write to him, and charge him with neglect of his promise:" and added, "that, in short, he wanted to be himself American consul in Syria, and charge himself with the care and interests of all Americans, who were then, or might afterwards settle, in Syria, or make it a visit." The reader is left to deduct from all this whatever he may consider as belonging to the usual *palavar* of such occasions; but, after all, Sheriff Pasha certainly acted and spoke in a very handsome manner.

The party, after this interview, proceeded to Mr. Farran's country-seat, where we were engaged to dinner. This is a very beautiful spot. It is quite near the foot of the mountains, in a north-western direction from the city, from which it is about two miles distant. The house stands within a large enclosure, and has in front a court surrounded by immense walnut trees intermingled with the orange and lemon, overhanging a large fountain. Directly under the windows in the rear rushes the Barraday, here undivided, and a full rapid stream of the clearest water. The grounds around the dwelling are laid out in good taste, and are covered by an exuberance of foliage, some of the trees being of prodigious magnitude.

The entertainment was in a style to correspond to all this; and after such a busy day, good appetites were not wanting to do it justice. It was, indeed, pleasant, away at Damascus, to meet with a hospitality so kind and agreeable, and society that beguiled the thoughts back to one's father-land: and the party were easily induced to remain till morning. Beds, in these countries, are easily provided, the broad ottomans only requiring a few sheets in order to make them excellent places of repose; and so they are generally used.

The next day was appropriated to a lounge among the bazaars; and we spent it agreeably, under the guidance of Mr. and Mrs. Farran, in looking at the great variety of oriental productions. I have always taken great pleasure in lounging in a Turkish bazaar; and it struck me that these of Damascus, though perhaps less splendid, are more pleasing than even the great bazaars of Constantinople. One very pleasing characteristic of them is their great loftiness; while those of the Turkish capital are low. The reader will imagine a street, or any succession of streets, or rather a labyrinth of streets, about fifteen feet wide, and covered at the height of fifty or sixty feet by a wooden roof, generally tight, but sometimes allowing, through the interstices of the covering or of a huge spreading grape-vine, the sunbeams to fall in a gentle and chequered light. The sides of this street are composed entirely of shops, not very large, and quite open in front; so that the passengers can easily distinguish every article upon the well-filled shelves. The floor of the shop is raised about three feet, and is carpeted; and in the centre sits the lord of the little domain, ready for the call of customers, and in the intervals helping away the time by means of a book, or a pipe, or it may be by a nap. From the sides of partitions between the stores bits of wood project into the street, and on these are hung specimens of the articles for sale, silks of various dye, handkerchiefs covered with vines or with sprigs of gold embroidery; towels ornamented at their ends in a similar showy manner; and cashmere shawls, rich enough to turn almost any brain, except, of course, those of the reader and myself. Here, as in other oriental cities, the shops are not mixed up together in the manner usual with us; but streets, or parts of a street, are appropriated to the sale of a particular article. One street has cobcobs; another has slippers; another jewelry; another arms; another dry goods; another drugs. We came to one lined with manufacturies of cutlery, and at once scattered along it in search of something that might be tortured into the boast of "a Damascus blade;" but all to little purpose. The gentlemen, seated cross-legged before their anvils, stared at our questions, and seemed now, for the first time, to become aware of the celebrity of their manufactures: and the nearest approach that we could find to the articles of our search, were some huge, coarse knives, and a handjar or two. They had, however, the delicate waving lines of yellow and blue along the blade, which was one of the characteristics of the

Damascus swords, and was occasioned by their being made of alternate pieces of iron and steel wire; the former to give them toughness, the latter hardness and edge.

Here and there, at the corners of streets, we came to fruit-stands, and in some of the well-filled baskets I noticed peaches, which I think were the largest that I have ever seen.

The appearance of such a large party in the French dress seemed to rouse the people from their natural apathy, and the streets sometimes became so crowded as to be uncomfortable. We were, however, always treated with politeness, and found them ready to gratify our curiosity with regard to their wares: if we purchased, well: if not, well: the muscles of the dignified and composed features of the merchant were equally unmoved.

We might have spent a much longer time very agreeably at Damascus, and were urged also to proceed on to Palmyra; but our time was limited; and towards the close of the second day we bade adieu to the hospitable family of Mr. Farrah, by which we had been so kindly entertained. Our faces were now turned towards Balbec, which was not far out of our way back to the ship; and as Mr. Farran's house was on the road to that city, he had insisted on our coming out this evening and spending the night under his roof.

Having filed out at the north-western end of the city, we came, soon after leaving it, to a large burying-ground, where the graves, covered with solid masonry, which was plaistered and whitewashed, showed a pleasing attention to the dead. The whitewash looked as if frequently renewed, and every part of the ground was clean and in good order. The appropriate cyprus, however, was wanting; nor was there any other tree, or even a shrub. Beyond this, we entered among the gardens once more; and were immediately surrounded by trees of venerable appearance and majestic growth, and by cottages and country-houses, and gushing streams. In our own country, majestic forest trees and streams of all dimensions are common things, and the reader may wonder at the enthusiasm which we felt when such objects were met with in our journeyings: our enthusiasm was owing to two causes—the rarity of such things about the Mediterranean was one, and the other cause was the fact that they are common at our home: they brought home to our minds, more vividly perhaps than any other objects could have done; and no one who has not made the experiment can tell how dear, at the end of a few years' absence, our father-land becomes.

Alighted at Mr. Farran's, however, we could not feel that we were in a strange country. A pleasant evening succeeded an agreeable day, and when we stretched ourselves on our couches, the gurgling of water on either side of the house lulled us to repose.

CHAPTER XXIV.

Sunrise on the plain of Damascus. Mountain Mosque. Superstition of the natives of Damascus. Mountain course of the Barrady. Tomb of Abel. Fountain of Rosalyn. Toils of travel. Comforts on the road to Pompeii. Ruins of Balbec. The great Temple and its courts. Stones of prodigious size. A gem in Architecture. The circular Temple. Gleanings with regard to their history. Pasha of Balbec. Marshal Bourmont. Cedars of Lebanon. Town of Zahle. Night in our tents on Lebanon. Attack by the natives. Return to the ship.

EARLY dawn on the 6th of September found us prepared for our journey. We took an early breakfast, and then, accompanied by our kind host and his lady, began to wind up the steep ascents that lie just back of his house. The scene was strikingly oriental. Two negro lads, attendants of Mr. Farran, dressed in the gay and fanciful costume of this region, and mounted on spirited animals, were amusing themselves with making their horses fly at full speed up the precipices, and with darting to and fro across our path. The air was perfumed with the odors of the orange and jessamine: the gardens had been steeped in dew, and seemed to welcome the god of day, which now rising on the edge of the boundless plain, filled it all with glory, and hung the mountain sides with splendid purple and roseate hues.

At the summit of the eminence, we passed a little out of our way, to examine a religious edifice of the Moslems, erected, I think, on the spot where Mahomet is said to have alighted to take once more a look at Damascus, while on his way to heaven. In the estimation of Mahommedans, Mecca is first in sanctity: next is Jerusalem; and next is Damascus, which they call the Prophet's Heel: the plain adjoining this city is the rendezvous for the great northern caravan of pilgrims for Mecca, and in the gains which the citizens draw from this source, together with the fresh and ardent zeal which the pilgrims bring with them and diffuse around, we may find the cause of the proverbial fanaticism of this city.

I saw a curious specimen of their superstitions the second day of our visit, while I was traversing one of the principal bazaars. The street had been well filled, but it suddenly became thronged; and turning to see the cause of this, I found a party of them leading a horse, on which was seated a young man, without any clothing, looking around him with a wild and vacant stare. He was an idiot, and was regarded by them as a saint; and they were leading him about to receive the homage of the people. As he passed slowly along, all treated him with the highest respect.

At the Mountain Mosque we took leave of Mr. and Mrs. Farran, with many sincere thanks for their kindness; and then set ourselves adrift once more on the broad range of Anti-Libanus: the relative of our Armenian host, however, still keeping us company and acting as a guide. Our road was considerably to the northward of the one by which we had come to Damascus; and followed up the course of the Barraday, which here, far down in a narrow glen, was spluttering impatiently among the rocks. At intervals the precipices receded from its banks, and left a level spot, which was always occupied by cottages and trees. This route across the mountain was, indeed, in fertility and beauty, the very reverse of the one by which we had come; and our ride was far more pleasant than we had anticipated. At the distance of five or six miles from Damascus we came to the green valley which had attracted our attention a few days before, and we found here a large village quite imbedded in verdure. By noon the river had lost three fourths of its magnitude; but it still kept up a streak of verdure and of profitable cultivation amid the mountain solitudes.

The route which we were following no doubt passes over the ground occupied by the ancient highway from Damascus to Balbec, and must have been once much travelled. We passed, about noon, along the sides of a romantic and deep ravine, where the road had been cut with great labour among the rocks of calcareous tufa; and here we had for our contemplation and antiquarian speculations an ancient aqueduct, carried among and sometimes through the precipitous rocks. In the face of the opposing cliffs were a great many openings to artificial subterranean chambers, probably in old times the dwellings of anchorites, to whose taste the wild and desolate grandeur of the place must have been well adapted. After passing several villages during the day, we came, after dark, to another at the side of a large and beautiful fountain; and here, amid the barking of dogs and the jabbering of the wondering natives, we stopped and pitched our tents under some venerable looking olive trees. The reader may form some idea of the security which we felt in these exposed encampments, when I mention that we never set a guard, or took any particular precaution with regard to our baggage; nor was a single article ever stolen.

About eight o'clock of the next day, we passed, among an amphitheatre of hills, the head waters of the Farrady, which here bursts into daylight amid a little paradise of verdure; thence our course was generally over high and barren ridges, deserted by the very insects. As we approached once more the plain of Coelo-Syria, we reached another stream, and soon after this we passed on our left the *Tomb of Abel!!* still in good repair. As such, at least, is regarded, both by Musselmen and Christians, a grave-shaped mound of earth, 113 feet in length. Near it are two pillars, on which Abel is said to have presented his offerings; and they tell us that yearly, in the month of December, fire descends from heaven and rests on their summit. "As I did not see this," says El Devoto Perigrino, "and it is told me by Christians who are not very scrupulous, I have not given it much credit."

Proceeding on, again over bare and desolate ridges, we came, at 1 P.M. to where a gorge in the mountain obstructed our path, and casting our eyes to the left, we saw, just beyond its outlet in the plain of Coelo-Syria, a profusion of majestic ruins.

These were the temples of Balbec.

At the head of the little valley at our feet we saw also a fountain, so large and clear, and cool-looking, that it immediately acted as a magnet, and we determined to be the companions of the Naiads during our visit here. So our tents were pitched beneath some fine spreading trees, on a green island formed by the branching of the waters, a few yards from the fountain.

This fountain, called Rosalyn by the natives, is about fifty feet in diameter, and lies embosomed among gently sloping hills, the only opening being on the west of it, where the eye rests on the ruins of Balbec, and beyond them, on the snowy summits of Lebanon. Towards one side of it is a small island, on which, and also on the main land adjoining, are ruins, apparently of an ancient temple; but at present it is impossible to determine their character.

Having pitched our tents, and disposed our baggage, and cooled our feverish faces in the stream, we prepared—to visit the ruins? no, but to take a nap. And there was good philosophy in this; for he who, after a long journey to see an interesting object, rushes up with eyes full of dust and faculties all jaded, does injustice to it, and gets but a modicum of satisfaction himself. If he would enjoy it to the full, let him first get a comfortable meal and then a little repose: the world, and every thing in it, will then be quite a different affair. If the reader's journeying has been altogether in fancy or in books, he can have no idea how much the traveller's pleasures are curtailed by these every day wants and feelings; and how often, when he expected to be in raptures, they keep him in incessant torments. "How magnificent are those ruins," says enthusiasm to him: "yes, but how burning hot this sun," says his poor, red, scaly face: "why don't you break out into rapturous exclamations at this splendid colonnade?" cry upbraidingly, reason, and taste and fancy, all combined. "Why, I can't," he groans pettishly; "don't you see my mouth is parched up with thirst, and my tongue is as dry as if it belonged to a mummy." "Come, come, look," exclaims his guide; "here, this way is something truly wonderful!" "What! away there," he answers; "why I am already almost inanimate from fatigue, my feet are blistered, and that roll down yonder precipice has left me in the state of a mere jelly."

The reader has doubtless often thought that he would like to walk the streets of the disentombed Pompeii, and has been in raptures as he imagined himself amid its remains. Yes, but let him first imagine himself *on the way to it;* for travelling does not give one the power of the magic Arabian lamp. Well, let us suppose him making the experiment of getting there. In the first place, if he does not desire the comfort of being cheated out of four times the honest price for the conveyance, he has to bargain at Naples—no, that is not the word—he has to get angry, and scold and quarrel, or at least to go through the appearance of all this, about his carriage; also about the fare to him who drives, and to him who rides behind; and perhaps about the price of the horses' feed. You start at length; and, except that in the thronged road one is in constant dread of jolts or an upset, all goes on well for a little while; but the beggars,—here they come: they mark the foreigner at a distance, and are really such pitiful objects that one's heart bleeds for them. The way up hill is occupied by the aged, or by cripples, or by the blind with a boy to lead them: the level spots by the more robust: and the descent by children, who start from the side of their haggard parents, and cry "miseracordia, famine, sickness," till your ears tingle, and your fancy is filled with all kinds of diseases and their associations. And the dust, the dust! you are now off from the paved streets of Resina, and a hundred vehicles besides your own are kicking up dust enough to satisfy the ambition of twenty Napoleons: it settles on your new coat, and fills your eyes, and sets you to sneezing; and still amid it all you hear the cry of "miseracordia," "orphans," "famine," "disease." Next comes a long level spot, and here the beggars leave you; and now start up a dozen urchins, who seem so many Mercuries with winged feet, so rapidly do they follow your godship as you sail along in the cloud—of dust. They would pick your pockets, too, if they could. And now look at them; they turn heels over head, and making a wheel of their extended arms and legs, whirl along by your side: they make music for you by chuckling their chin with the fist; they pick up the dust, and, rubbing it all over their faces, then grin and wriggle, and look like so many imps escaped up from the flames of Vesuvius: and you try in vain to bribe them to stay behind by tossing them some money. They pick it up, and follow you for more. At last you are at the gate of Pompeii, and your carriage comes to a halt; but here, children, with all kinds of deformed limbs, crawl about, and dragging themselves to your feet, call upon you for compassion. And while you yield to pity and think you are doing a charitable act, you are filled with horror on being informed that, in the opinion of physicians who have examined them, their limbs have probably been distorted thus on purpose, in order to make them objects of charity; and that you have been only encouraging their inhuman masters in their iniquitous gains. But at length you are in the city, and you hope now to be at peace. No. You are accompanied all through it by a soldier, who tells you plainly, by his looks and by his manner of watching you, that he believes you only want an opportunity to turn thief and steal some of the relics; and he expects too to be paid for his strict attentions. And you will find a dozen official showmen there, expecting to be paid, and they would not be satisfied if you were to spend a fortune in presents to them. And no matter how liberal you may have been, when you go away you leave behind you faces, looking at least, as if they thought you mean. The rogues! how indignant you feel at them! And this is the strongest feeling which you carry away with you, and it ever afterwards is associated in your mind with Pompeii.

Yes, this is a plain account of a visit to Pompeii. How greatly obliged, then, are the public, to those writers who enable them to travel without the vexations of travel; and to grow sentimental or to grow wise, without growing—hungry; for I will warrant to every man by the time he gets from Pompeii to Naples, not only a good covering of dust, but a famous appetite.

And yet, I suppose the reader is scolding because I have not already set him down quietly among the ruins of Balbec, forgetting that we ourselves had yet a walk of two miles through the hot sun before we could reach them.

These ruins of Balbec, which stand here without a history and without a name, are indeed worthy of all the admiration that has been bestowed upon them. They are at one side of the present village or town of Balbec, a miserable place of a few hundred hovels, and in no wise diverting the attention from them as we approach: its squalid appearance, perhaps, heightens their effect. They rise high above all other objects, so as to be conspicuous at a great distance; and as we approach, our wonder and admiration are mingled with sadness to think that such magnificent edifices should have been so mutilated by the hand of violence and of time; and yet this sadness increases our interest in them.

Our attention was first directed to the most perfect of the temples; but, as we entered at the wrong end of the structures, and soon got our ideas confused amid the masses of ruins, I believe the reader would rather be excused from accompanying us; so I will first state their appearance in ancient times, when there was great regularity and symmetry in them, and then describe them as they are at present.

They stood, then, on an artificial platform of stone, raised on the plain of Coelo-Syria to a height varying, according to the inequalities of the plain, from thirty to forty feet. This was about half a mile from the chain of Anti-Libanus. The platform was adapted in shape to the structures upon it, the complete length being 900 feet and the greatest width about 420. The entrance was from the east. At that end was a flight of about fifty steps, 180 feet in length: at the top of this was a range of twelve columns, each fifty-one inches in diameter, with an interval of nine and a half feet between. The visitor was admitted between them into a covered vestibule,

250 feet in length by 36 in width; this was adorned at the extremities with square columns, while the side opposite to him was ornamented with semi-columns, and also with niches, and, above these, with tabernacles; both the latter being occupied by statues. Crossing this vestibule, he might leave it either by a large central passage or by a smaller one at each side of this, and would then find himself in an open hexagonal court, 150 feet wide and 200 at its greatest length. This court had at its sides, on his right and left, four exedrae, or chambers for schools, open in front, and ornamented each with four columns and pilasters: the intervals between these were taken up with chambers for the high priests and with niches for statues. The whole court was thus surrounded by columns and pilasters, except in the front. In this part was a passage 78 feet wide, with two side passages, giving admittance into the great court of the temple. This court was 380 feet square, and, except in the front and at the entrance, was surrounded by square exedrae, alternating with others of a semi-circular shape: the former had each four columns and two pilasters, and the latter two columns with pilasters at their front. At the entrance into this court were colossal niches, and at the angles were chambers for the priests.

The great temple, which stood at the further end of this court, and facing the visitor as he entered, was 290 feet long by 160 in width. It had ten columns at each end, and nineteen at each of the sides;* they were seven feet in diameter, and the details of the whole edifice were of the same colossal proportions: they allowed eight feet ten inches for the intervals between the columns. There are still remaining three rows of stones, supporting the platform on which this temple stands, which are of remarkable dimensions. In the lowest tier they measure severally 35, 33, 32, 31, and 38 feet in length; with a height of thirteen feet and a breadth of ten feet five inches, exclusive of their mouldings. In the second row, which is twenty-seven feet from the ground, they are generally of the same size, but here are three measuring 64, 64, and 63 feet in length, with their other dimensions to correspond. In the quarry on the side of the mountain adjoining this, is a stone cut loose, that measures seventy feet in length by fourteen in width, and fourteen feet five inches in depth: the weight of this is estimated at 1,135 tons.

Of this colossal temple, nine of the columns of one side, with a portion of their entablature, are all that now remains: its foundations may still be traced, and a few huge fragments are scattered about; but if it was ever completed, it has served as a quarry for more modern structures, perhaps for some that were erected by Constantine, for its area and the environs are pretty well cleared: but the great columns, standing thus naked and alone, pro-

* Or was intended to have, for it is doubtful whether this temple was ever finished.

duce a very powerful effect. Of the ranges of exedrae, columns, &c., which formed the sides of the square and hexagonal courts, and of the vestibule, there are still large remains; but so broken and defaced by time and human violence, that it is often difficult to ascertain their shape or proportions. The ground is covered over with their ruins. In one corner of the square court are some large columns of the red Egyptian granite: they are of peculiar beauty, and though they have been exposed to the weather for so many centuries, their polish has scarcely been at all affected.

It is sad to walk over this great platform and mark the desolations that have been wrought amid such architectural beauty. A few yards, however, from this is a temple of the same age, still almost perfect, and probably the most splendid specimen of the Corinthian order of architecture that the world now can boast. It stands also on a platform of stone, and was reached by a stair-way of thirty-two steps: it is about twenty-five feet from the south-west angle of the great court just described, and also faces the east. It is peripteral; that is, with a range of columns quite around, and has also another range at the front, forming a vestibule: the length is 280 feet, the breadth 122. There were fifteen columns on each side and eight in front (the angular columns counted twice), or forty-two in all; to which we are to add eight for the vestibule, six in front and one at each side. Of these, thirty-three are now entire and erect, and nine in a ruinous condition; the eight front columns are missing, but those of the vestibule remain. The sides of the interior were also ornamented with half columns, six on each side; between these were niches for statues, with ornamented lacunari (arched coverings), and above the niches were tabernacles, also for statues. The further end was occupied by a platform, reached by a broad flight of fifteen steps, and on this was placed the statue of their divinity. The interior is also in tolerably good preservation. This temple belongs to the florid age of architecture; its ornaments are exuberant and exceedingly rich; the doorway is decorated with vines and foliage, amid which children are sporting; the pannels of the ceiling are occupied by figures of gods and goddesses in relief; in short, Sculpture has here joined her graver sister Architecture, and they have worked together harmoniously, and have produced—what is very seldom produced—a building where great exuberance of ornament is united with delicacy, and chasteness, and simplicity. This building is, indeed, a gem in the art.

South-eastward from these, at the distance of about 300 yards, is a pretty little thing, though of more objectionable taste. It is a temple, circular within, the diameter being thirty-two feet. It is on an ornamented platform or substructure, and the floor was reached by a flight of about fifteen steps; the front presents this flight of steps and a large door-way, with two Corinthian columns at each side. The rest of the exterior is formed by a succession of great niches for statues, five in number, with a Corinthian column at the sharp angles between them. The exterior diameter of the building, from column to column, is sixty-four feet. The interior is highly ornamented, and has a double range of semi-columns one above the other, one range Ionic, the other Corinthian. This little temple answers very well by way of variety, and for employing the power of contrast; and is placed just at the proper distance from the other colossal structures to make the effect very good. Winding around its foundations, and murmuring amid its broken, prostrate columns, is the clear brook from the fountain of Rosalyn. As we listened to the sound of its waters, we could almost imagine it to be the voice of pure and holy Nature chanting the dirge of the unhallowed worship that once was prevalent here.

It is very strange that, in order to learn the origin and design of these splendid structures we are compelled to turn over a variety of ancient books; and that, after all, the information we glean is sufficient only to tantalize, and not to satisfy our curiosity. Its whole amount, I believe to be as follows:

Macrobius informs us that

"In the city called Heliopolis* the Assyrians worship the Sun with great pomp, under the name of Heliopolitan Jove; and the

* "City of the Sun"—the Greek name of Balbec. Balbec is Syriac, and means the Vale of Baal. Balbeit signifies the House of Baal.

statue of this god was brought from a city in Egypt, also called Heliopolis, when Senemur or Senepos reigned over the Egyptians, by Opias, ambassador of Delebon, king of the Assyrians, together with some Egyptian priests, of whom Partemetis was the chief; and it remained long among the Assyrians before it was removed to Heliopolis. * * The statue is of gold, representing a person without a beard, who holds in his right hand a whip, charioteer-like, and in his left a thunderbolt, together with ears of corn; all which mark the united powers of Jupiter and the Sun."

From this he infers that the divinity was both Jupiter and the Sun: he adds that the temple excelled in divination, and that Trajan consulted it about his Parthian expedition. Macrob. Saternalia, lib. 1.

Lucian, who was a native of Syria, speaks of a great and ancient temple in Phœnicia, the rites of whose worship were brought from Heliopolis in Egypt; and adds, that "many persons assert that this temple was erected by Deucalion, the Scythian; that Deucalion, in whose days the grand inundation of waters took place."

All this refers to this spot and to the origin of these temples, but not to these temples themselves: the structure to which Lucian refers being evidently of more ancient date. The first clear and authentic information which we have of the edifices now standing, are in John of Antioch, surnamed Malala; who says, that Aurelius Antoninus Pius erected a great temple to Jupiter at Heliopolis, near Libanus in Phœnicia, which was one of the wonders of the world.

The Chronicon Paschale informs us, that Theodosius converted the great and famous temple of Heliopolis into a Christian church.*

The florid architecture of these edifices corresponds exactly to the times of the Antonines; and I think we are at liberty to infer, from what we can gather on this subject, that there was here, in very ancient times, a famous temple, containing the statue of Jupiter Igneous, if I may use the term; and that its celebrity led the first of the Antonines, who distinguished himself by building up decaying cities, to erect these vast and beautiful structures. Close adjoining them on the south, is a dark, heavy, and ancient looking building, without windows, and composed of stones, pannelled like those which I saw at the foot of Mount Moriah; and this may, perhaps, be the original temple noticed by Lucian.

The modern Balbec contains about 200 houses. It is protected by a low wall, but not more than half the enclosure is occupied by the dwellings, which are small and miserable looking hovels. As we were leaving the ruins in the evening, we received an invitation from the Pasha to make him a visit, which the lateness of the hour led us to decline. But his house was adjoining our road back to the fountain; and on approaching it, we found the gates wide open, and a train of attendants marshalled for our reception; so there was no help for us, and our party entering, filled his little hall of audience. He seemed

* Vide "The Ruins of Balbec," by Robert Wood.

disposed to be sociable, and regaled us with pipes, coffee, and apples; and we regretted that our time would not permit a longer visit.

It was now dark, and on leaving his house we found that he had had the politeness to have torches provided for us. They consisted of bits of pine, piled up in small baskets made of iron hoops, and elevated at the end of a long pole. As we wound around or over the undulations of the valley, the effect of the broad lights and shadows, the dancing waters in the pebbly brook by our side, and the oriental costume of the natives, numbers of whom were accompanying us, was very fine.

During the day some other travellers, in the native costume, stopped for an hour or two by our fountain. We had no conversation with them, but were afterwards informed that they were probably the French Marshal Bourmont and some friends, travelling in disguise.

September 6. We stopped again, an hour or two, at the ruins, and then commenced re-crossing the plain of Coelo-Syria, directing our course transversly so as to strike our former route over Mount Lebanon. Had our time permitted, we should have visited the cedars of Lebanon, which are about half way between Balbec and Tripoli; but as the autumn was advancing, and the Commodore was anxious to get away from this unknown coast, the project was relinquished. Mr. Chassaud was good enough, however, afterwards to procure some of the wood for us, and

32*

to forward it by way of Marseilles to our wintering station at Mahon. I have had my portion of it cut into veneers, which are greatly admired by cabinet makers, both for the color and odour of the wood; the interior of the block is of a golden yellow color, and some portions, which are sprinkled over with small black specks or knots, are very beautiful. The number of the old trees has been gradually diminishing since the mountain first began to be visited by travellers, and but seven or eight are now remaining. The largest of these are ninety feet in height, and they have in one or two cases a circumference of forty feet; which, however, like that of the great chesnut on Mount Etna, is not the circuit of a single tree, but of the generation that has grown around the original trunk. The natives have an annual religious festival beneath these venerable fathers of the forest. There are groves of a younger growth around these, containing altogether about 400 trees. A fine large tree of this species may be seen in the garden of plants at Paris; and in Mr. Prince's garden at Flushing is a young one also, in a flourishing condition.

About half way across the plain, we came to another large fountain, and smaller ones occurred at intervals; but the ride was wearisome enough: in the whole distance we passed not a house, nor a tree, nor a speck of cultivation; a withering and blighting influence has been for ages upon all this region. About three o'clock, we reached the village of Zahle, at the foot of Lebanon. It has rather a modern appearance, having grown up lately in consequence of some violence and exactions on the other side of the plain, from which the inhabitants have taken refuge under the wing of the princes of Lebanon. It is quite refreshing to an American traveller to see a modern town, and this of Zahle is also particularly pleasing from its situation. It is built on unequal, broken ground, and is bordered on one side by a deep, shaded ravine, along the bottom of which dashes a torrent, singing and making melody in its joyful course. We found near its banks a convenient spot for satisfying our now ravenous appetites, and then, although we had no ruins to inspect afterwards, we again sought the reviving effects of a nap.

And well it was for us that we did so, for we were destined on the following night to have no repose. Having travelled on from Zahle in the coolness of the evening, we came at dusk to our breakfasting place of the 2d., and here determined to pitch our tents. But that was to be a night of fighting and not of sleep.

There is a set of natives on this mountain, the most thievish beings in all the country, with the reputation also of being blood-thirsty and merciless, and waiting to pounce upon every unprotected traveller that may come in their way. They are a small race, but are said to be numerous; and the traveller across these mountains must be on his guard, or he will be very apt to be plundered by them. They carry a concealed dagger, with which they are very expert, and which they do not hesitate to use when there is occasion for it. They are cowardly, and seldom make their attacks except in covert places or by night: and their cunning and malevolence are said to be equal to their cowardice. We had met them occasionally, and had generally been on our guard; but there seemed to be no particular danger this night, and we took no unusual precautions.

But they were lying here in ambush; and we had scarcely blown out our lights, and wrapped ourselves in our blankets for repose, when they made a sudden attack—how many there were, we could not tell in the darkness, but their number must have been very great. We sprung up, and seizing such weapons as were handiest, repelled our assailants, and forced them to a speedy retreat; but not before several wounds had been given and received. I think it probable that some of the enemy were killed. And now we sat down to consult upon the best mode of preventing another attack. Some advised shifting our encampment; some concluded to sit up; and others, amid the confusion of counsel, again yielded to drowsiness, and tried once more to seek repose. But hope of repose was vain: we carried on a skirmishing with them all night, and, notwithstanding our resistance, many of the enemy in the dark succeeded in carrying off the plunder, which was their object.

I should certainly caution all travellers over Mount

Lebanon against pitching their tents, as we had done, in an old stubble field swarming with fleas.

As may be supposed, we made an early start on the morrow. Our journey back offered nothing new, and after stopping to pay our respects to Mr. and Mrs. Smith, and to thank them for their kindness, we picked our way down the mountain, and towards evening took up, once more, our quarters in the Delaware.

CHAPTER XXV.

Sensation produced by the Delaware. Effect of this visit on the cause of Missions in Syria. Service on the Sabbath on board, and the crowds attending. Crowds attracted by this ship during her whole cruise. Appearance of the ship. Her effect on the visitors. Progress of free principles throughout the world. The cause of humanity secure. Our own Country, and its prosperity. Adieu to the reader.

We found, that during our absence the ship, having taken in water, had changed her anchorage, and was now lying abreast of the city, and but a short distance off. A vessel of her class had never appeared along this part of the coast before; and on her arrival she immediately began to attract observation. A few of the citizens visited her, and found no difficulty in getting admittance on board: they carried news of this to the shore; other visitors came; her fame soon spread far and wide; and in a short time she was all the rage. Mr. Chassaud's house was thronged by applicants for tickets of admission (the impression having gone abroad that they were useful), and the street to it was so crowded, that it was often difficult to get along. He computed the number who visited the ship here at 40,000; but, although this was perhaps above the reality, it was still prodigious. Some persons came two days' journey simply for this purpose; and the city was thronged to such a degree, that provisions rose to double their former price. They came, old men, women and children, Druses and Mahommedans, princes and laborers: all seemed to be seized by the mania; and, until the day of our leaving (the 11th of September), there was a constant throng from early in the morning till dusk. Such a sensation had probably never been produced here before by any object of curiosity.

I believe our visit has been beneficial to the interesting mission at this place. Mr. Bird, at my request, preached on board on the first Sunday of our stay here, and Mr. Smith on the second; and during the latter service, the visitors from shore were suffered to be present. Generally, visiting was not permitted on the Sabbath till public worship had been concluded; but on this occasion they were admitted, and allowed to stay; and when the crew were called up to worship, they came up also to witness the services. Our upper deck has a clear sweep of 225 feet in length: the whole is covered by an awning, elevated twelve or fifteen feet, with side pieces of canvass reaching down to the hammock-cloths, and thus forming a complete chamber. The poop-deck, on this occasion, is occupied chiefly by the band in their uniform: the officers stand by the capstan, and from this aft, on the starboard side: the larboard side is occupied, in front, by the ship's boys, with prayer-books; then by the marines in full uniform; and, back of these, by the seamen, who also stretch along by the mainmast on either side. All are in their "first best" clothes; and our ship on these occasions presents an air of thorough cleanliness and neatness which, I do not hesitate to say, I have never yet seen a church on shore present. Mr. Smith's discourse was suited to the occasion, and was listened to by officers and seamen with deep interest; and I have no doubt that the scene made an impression on the minds of the mountaineers which will materially advance the success of the mission.

Probably no ship has ever floated on the water that has attracted so much attention, or drawn so many visitors, as the Delaware during this cruise. The number of visitors, I think, may be safely estimated at about 200,000. At Naples, at Palermo, and at this place particularly, there was a constant throng from morning till night. No one was denied admittance; they were allowed to go freely through the ship, and, when the Commodore or Captain were absent, were admitted also into their cabins. At Naples the visitors were from all parts of Europe, a very large portion of them being from the interior of Germany. They saw a vessel, not only effective as regards her battery, but every where showing a neatness and a completeness of finish that must have astonished them. This ship, like some others of our seventy-four's, has a deceptive appearance at a distance, seeming to be smaller than she is, and less effective. When they got on board, they found a battery of ninety-four guns, the greater portion of them of the largest calibre; the decks high and wide, and in every part scrupulously clean; and a sufficient attention to ornament, which was all, however, made subservient to the main design of efficiency. She is a very powerful ship, and so she appeared on inspection; and was also a very handsome vessel. The most perfect order also prevailed in every part. The impression which she gave must have been a favorable one; and I believe that the Delaware, in this cruise, did more towards advancing the rights of man, than if she had come home with a dozen captures of bulk and power equal to her own. Around the world the voice of freedom and of humanity is beginning to make itself heard. In many places it is only a still small voice, but it is yet heard; and though people often scarcely know what it means, yet there is a feeling in their breasts that more or less responds, and tells them that what it says is the truth. They have heard, too, that there is a republic somewhere, in a distant land,—a country of free principles and equal rights. They cannot tell how the system operates; but this system, as far as they know it, is a beautiful one, and they would like greatly to know more of it. A ship comes among them from that far country, and their vague floating visions now take a more substantial form. It is a vessel bearing signs of wealth and power, marked by good order and efficiency: the

33

country that has sent out this ship must be wealthy and prosperous, enterprising and successful. This is the lesson which is taught by all our ships wherever they go; and taught in a manner that is intelligible to the lowest capacity.

And to this noble and glorious cause of humanity we bid prosperity and success. Yes,—may Heaven sustain and bless it! I am not a politician, but I hope I am a philanthropist; and, next to religion, I love my country and its institutions, for I believe that in them is the regenerating principle that is going to awaken and vivify the world. These plains that we have just been passing over, abounding in a rich soil and under a prolific sky, why are they not cultivated? But they *will* be cultivated, and this people here will be intelligent and intellectual: the *mind* will rouse up, and claim its high pre-eminence; woman will be elevated to her proper lofty sphere; brute force will yield to moral power; and smiling plenty, and security, and happiness, will prevail; and from our country will come the power that is to effect this mighty change.

It is good sometimes to get far off from our land, so that, as from an elevated spot, we may look over the whole country; and, away from the influence of local prejudice, and interest, and alarms, may scrutinize our institutions and examine into their permanency, and see what strengthening and what counteracting influences are at work to promise them security. For myself, I have no fear for them.

They are built on *knowledge;* and, till we can destroy for ever our printing presses, and can roll back the age of ignorance, they are safe: they may change their *forms*, but the substance will remain; and always, and in every form, will liberty and humanity be secure.

It is good also, sometimes to get away, and to be able to compare our own country with others, and be able thus to calculate the amount of prosperity and happiness which we enjoy. In the clashings of enterprise and rivalship among us, angry feelings sometimes will arise. Europe is disgorging upon our land the inmates of her prisons, and there will be crime: the poor, the ignorant, and the oppressed of her population find refuge here, and abundance; and, in the wild joy at their newly-acquired comforts and their freedom, they may run into riots and disorders; but nowhere in the world is so much virtue to be found as amid our population; and virtue is happiness. We are a nation but of yesterday; and our rail-roads, and canals, and steam-boats, and commerce, are already a subject of astonishment; and what will they be a few years hence?—and a century after that?—and why may not the whole world be like it? There is nothing, surely, to prevent this, except Ignorance, and its twin-sister, Vice; but knowledge, and with it virtue, are gone forth conquering and to conquer, and their triumph will be complete. It is a glorious thing to live in such an age as this.

And now, reader, I turn and offer you my hand, for the time when our companionship must cease has at length arrived. I hope that we have been friends during these journeyings, and that we part in kindness. May Heaven bless you! Adieu!

THE END.

Zeitfracht Medien GmbH
Ferdinand-Jühlke-Straße 7
99095 Erfurt, Deutschland
produktsicherheit@kolibri360.de